Praise for Joseph Goodman's WE WANT BAMA

T0028776

"Joseph Goodman's WE WANT BAMA is a book about sports, sure. But it is far more than that. It is a stunningly stylish take on psychology and success, a free-wheeling but deeply reported look at the culture—some might say the neuroses—that makes phenomena like the University of Alabama possible. This is a sports book, sure. But not like the others you've read."
—John Archibald, Pulitzer Prize-winning columnist, *Birmingham News*

"Alabama football might be a larger unifying force than Jesus in some parts of the South. For three hours on a Saturday the state stops spinning. Joseph flawlessly dissects the people and the catalysts for this phenomenon and flawlessly walks us through the one thing that unifies every fall in Alabama. Win or lose, football is religion. On Sundays we pray to Jesus, on Saturdays it's Nick Saban."
—Roy Wood Jr., *The Daily Show* with Trevor Noah

"Joe Goodman—Alabama man, sports fan, and one hell of a writer—takes the reader along on a deep dive into the fascinating, complex, and wildly passionate pool of crazy that is Alabama Crimson Tide football."
—Dave Barry, Pulitzer Prize–winning humor writer

"Joseph Goodman on Alabama's best season ever—and all that went with it—is exactly what I'd expect from him. It's smart, it's funny, and it's a bit out there. If you're an Alabama fan, a college football fan, or someone who wants to enjoy an unconventional approach to a sports book, you'll love this."
—Pat Forde, National College Football columnist for *Sports Illustrated*

"Covering Alabama Football over the years, you discover early on the importance of 'team' to Nick Saban. In a year filled with so much strife, seeing the 2020 Crimson Tide come together to win in the most unpredictable of seasons inspired so many Alabama faithful. Goodman's focus on the significance of togetherness through adversity is something that can ring true for us all."

—Laura Rutledge, ESPN/SEC Network host & reporter

"WE WANT BAMA isn't just a story about a great college football team—this is also Joe Goodman's love song to the state of Alabama: its flaws, its charms, and its wonders. With an unflinching, biting, and humorous style, Goodman shares the economic, political, social, and historical factors that converged for the Crimson Tide to thrive through an unforgiving and unforgettable 2020 season. A must-read for every college football fan—but especially Alabama lovers and haters—who wants to understand what's required for excellence." —Michael Lee, *Washington Post*

"OMG. Read this book. Now. Joseph Goodman's fever dream about our great and terrible state recalls Hunter S. Thompson, Charles P. Pierce, and W.J. Cash on a good day, which is to say, Game Day."

—Diane McWhorter, Pulitzer Prize-winning author of
*Carry Me Home: Birmingham, Alabama: The Climactic
Battle of the Civil Rights Revolution*

"If David Foster Wallace was from red clay country and liked football instead of tennis, he might have approached Goodman's gonzo-lashed prose. An outstanding work of sports journalism that far transcends mere sports. Roll Tide." —*Kirkus* (starred review)

WE WANT BAMA

A SEASON OF HOPE AND THE MAKING OF NICK SABAN'S "ULTIMATE TEAM"

JOSEPH GOODMAN

GRAND CENTRAL
PUBLISHING

NEW YORK   BOSTON

Grand Central Publishing

Hachette Book Group

1290 Avenue of the Americas, New York, NY 10104

grandcentralpublishing.com

twitter.com/grandcentralpub

First published in hardcover and ebook in November 2021

First Trade Paperback Edition: November 2022

Grand Central Publishing is a division of Hachette Book Group, Inc. The Grand Central Publishing name and logo is a trademark of Hachette Book Group, Inc.

The publisher is not responsible for websites (or their content) that are not owned by the publisher.

The Hachette Speakers Bureau provides a wide range of authors for speaking events. To find out more, go to www.hachettespeakersbureau.com or call (866) 376-6591.

Map on page xxviii by Jeffrey L. Ward

The Library of Congress has cataloged the hardcover as follows:

Names: Goodman, Joe (Sports columnist) author.

Title: We want Bama : a season of hope and the making of Nick Saban's "Ultimate Team" / Joe Goodman.

Description: New York : GCP, [2021] | Includes index.

Identifiers: LCCN 2021025408 | ISBN 9781538716298 (hardcover) | ISBN 9781538716281 (ebook)

Subjects: LCSH: Alabama Crimson Tide (Football team) | University of Alabama—Football. | Saban, Nick.

Classification: LCC GV958.A4 G67 2021 | DDC 796.332/630976184—dc23

LC record available at https://lccn.loc.gov/2021025408

ISBNs: 978-1-5387-1627-4 (trade paperback), 978-1-5387-1628-1 (ebook)

Printed in the United States of America

LSC-C

Printing 1, 2022

To my older brother Kevin and our family.
And in the eternal spirit of his godson.

CONTENTS

INTRODUCTION

The yellowhammer is a bird of striking savagery.

That's an ornithological salute to a subspecies of woodpecker that eats ants and then rubs the formic acid from those same swarming, hateful devils all over its feathers to protect it from the world's bullshit. Yellowhammers are resourceful soldiers in the fight against the universe, in other words. Their armor is the bodily fluid of their breakfast.

This book was inspired by one of the most culturally significant college football teams that has ever played the game, and understanding why requires an appreciation for what it represented in the Foul and Venomous Year of Unholy Universal Biting Bullshit that was 2020. That bastard of a year was like a horde of zombie fire ants sent by Lucifer himself to carry us all down into the tunnels of a sadistic and jealous hell. It was a year that none of us will ever forget, and one that we're all duty bound by acid burns to pass on with stories and wisdom so that future generations may somehow avoid our mistakes. In that year, the University of Alabama Football Crimson Tide of the Yellowhammer State defeated the universe with resourcefulness, achieved historic perfection during the COVID-19 pandemic, and, most poetically, leveraged its power and influence born of Southern pride to push back against the country's hateful legacy of racism that Donald Trump exploited to divide America.

Was Alabama in 2020 the greatest team of all time? It's such an overvalued and played-out question in an era of media oversaturation. Maybe so, but who's to say? The only thing we know for certain is that we should all dry heave at the phrase "media oversaturation," and then seek out a shower, drink some bourbon, turn off our phones, take a walk in the woods, and also maybe burn one all the way down to our lips to cleanse our senses and our souls. There have been some great football teams through the years, and they all deserve respect. Here's what we know for sure. They all would have been appreciative of what this Alabama team represented, and proud of what it accomplished under the most difficult set of circumstances ever thrown at a national champion.

Would Miami's all-time collection of talent have opted out in 2001? Did USC in 2004 have to worry about navigating a plague? Did Hall of Fame coach Tom Osborne test positive for a potentially deadly virus the week Nebraska played Colorado in 1995? LSU quarterback Joe Burrow didn't win 11 games against SEC opponents in 2019. Maybe he could have, but he didn't. Quarterback Mac Jones and Alabama did in 2020, and a team might never accomplish that feat again.

Alabama in 2020 captured something special that moved it beyond the conversation of best ever, and into the place reserved for most important of all time.

With a star running back from Northern California who idolized Colin Kaepernick and Megan Rapinoe, a former child model from Florida at quarterback, a down-home country karate black belt Eagle Scout at center, a brilliant artist from L.A. at offensive tackle, and an overachieving, majestic receiver from small-town

Louisiana, Alabama football in 2020 was a picture of what America can be when it comes together under the vision of strong leadership.

(And, by the way, when people from the Deep South say "L.A.," they don't mean Los Angeles. They mean Lower Alabama.)

But we all love the real L.A. down here among the dogwoods, too. That's where some really great future defensive end who runs a 4.6 in the 40-yard dash and has a 39-inch vertical jump is going to one day test his 6-foot-4, 265-pound frame against America's best. He wanted to go to Alabama, but Saban got the kid who was an inch taller and a tenth of a second faster.

That five-star recruit, who beat out the guy from the real L.A., had to wait four real and whole years to start a single game, but then won a natty, earned two degrees, and went in the first round of the NFL Draft.

Alabama, as they like to say inside the Mal M. Moore Athletic Facility until everyone believes it like some blood code, just "isn't for everyone." Those three perfect words make competitive people demand it even more, and have given us another turn of phrase that has come to define the pursuit of archetypal perfection. Everyone wants Bama. They want Bama. She wants Bama. He wants Bama. Y'all definitely want some Bama. Through a decade of dominance, "We Want Bama" became America's college football battle cry, but then it transformed into America's meme that represented testing yourself against the best in every walk of life. In the challenging year of 2020, "We Want Bama" meant something else for people who still believe in things like a new hope. Truly working together still has great power in this country, and, friends, Alabama set out to show everyone what that meant with cold fists of fiery rage.

Coach Nick Saban said it best when he called 2020 Alabama

"the ultimate team," and those players cemented their coach as his sport's best to ever do it. Saban would later call his group in 2020 "the best team." For a coach who loathes reflection on past accomplishments, his pull to look back and celebrate that team again and again says it all. For Saban, it was a hellish and beautiful ride to earn the undisputed title of greatest of all time. He has the seven rings now to prove it, the staying power to back it all up.

Because here's the thing about Saban: His rare affliction for a greater standard goes far beyond football now. A year like no other also framed him as the country's greatest living leader. He passed former Alabama coaching legend Paul "Bear" Bryant for the most national championships in college football history, but before the historic seventh of his career, Saban defended what was right when the hour of truth demanded it. He chose to speak out against the rekindled politics of white supremacy embroiled so deeply in places like Alabama that they even use woodland creatures like the yellowhammer as metaphorical Confederate statues.

———

History will remember what Saban represented in 2020 long after those who are spiteful of his greatness and courage melt away like trollish gremlins in the sun. Saban's call to respect Black lives spoke to people enthralled by Trumpism. "Until I listen with an open heart and mind, I can't understand his experience and his pain," he said in a video produced by Alabama athletics in 2020's summer of protest against white supremacy, racial injustice, and police brutality. His calming refrain was a universal message we've heard before. In another time, in another wicked world, in a book about a different kind of bird in Alabama, it was Atticus Finch who said, "If you can learn a simple trick, Scout, you'll get along a lot better with all kinds of folks. You never really understand a person until you consider things from his point of view...until you climb into his skin and walk around in it."

History will remember 2020 as the year Trump pulled the sports world into his toxic underworld like he did with everything else, but the truth of it all is that when America needed real leaders in the face of so much hate, the sports world answered the call and fought back for the soul of the country. LeBron James, long an activist for civil rights, was the leader of America's team, a collection of athletes from all sports who protested together. For many, though, it paid to be silent. In Alabama, one former college football coach, Tommy Tuberville, called Trump "sent by God" to save America. It bought him an election to the U.S. Senate. Remember that, too, about the division bells of 2020 to fully understand the power of college football in the South. Under that backdrop, Saban's "ultimate team" from Alabama showed what people can accomplish when they fight together for a just cause in the name of unity. To underscore the importance of their union and its message, Alabama then went out and kicked the ever-living hell out of everybody. They could not lose, and they did not lose.

What makes the "ultimate team"?

Alabama stood for strength and toughness by wrecking an unprecedented schedule in the ultra-competitive Southeastern Conference. It stood for brotherhood by freely committing to a season many will say only happened to bail out a system that exploits unpaid athletes. Most important, though, the team and their celebrated coach stood in the schoolhouse door made infamous by a populist bigot who championed white supremacy. In 1963, Alabama governor George Wallace used the forced desegregation of the University of Alabama to launch himself into the national consciousness and pour gas upon a country on fire.

"Segregation now, segregation tomorrow, segregation forever,"

Wallace said in an inauguration speech that invoked "Jefferson Davis," the "Cradle of the Confederacy," and "this very Heart of the Great Anglo-Saxon Southland." A few months later, he stood in front of Alabama's Foster Auditorium in defiance of federal law. Really, he was just whistling Dixie to generations of white Southerners who saw the civil rights movement as a political, social, and economic threat and were happy to vilify Black students who were "fighting" for nothing more than equality.

George Wallace, a political moderate at the beginning of his career, turned hard right to win his first election. He was backed by the Ku Klux Klan and was officially endorsed by the Klan's favorite son, Birmingham commissioner of public safety Bull Connor. By allowing Wallace to grandstand in front of Foster Auditorium and demonize the state's Black population as the enemy of white supremacy, the University of Alabama let all of its strength and power be wielded as a tool to further divide the state and embolden the Klan's use of police-aided domestic terrorism. This is the "Alabama" that much of the world still sees, and the Alabama that haunts the entire state even today.

The sum force of Alabama's fascinating culture, and its artful beauty and intense pain produced in equal measure, was built around a pyramid of white supremacy dating back to the failed end of post–Civil War Reconstruction. It is easy to see when viewed from afar, but up close, the pyramid, now covered with dirt and kudzu and privet, just looks like a natural part of the topography segregating neighborhoods and schools. It is not natural. It was engineered by the hatred of white men for Black, and then built with laws and law enforcement. First came the fraudulent state constitution of 1901, then Jim Crow laws, and then new municipalities and school districts throughout the state. George Wallace's 1963 "stand in the schoolhouse door" was actually just another speck of dirt in the state's Mound of Unholy Biting Fire Ant-ed Bullshit.

In the summer of 2020, the Alabama football team dug its cleats into that scratch of venomous earth in front of Foster Auditorium and flexed its power during a revolutionary summer of protests across the country. With America's professional athletes rallying to make their own stand against police violence, the most powerful entity in modern-day Alabama joined the cause and players used their voices to create a conversation to last long after the historic 2020 football season. Speaking as one, and with their famous coach in tow, Alabama football players asked how the state could be strengthened with the same values and blending of different voices that made their team the best in the country. They called for an acknowledgment of systemic racism that pulls people apart and the devastating instruments of that system: overpolicing, profiling, and their inevitable upshot, police brutality.

These are not easy words, nor should they be. It's easier just to call something fake news, and much more satisfying to ignore everything and retreat to corners of the internet with guys like 2020's Opportunist of the Year, Clay Travis. A popular voice for expressing the mythos of Southern white men who feel attacked by popular culture for simply being Southern white men, Travis, a talented communicator with a law degree from Vanderbilt, is a commentator for Fox Sports and the operator of his own website, Outkick.com. Like many members of the media, he cashed in during a bitter presidential election year featuring an incumbent whose playbook was about as obvious as his painted-on tan: divide and conquer. The sports world, for decades one of America's great unifiers, was not off-limits for Trump. Throughout his presidency he labeled outspoken Black athletes as the enemy, and guys like Travis just went along for the ride. He even sold T-shirts on his website featuring LeBron James as a communist and others with catchy slogans like "Defund the Media" and "60 Minutes of lies." It's an old grift. Southern sports commentators have always found success playing the contrarian's victimhood song. The verses in 2020 were:

1. Racism isn't the problem. Talking about racism is the problem.
2. The outside agitators and "media" are to blame.
3. Sports journalists worried about COVID-19 obviously hate sports and want all sports to die.
4. Look how tough we are if we refuse to listen to people hurting.
5. I love Morgan Wallen.

There will be no servicing of political narratives here to sell you T-shirts. We'll figure out other ways to sell swag. The 2020 football season didn't happen in a political vacuum, and everything that happens in this world is connected. The uncomfortable corners of the internet cannot be ignored in the search for truth in Alabama and the Deep South. Here is a light in the dark to guide the way: The South is a place of perpetuating tragedies, but it's also beautiful and important in ways no other region of the country could ever be. I'm not talking about the food and the bourbon and the Southern hospitality either. People in the South care, and the true potential of a country united is hidden down there in those pine trees.

On Saturdays in the fall, when the summer's humidity finally breaks and the fire ants start planning their retreat, a portrait of what really makes America great is celebrated by everyone in the South. It's not some misty, romantic phantasma about mossy oaks,

Solo cup tailgating with chandeliers and seersucker shorts. This isn't some storybook simpleton Disney movie like *Remember the Titans* either. Yes, *Remember the Titans* is great because it teaches an important lesson, but college football in the South in the early decades of the third millennium of recorded Christian history is a window into the heart of America because it's a savage desire for dominance at all costs.

And there is so much money to be made by a university whose alternative fight song is about yellowhammers.

The maniacal pursuit of college football perfection is an American drug, and people pay thousands and thousands of dollars every year to be a part of that high. In that world, there is not a more American place than Alabama. In "Alabama the Beautiful," it is football at all costs all of the damn time. Even during a pandemic. The best players from around the country (and one from Canada who will clean knock your teeth out) devoted their lives to one another, what they believed in, and the love of football at the University of Alabama in 2020.

And for a maniacal coach who controls everything in his bubble, a pandemic isn't a crisis. It's an opportunity to find every advantage possible.

It's your choice to either hate that or love it, but know that everyone in Alabama—and for that matter, everyone in the South—regardless of their political affiliation or philosophical trappings or, more important, college football team loyalty, understands the game and loves it for how unbelievably unifying it is in its craziness.

At least they tested college players and coaches for COVID-19 multiple times weekly beginning in the summer of 2020. Would the players have been safer at home? Doubtful. High school athletic associations in Alabama and other states went full-on reckless in 2020 and played football games without testing players even when many of those players' physical high schools were closed and classrooms were virtual.

Yes, we are a football-mad nation, and the politics of football in an election year cannot be discounted either.

When conferences around the country were canceling college football in August 2020, pretty much everyone in the South understood that the game was going to be played by the schools in the SEC. The conference planned for it all along and didn't blink when the Big Ten and Pac-12 announced fall football was a wrap because of "new research" linking the coronavirus to cardiomyopathy. In 2020, those conferences tried to act elite like they always do, but the ironic thing about their rush to force the hands of the SEC, Big 12, and ACC was that Trump used it as political leverage. The Big Ten reversed course after that and looked like chumps. The Pac-12, of course, followed like some idiot sidekick from a cartoon. SEC commissioner Greg Sankey was the guy credited with saving the season, but the truth is that college football was simply too big to fail.

Someone had to pay Saban's 2020 salary of $9.1 million (before the bonuses, of course).

He's worth every penny, by the way, and the reason is not because of winning so many football games, but rather the enormous wealth all that winning has brought the University of Alabama in student enrollment, alumni donations, and national clout.

Across the country, but especially in the SEC, selling the college experience is tied directly to football. No one has done that better than the University of Alabama since it plucked Saban and Mrs. Terry away from the Miami Dolphins. The University of Alabama's student population grew from 25,580 in Saban's first year in Tuscaloosa (2007) to 38,103 in 2018. That's so much damn cornbread for a poor Southern state.

The "Saban Effect" is well known, and takes its name from the "Flutie Effect" after Boston College's student applications spiked 30 percent in the year following quarterback Doug Flutie's Hail Mary against Miami in 1984. Look inside Alabama's enrollment numbers and there is a more revealing trend for why football had to be played in 2020. Since 2011, out-of-state students at Alabama have outnumbered in-state students. From 2009 to 2015, according to one report, in-state enrollment for incoming freshmen declined from 3,103 to 2,508 while out-of-state enrollment for that group jumped from 2,013 to 4,706. In 2018, out-of-state enrollment made up 58.1 percent of the student body.

They weren't there for the degrees in math and science. Rich kids from Texas, New Jersey, Georgia, and Florida were paying double tuition for the football. Happens everywhere, but no place has more tied to football than Alabama. It's a national brand for a reason, and the reason is that Southern pride demands it, and it's stitched into Alabama's culture and ethos of rebellion all the way down to the egregious exploitation of that badass little bird known as the yellowhammer.

For Alabama, not having a season in 2020 simply wasn't an option. On top of the enrollment that had to be protected and saved, the university's famous football stadium also underwent a massive $107 million renovation during those frightening early summer months of the pandemic. Construction never stopped despite multiple outbreaks of COVID-19 on the job site. Pre-booked multimillion-dollar luxury suites had to be finished before the first home game.

And they were.

Everyone wants a spot in those suites, and it's because the aura of American exceptionalism at an Alabama football game is seductive in the same way that the perfect Italian sports car will give every dude an erection and get even the ugliest nerds laid.

In the fall of 2019, before the stadium's renovation and long before the protest march by Saban and Alabama's players, Trump and Melania watched from the presidential suite in Bryant-Denny in the latest "Game of the Century." What a shitshow that was. *ESPN College GameDay* was there, too, and ESPN's flagship college football show is the one thing that really launched the mythology of Saban's Alabama into the mystical ether. All you gotta say is three perfect words: "We Want Bama."

But, yeah, having been booed everywhere else, Trump wanted Bama in 2019, and that sherbet philistine cursed the Tide in the first quarter when the cameras showed him up there look'n like a radioactive roast beef and cheese. Everyone either cheered or booed, but there were, let's be honest, far more cheers than boos. Then it got real quiet real fast, though. Alabama quarterback Tua Tagovailoa fumbled running into the end zone on the very next play, and after that sequence of events Alabama's season was never the same. As long as Saban is the coach at Alabama, Trump will never be back at Bryant-Denny Stadium for a game.

———

No. 2 Alabama lost to No. 1 LSU 46–41 in that 2019 "Game of the Century," and no one came close to beating LSU for the rest of the season. Can those Tigers be considered possibly the best team of all time? Sure, why not? And good for them. Here's the thing about Alabama, though. It was bigger news that Alabama lost on that day—Saturday, November 9, 2019—than it was that LSU won, or even that the most powerful person on Planet Earth was in attendance to be fellated on national television. That was the first time Alabama lost in its home stadium since 2015, and the first time in 32 consecutive games that Alabama's fans couldn't sing about the badass yellowhammer bird in the fourth quarter of victory.

When Saban's Alabama loses at home, that Alabama mystique makes the rare giant slayers national celebrities for life. Johnny Manziel in 2012. Hugh Freeze in 2015. Burrow and LSU coach Ed Orgeron in 2019.

But here's why Bama is Bama, why "We Want Bama" has defined the gold standard of archetypal alpha villainy for a generation of American sports fans, and why Nick Saban is the greatest SOB ever to blow a whistle: The year after LSU shocked the Tide in 2019, the Tigers went 5–5 and their season highlight was actually a personal foul committed by a Florida defender when he had potted meat for brains and threw the shoe of an LSU player 20 yards downfield to ultimately lose the game. In 2020, Alabama went 13–0 during a pandemic, scored 107 points combined against LSU and Florida, watched another Auburn coach get fired, and followed all that up with the top-rated signing class not just for 2021 but ever since they've been assigning value to the endeavor.

That's why they flock from all over the country to Tuscaloosa, Alabama, to sing a fight song about a bird that's not even yellow and a long-defunct campus gossip tabloid once edited by Harper Lee: *"Hey Auburn! Hey Auburn! Hey Auburn! We just beat the hell outta you! Rammer Jammer Yellowhammer give 'em hell, Alabama!"*

People hate that shit, but it's one of the best traditions in American sports. Made the bird famous, too, and that's why Alabama is one of the most confounding places in the universe for human behavior.

The yellowhammer is so revered in the Yellowhammer State

that it is now celebrated with a signature drink and tattoos. Businesses market the yellowhammer in their names, and children learn about yellowhammers in school. Why do people sing about the yellowhammer at football games, and name drinks after the yellowhammer at college dive bars, and needle artwork of this bird on arms and ankles and the smalls of backs? By all accounts, it's because yellowhammer romanticism inspires great pride.

It's not really for the love of birds, though. More than anything, it's just a metaphorical fuck-you to the United States of America.

Rammer Jammer Yellowhammer, who the hell are you? To know that answer is to understand the competing forces of power wrapped up in Alabama football amid the most brilliant dynasty in college football history, and after a summer of protest that set the Crimson Tide against its own state's sinister past.

Alabama became a state in 1819 but really never had any interest in all of that. White Alabamians just wanted to have Black slaves pick cotton forever, which sounds so completely insane when it's phrased that way, but that's the unfiltered, undeniable truth about it. It was even written into the Constitution of the Confederate States in 1861, and then Alabama went to war to defend it.

Confederate president Jefferson Davis and his slave masters are all burning in eternal hell now, but to this day, Alabama's disgusting loyalty to the political legacy of white supremacy is still being used to dehumanize Black Americans. White supremacy has adopted many forms through the years to remain in power, including but not limited to the American Civil War, sharecropping, domestic terrorism in the form of lynchings, bombings, burnings, hangings, draggings, and so on, rigged elections, discriminatory lending practices, religion, a rewritten constitution in 1901 to guarantee that Blacks can never help govern the state or themselves, convict-lease systems, Jim Crow laws, cowards, con-men, the Klan, the Lost Cause, a shitload of statues, state holi-days, state-sponsored revisionist history, Dixiecrats, Sons of the Confederacy, shadow governments, voter suppression, redlining, profiling, white flight, the "war on drugs" and the prison indus-trial complex, payday lenders, opting out of Medicaid expansion, and systemic educational disenfranchisement that has held back the potential of a still-wondrous state for generations.

That's just a warm-up.

In effect, nearly every major aspect of the economy and Confederate-loving government in Alabama for hundreds of years was engineered to either own, oppress, or exploit African slaves or their American-born descendants. This is not an exaggeration, and the state of Alabama would vouch for that statement of fact. Because here's what happened in 2020. On the 175th day of that sordid year, the Alabama Department of Archives and History issued in writing this gobsmacking mea culpa:

> As our state and nation struggle to navigate through a place of contention, fear, and uncertainty, the Alabama Depart-ment of Archives and History (ADAH) recommits itself to the mission of illuminating the path that brought us here, and thereby equipping all of us, together, to build a future characterized by justice, human dignity, and a commit-ment to the wellbeing of all people. Our recommitment includes acknowledgment of these truths.
>
> 1. Systemic racism remains a reality in American soci-ety, despite belief in racial equality on the part of most individuals. Historically, our governments, our economy, and many private institutions seeded or perpetuated dis-crimination against racial minorities to the political,

economic, and social advantage of whites. The decline of overt bigotry in mainstream society has not erased the legacies of blatantly racist systems that operated for hundreds of years.

2. The ADAH is, in significant part, rooted in this legacy. The State of Alabama founded the department in 1901 to address a lack of proper management of government records, but also to serve a white Southern concern for the preservation of Confederate history and the promotion of Lost Cause ideals. For well over a half-century, the agency committed extensive resources to the acquisition of Confederate records and artifacts while declining to acquire and preserve materials documenting the lives and contributions of African Americans in Alabama.

To which everyone said, "No fucking shit, Alabama." Still, that's quite the official admission of guilt from a state that has done more to destroy the lives of its Black population over the last 200 years than perhaps any other political entity on Planet Earth. This cultural homicide that Alabama has played with itself for generations—now a matter of official public record, according to the Alabama Department of Archives and History—includes the yellowhammer woodpecker that eats ants and is championed after every Alabama victory.

Saban had a win-loss record of 170–23 through his first 14 seasons at Alabama. That's a lotta yellowhammering. The yellowhammer is the state bird of Alabama because a band of soldiers from Alabama showed up to the Civil War with yellow cloth on their uniforms, so the story goes. That was just too much flair for the other troops to handle, so the guys nicknamed the fancy Alabamians after a bird. The official record in the Alabama Department of Archives and History proudly notes that the person leading the troops who nicknamed the Alabama soldiers was General Nathan Bedford Forrest.

More from those hardworking archivists of ADAH down in Montgomery:

> The officers and men of the Huntsville company wore fine, new uniforms, whereas the soldiers who had long been on the battlefields were dressed in faded, worn uniforms. On the sleeves, collars and coattails of the new cavalry troop were bits of brilliant yellow cloth.
>
> As the company rode past Company A, Will Arnett* cried out in greeting, "Yellowhammer, Yellowhammer, flicker, flicker!" The greeting brought a roar of laughter from the men and from that moment the Huntsville soldiers were spoken of as the "yellowhammer company." The term quickly spread throughout the Confederate Army and all Alabama troops were referred to unofficially as the "Yellowhammers."

Forrest, a white supremacist who said God intended for white men to rule over Blacks, was later elected the first grand wizard of the Ku Klux Klan. Alabama's Lost Cause mythologists like the "Sons and Daughters of the Confederacy" helped glorify him as the greatest bastard ever to ride a horse.

A great bedtime story to tell the kiddies, right? The white supremacists sure thought so. As part of the ongoing Lost Cause of the Confederacy movement, when all those statues were going

---

* Not the contemporary actor of the same name, presumably, but "a great wag" nonetheless, according to a 1901 account in the *Birmingham Age-Herald*.

up to make people feel proud and heroic for defending slavery, Alabama's racists went with yellowhammer as the team name. To understand Alabama, and to appreciate why the University of Alabama's football team was so important to the state and the country in 2020, it all must be laid bare. Everything is connected.

Alabama is a wonder because it still finds ways to shine its light after so much hate. For all of its long history of apartheid, horror, and worse, hope remains. There have always been heroes among the villainy, and then in 2020 the greatest national villains of all were actually the heroes. That's why this book was written. It was written because there is an Alabama out there that is not so easily framed by its past, and is instead a picture of what the state can be if it tried to work together for common purpose. *That* Alabama is the University of Alabama Football Crimson Tide, a team everyone in the country loves to hate, but is a reflection of America's complicated culture all the same.

Nick Saban, antihero? He'd probably punch an American antihero right in the throat on national TV, but maybe even that image is too idealistic for post-Trump America. Anyway, understand this: Over the course of a few months, when the country felt more divided than at any time since Vietnam, and everyone else was experimenting with facial hair and hoarding Slim Jims and toilet paper, a college football team in Alabama showed people that the spirit of love, sacrifice, and togetherness can accomplish historic things even in hours of darkness and doubt.

WE WANT BAMA

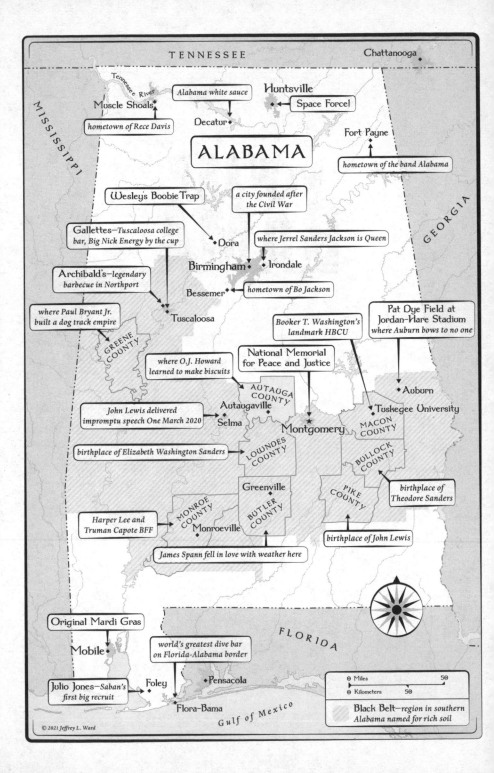

Chapter 1

THERE WILL BE RUM

The plan to bring together raging, quarantined 18-year-old hormones during a pandemic and then keep them separated like thirsty lab rats in a bank of stackable cages might have worked, but there was rum.

The official record will say it was Nick Saban and the "process" that built the University of Alabama into a mountain of gold, but that's only half of the truth. "Yellow Hammers" did the rest one golden pour at a time inside a redly brash and unapologetic college dive bar named Gallettes.

They got $2 beers for the boys, and "$5 32 oz wells" is painted on the side of the windowless brick building facing the road to the river and then on out to fuck-all Mississippi. Roll Tide. It's quite possible that Gallettes is more Alabama than the university at this point. It'll buy you a beer and then steal your girl, and that's for damn sure. The University of Alabama sells degrees, but educations for life are served up one night at a time at the roadside "Campus Party Store" that doesn't even have a proper sign outside to keep people from getting lost. Try not to get too sloppy, kid, but if it comes to that, then make sure to toast the ancestors. They're looking down with pride, and cringing.

Which is to say, Gallettes is not your Apple Store hipster's kind of ramrod two-bit phony pony wanna either quote or cancel Faulkner with a Southern pecan-spiced craft ale in our laps while we pretend to care about the world, but really this is all just ironic bullshit hung on a wall in the name of awkward maybe micro-agressive college sex although more than likely we'll cry together later listening to a song by Jason Isbell.

What's really impressive about Tuscaloosa, Alabama—and the reason it's the swollen beating heart inside the chest cavity of college football—is that everyone in that hipster bar, God bless them all, can easily name the Top 20 offensive skill players of Nick Saban's 14 years of Crimson Tide dominance, too. They are, in order: (1) running back Derrick Henry, (2) receiver DeVonta Smith, (3) quarterback Mac Jones, (4) receiver Julio Jones, (5) running back Najee Harris, (6) quarterback Tua Tagovailoa, (7) receiver Jerry Jeudy, (8) running back Mark Ingram, (9) quarterback Jalen Hurts, (10) receiver Amari Cooper, (11) receiver Jaylen Waddle, (12) running back Josh Jacobs, (13) receiver Calvin Ridley, (14) running back T. J. Yeldon, (15) running back Trent Richardson, (16) running back Eddie Lacy, (17) tight end O. J. Howard, (18) receiver Henry Ruggs III, (19) running back Damien Harris, and (20) quarterback A. J. McCarron.

To understand the evolution of offense at Alabama from 2010 to 2020, consider that A. J. McCarron, the Maxwell Award winner in 2013 and the starting quarterback of two national championship teams, is last on that list. What's more telling, though, is the number of rushing touchdowns by Heisman Trophy–winning running back Mark Ingram in 2009 compared to the number of rushing scores by Najee Harris in 2020. In 2009, Ingram ran for 17 touchdowns. In 2020, Harris had 26. Add in receiving numbers, and Harris had 10 more total touchdowns in one less game than

Alabama's first-ever Heisman Trophy winner. Najee Harris finished third in Heisman voting *among players on his own team*: 2020 Heisman winner DeVonta Smith and quarterback Mac Jones.

But no, man. Gallettes is not for nerds who like numbers unless by numbers we mean counting money. They cash in on the college crowd at Gallettes, and kids throw down.

Dudes can't wear hats, T-shirts, or tank tops, according to the old rusty sign on the wall, but those who are not dudes can wear anything they want. For a long time, the retro funk inside smelled of Joe Namath and Lane Kiffin sharing a pack of Kool menthols, but smart businessmen ripped out the walls for bay doors in 2017 right after No. 2–ranked Alabama slack-jawed LSU 24–10 with a defense that started nine players who would later be drafted. With the bay doors and a little rum, they can now fit more than 800 of America's youth in Gallettes on a Saturday night.

On average game days in the fall, Gallettes sells more Yellow Hammers than the total number of passing yards Alabama quarterback Mac Jones threw in all of the 2020 football season. It was exactly 4,500, which led the country and set a new school record. The bright mixing tanks of mystery punch rest on the business ends of a dark, prison-grade-strength bar top that looks like it was formed to withstand a biker gang swinging blunt weapons or maybe slightly unhinged professional football players who never really learned how to drink but come back to town in the off-season to test their strength against the best of the best. The gray concrete floors are wide open to cram in as many dancing sorority girls as possible, but out back is where it gets really wild.

It's unclear exactly what goes into the now-famous rum drink named for the lyric in the Rammer Jammer song, but it tastes kind of like "Dixieland Delight" sounds near the end of Alabama home games. The recipe for Yellow Hammers is a proprietary secret, and it's going to stay that way by the grace of God. They make a catfish pond's worth of that flowing sunshine every weekend, though. A man can only guess the holy formula, but it's like if a Rum Punch from the Flora-Bama and a Neptune's Monsoon from Port of Call on Esplanade in New Orleans met up in Tuscaloosa back in 1976 for a Jimmy Buffett concert and had a love child who never left. It's yellow, it's delicious, and it is now synonymous with Alabama's Southern football party culture like beads at Mardi Gras or the Mullet Toss down in L.A.

When football recruits visit the University of Alabama from all over the country, they may or may not go to Gallettes on The Strip one of the nights, but they definitely go home knowing it's there and, more pointedly, appreciating the fun that goes on in "The Back."

What, y'all thought that Saban, at 70 years old on October 31, 2021, recruited all those players by himself with only the power of his voice? That's not how this game works. The SEC is a marriage of carnal pleasures and the savagery of college football. It's not why Saban, the man, is so good at what he does. It's why "Saban," warrior deity, is allowed to exist inside his fantasy. Roll Tide.

The life force of college football—SEC college football—is the glorification of a Southern ethos that has been mythologized perfectly in the words sung by thousands and thousands of heroically horny students dedicated to Alabama football.

Gallettes calls their signature drink the Yellow Hammer, but the spirit of "Dixieland Delight" is what they're selling.

Students sing that fanciful country song by the band Alabama in the fourth quarter of home games, and it's one of the SEC's great traditions. The song is so intertwined with Alabama football that former quarterback Brodie Croyle (2001–2005), a second-generation Crimson Tide player, hopped up onstage during his 2007 wedding reception in fuck-all Mississippi and belted out a perfect rendition of the twangy tune. Roll Tide.

"Dixieland Delight" is the cultural highlight of every Alabama home football game. Seeing all those students sing that song on a Saturday night, and being in that sea of crimson love, makes anyone who experiences it—even the biggest preening hipster in that craft-beer bar—consider a lifestyle change that somehow includes more sex in rural places.

There's an important history lesson in all of this when considering what happened in 2020 to universities that rely so heavily on the college football experience to market higher education. In 2014, much to the dismay of students, fans, and most alumni, the University of Alabama forced the sound engineers at Bryant-Denny Stadium to stop playing "Dixieland Delight" at games because the song wasn't "family friendly." Now, an argument can be made that a song about making sweet hillbilly love in a pickup truck is the most "family friendly" form of music ever recorded by a white man, but that's probably a perspective that would go unappreciated by the Alabama System Board of Trustees.

Anyway, it was a big fucking mistake.

———

When the selectively principled Southern elitists up in their chandeliered stadium suites banned Bryant-Denny Stadium's minstrel fourth-quarter pledge to Appalachian moonwashed intercourse, they broke a sacred code: One does not fuck with the folklore. For a people so devoted to preserving an alternative history crafted to whitewash their white supremacy, this should have been obvious.

Without "Dixieland Delight" playing near the end of games,

the students really had no reason to stick around for the fourth quarter. They all just started leaving for the bars and house parties at halftime. The mass exodus from games wasn't just because Alabama 86'd the song, but cutting it from the program angered the student body and plenty of alumni, too. More accurately, the decision just further sanitized the product of Alabama football into something polished and grossly corporate. This ain't a royal wedding in Buckingham Palace, y'all. It's college football in Alabama. They ended the tradition of "Dixieland Delight" not because of the reference to passionate pickup truck lovemaking in the mountains of Tennessee. No, they cut the beloved timeout tune because the students peppered the song with bawdy alternative lyrics.

It's not fair to say students protested the decision, but why stick around for another masterfully boring 40-point blowout in the hot sun when an oasis of refreshing Yellow Hammers is right there next to the stadium? Gallettes has no problem playing the hell out of "Dixieland Delight," by God. For the first few home games of the 2018 season, the enormous student section inside Bryant-Denny—expanded to 17,000 seats in 2010—was mostly cleared out midway through the third quarter. Student attendance had been a "problem" for the university since as far back as 2013, but in the years without "Dixieland Delight," the south end zone looked like the empty seats in Psych 101. Understand, most Alabama football games are not really a competition of athletics inside the big 100,000-seat stadium as much as they're worship services of predictable routine.

For the elites, it was all incredibly embarrassing. They expanded the stadium for this? For Saban, the empty seats were problems. The illusion was broken. No students? What are the recruits going to think? For Saban, above all else, it's always about recruiting. They tried to say it was Greg Byrne who brought back "Dixieland

Delight" for that second home conference game in 2018, but the "inspiration" came from Saban, the Exalted Supreme Leader.

Saban's magma chamber popped on October 3, 2018, four days after Alabama fans attempted and failed to appease the God of Fire during a 56–14 sacrifice of Louisiana-Lafayette. Alabama built a 56–0 lead on the Ragin' Cajuns, but many of the students didn't see backup quarterback McCorkle Freaking Jones and backup receiver Jaylen Waddle connect on a 94-yard passing play with 1:30 left in the third quarter. It was a dominant victory for Alabama, but afterward Mount Saban still blew its top.

It was a Wednesday news conference inside the Naylor Stone Media Suite, which is the room inside the Mal Moore Athletic Facility where Saban and his football players field questions from reporters during the week. Saban was asked a question about the fans' love of starting quarterback Tua Tagovailoa: "How cool is it to see your fans kind of support him with things like leis and Hawaiian shirts on game day?"

How does one effectively answer that question? *Soooo cool, man.*

The following is Saban's answer in full, and this transcript was chosen as the first glimpse into his world for an important reason. Who is Nick Saban? Why is he such an incredible leader? What makes him so successful? Like all geniuses who can't really help but be great at what they do, he's a little crazy.

Like a volcano gathering energy from the naturally occurring elements inside our ever-moving earth, the words of a "Saban rant," like the constant transformation of his teams, start gradually but build and build and vent steam and heat until raw, uncut, molten vehemence spews forth into a violent upchuck that marks the beginning of new paths from the destruction of old and tired things.

"Well, I think it's great, you know, I think what makes this a special experience here is when we have great support from everybody in the program, everybody who supports the program, all of our fans, all of our students."

Indeed, and sometimes to the shock of everyone in the country, there isn't a more fervent and unhinged SEC fanbase than the one for Alabama. Never forget that in 2011, an ex-cop from Texas who named his children Bear Bryant Updyke and Crimson Tyde Updyke decided he needed to kill Auburn's sacred Toomer's Corner oak trees with industrial herbicide and then phone into the Paul Finebaum radio show to brag about it. That guy's gone now—he left us during the summer of the COVID-19 pandemic—but crazy ol' Harvey Almorn "Al from Dadeville" Updyke Jr. (October 9, 1948–July 30, 2020) wasn't as much of a rogue outlier as the University of Alabama would like people to believe. As noted by Finebaum in his 2014 memoir, Updyke signed autographs for other prisoners in the Lee County Detention Center in exchange for honey buns while serving time for killing the trees.

The "Updykes," that proud sect of Alabama faithful who are too extreme in their fandom simply to be known as everyday "Gumps," understand exactly what Saban means when he says "all of our students."

Those entitled shits who leave early for Gallettes, in other words.

Look, if we're going to annotate a Saban rant, then we must leave nothing out. There is always a preamble before the rage. Saban continued:

"I can honestly say I was a little disappointed there weren't more students at the last game, and I think we're trying to address that. I don't think they're entitled to anything either, aight, and me personally, I think it ought to be first come–first serve, and if they don't want to come to the games, they don't have to come, but I'm sure there's enough people around here who'd like to go to the games, and we'd like for them to come too because they support the players."

Saban was speaking to the Updykes, those loyal minutemen who can no longer afford entry into Bryant-Denny Stadium. *Yes, give us those tickets, dammit.*

"So, I've never said anything about that before," Saban divulged, and this is the point in the rant where everyone knows what comes next is going to make ESPN's *SportsCenter*, or at least go viral on Facebook and Twitter.

"You know, when I first came here, they used to play that tradition-thing up there [videoboard], and everyone was cheering and excited and there was great spirit, aight, and now they don't even cheer."

Saban was referring to a video montage of Alabama football history that is played before the games. To be clear, the headspace where Saban berates his own fans, who are born into one of the poorest states in the country, and are taught from birth to love the Alabama Crimson Tide and all of its traditions, and then when they die maybe even bequeath a substantial amount of their life savings to the football team of a university they never attended, that boiling brain of competitive pyroclastic flow is a firepit of charred mastodon carcasses and forever smoldering crazy. This is not how a national championship is won. This is how the record-breaking seventh national championship for the greatest coach to ever do it was willed into existence during the worst pandemic in 100 years.

But there's more to come, of course. Iron sharpens iron, the players like to say inside Alabama's locker room, but it's also the crushing weight of the iron at the center of the world that sets all that geology to spinning.

"They introduce our players and nobody even cheers," Saban said, and then he caught himself because maybe he had gone too far by bringing up the players. Do y'all not understand what hell we put our players through just to find out who's going to start?

"So, um, I don't know," Saban said. "Maybe there's something else somebody ought to talk about. Maybe I shouldn't talk about it. Maybe I already talked about more than I should. So, y'all can beat me up for that if you want, but, look, our players work too hard, aight, and they deserve to have everything, and people supporting them, and have people supporting them in every way, and have tremendous spirit for what they've done, and they may not be able to continue to do it."

People passionate for their work appreciate when others take notice. Compromised people desperate to keep students in their seats to appease the angry God-Coach design a smartphone application to track students with Bluetooth technology during games and award more "Tide Loyalty Points" to those who stay for the fourth quarter so they can be eligible for postseason tickets. Yep, that happened for the 2019 season after this 2018 meltdown by Saban.

"We're going to work hard to try to continue that, um, but, there's a part of it that other people need to support them, too, and there's got to be a spirit that makes it special to play here because that's what makes it special to be here, and if that's not here, does it continue to be special to be here or not?"

The recorded attendance for the victory against Louisiana-Lafayette was 101,471.

"That's the question everybody's got to ask, and I'm asking it right now. So, um, I'm hopeful that—we've always had great people travel on the road with us, and had great spirit on the road, and we've got great fans, so I appreciate that, but to see half the student section not full, I've never seen that since I've been here before."

Aight?

With those 387 ranting words, Saban kicked open the door to bringing back the song about sex in the bed of a pickup truck. New York has the Statue of Liberty. Colorado has the Rocky Mountains. The Yellowhammer State's towering beacon of American pride is Alabama and Auburn football. Roll Tide and War Eagle.

To keep students in their seats for Saban's second-half tooth extractions, Alabama athletics director Greg Byrne convinced enough of the puritans up in their gilded party boxes that "Dixieland Delight" needed a revival. Byrne even made a PSA-style video about it featuring Terry Saban, the wife of the coach, star Alabama running back Damien Harris, and SGA president Price McGiffert.

"We're going to do our part here and try this one more time, so we need you to do yours," Byrne said in the video, perhaps in the spirit of Pee-wee Herman trying to convince a band of alcoholic pirates to pay him money for moonshine from the Playhouse, and hold those bottles of devil-water in their fists, and raise them to the moon, but then never taste a drop.

"There's nothing like college football: the band, the cheerleaders, the students, the fans, the big rivalries, the traditions," Terry Saban said. "We're proud to invite everyone to Bryant-Denny Stadium, and happy to bring back this other tradition, 'Dixieland Delight.' Let's do it right."

On October 13, 2018, the fiddle-playing ballad to hillbilly sex returned to Bryant-Denny Stadium, but with a prophylactic. They dubbed in "Beat Auburn" and other nonsense to drown out the students' callbacks of Southern graffiti. In proper honor of those long-haired Alabama country boys from up in Fort Payne, and the rum-drunk lyrical vandals who scream even louder now to overcome the stadium's speakers, here are the forbidden words to Alabama's version of "Dixieland Delight." Pass them all down to future generations, and may they all be conceived in metaphorical sheltered coves of Appalachian mountain laurel.

> Spend my dollar (ON BEER),
> Parked in a holler 'neath the mountain moonlight (ROLL
>   TIDE),
> Hold her up tight (AGAINST THE WALL),
> Make a little lov'n (ALL NIGHT),
> A little turtle dov'n on a Mason-Dixon night (FUCK
>   AUBURN),
> Fits my life (AND LSU), oh so right (AND TENNESSEE,
>   TOO),
> My Dixieland Delight.

This is the stuff that makes modern SEC football the economic engine for entire universities and the states they occupy. This is what the tuition buys like a ticket to the party. Game days on SEC campuses are absurd, grotesque heaven-scapes of hedonistic beauty wearing miniskirts and cowboy boots. College football is American bloodlust played by unpaid gladiators, and game days in the Deep South are the feasts before the altars of decadence. Saban sells it by the ring, and Gallettes by the 16-ounce collectible plastic cup.

The Yellow Hammer—and if you call it the "Yellow Hammer Alabama Slammer," so help me Sweet Home Lynyrd Skynyrd Saban Halloween Birthday Party Vampire, I, the author of this degenerate's COVID-fogged gamble of cabin-fevered, pandemic Southern shenanigans, will track you down with a pack of 18 underfed Catahoula Leopard Curs, force narcotics under your eyelids, and make you watch reruns of the 1992 Sugar Bowl—is the perfect drink for innocent kids who grew up on country roads in places like Autauga County, Alabama, or learned about the world through the filter of an insulated reality in the suburbs of Birmingham, Atlanta, Houston, or Dallas. If those pristine pups are the offspring of Alabama fans, then they imagined their whole lives about going to "The University," singing "Rammer Jammer Yellowhammer give 'em hell, Alabama," and maybe finding life-long companionship in sorority houses that over the last decade have started to all look a lot like mansions from *Gone With the Wind*.

This is how higher education is marketed in the land of obscene student debt, and the home of a system that really never wants it to be reformed. It wasn't the fault of the teenagers that they wanted to party when they all got to college in the summer of 2020. How can those students possibly be blamed for anything after arriving at the promise of their dreams, and their parents' dreams before them, and after having their senior years of high school abruptly ended because of the coronavirus?

They shouldn't have been, but they were, and the adults in charge set the stage for the scapegoating before the first can of black-cherry-flavored White Claw was ever cracked.

CHAPTER 2

GROG MUTINY OF THE UNREAD

No one will ever admit this, but in the summer of 2020 "covering thine ass" was the playbook in Alabama so students could return to campuses during the pandemic. If at some point in 2020 there was a sense that the SEC wasn't going to play football because of the pandemic, then it was unfounded conjecture based upon that Trumpian catchphrase that probably contributed to more deaths of Americans during the COVID-19 than any other social factor: fake news.

Regardless of what anyone ever reported, they were playing football in the SEC with or without anyone else in the country. The conference's decision to close ranks and play regular-season schedules of 10 intra-conference games was to ensure that no matter what happened around the country in the other leagues, the SEC football teams were going to line up on Saturdays in the fall of 2020. When the SEC made "It just means more" the league's slogan in 2016, buddy, they weren't kidding around. That's the red-ass truth, and could be the title of this book. Unintentional or not, the SEC's biting commentary of itself and the Deep South might be the most honest thing it ever said. College football, in other words, means more than pretty much everything.

And that includes entrenched political ideologies that reach back before the Civil War and have shaped history in the South every step of the way. They might vote red in Shelby County and blue in Jefferson, but when it comes to football everyone moves in the same direction and with SEC speed.

In 2020, the state of Alabama left no doubt when it pulled off a feat of organized social health care that would impress systematization experts in the People's Republic of China.

On short notice, Alabama, which proudly celebrates its middle-finger, yellowhammered state motto of "We dare defend our rights," planned and executed a most remarkable government-sponsored and government-mandated logistical triumph that helped clear the way for a return of SEC football. While U.S. Senate candidate Tommy Tuberville (R), a former Auburn football coach, was on the campaign trail telling Alabamians it should be their God-given right to refuse the wearing of masks in public, the governor of the state, Kay Ivey (also Republican; also pro-Auburn), took part of the $1.9 billion given to Alabama for the CARES Act and directed the state to test everyone registered to attend an Alabama college or university in the fall of 2020. The University of Alabama at Birmingham, the University of Alabama System's internationally renowned regional medical center in the state's largest city, was put in charge of the enormous task. From UAB's website announcing the news:

> The sheer scale of the GuideSafe Entry Testing initiative is staggering. Part of the multi-tool GuideSafe platform— a partnership between UAB and the Alabama Department of Public Health that has received more than $30 million in CARES Act funding from Gov. Kay Ivey—Alabama's GuideSafe Entry Testing is the largest higher-education testing initiative in the nation.

The testing is free—and required—for any student attending a public or private four-year college in Alabama and all two-year college students who reside on campus. That is more than 200,000 students, who will be tested at 15 locations around Alabama—in addition to thousands of out-of-state students, who will use at-home collection kits mailed to their homes.

They did it, too.*

The idea to test every college student in Alabama was hatched in May by the Birmingham-based company Event Team Bruno during a conference call with medical experts at UAB, state officials, and other key administrators. ETB runs and operates sporting events around the country, including football game days at Alabama and UAB. The large-scale event planner deserves some credit for saving college football, in other words. Their plan saved hundreds if not thousands of jobs around the state, and maybe the entire season.

Now, did the tests keep COVID-19 off campus? No, of course not, but that wasn't the point. At best it was for metering out the spread. A completely cynical person might call the $30 million emergency project superficial spackling to cover over cracks in the wall of a house with a compromised foundation. Should it have happened at all and was it a waste? See, that's a missing-the-point question for liberal reductionists who don't understand the Deep South. For poor states below the Mason-Dixon Line, state universities are some of the biggest economic engines, and college football, without question, is too big to fail. The progressive takeaway, for those familiar with Alabama's history of division and grinding obstructionism, was that in a window of little more than a few weeks, the state of Alabama

---

* If only vaccines would have been such a priority a year later.

proved to the world and itself that, yes, it can actually get together and accomplish an enormously challenging task for the health and benefit of the state.

Can't have college football without students on campus.

With the state of Alabama aggressively committed to opening schools in the fall, the rest of the SEC pushed forward with their own plans for the return of students. Reopening campuses wasn't just about football, of course, but to understand the reckless demand for the sport in the Deep South, the lengths that Alabama went through to ensure a season of college football don't properly frame the maddening addiction to the game. In high schools throughout the state, they practiced football and played games throughout the summer and fall without any required testing. In some places, the football coaches were pressured to field teams even when schools were physically closed to prevent the spread of COVID-19. Don't blame the coaches who supported playing, either. In reality, they didn't have a choice. It was the cowardice or stubbornness—or both—of Alabama's elected state and local officials, boards of education members, and leaders at the Alabama High School Athletic Association who put players, coaches, families, and vulnerable communities at risk. Steve Savarese, the executive director of the AHSAA, had a tough year if he attended all of the funerals of Alabama high school coaches who died during the pandemic. He did not.*

How does something like that happen? Football in the South is deeply tied to state and local politics, and no one wanted to be the elected official who canceled the season. High school coaches throughout the state contracted COVID-19, and many were hospitalized and died. To understand the scope of tragedy in Alabama

---

* After allowing sports to be played without testing in 2020, Savarese announced his retirement on April 21, 2021.

during the height of the pandemic, eight employees of Montgomery Public Schools died over a two-month span between November 2020 and January 2021. Montgomery's Robert E. Lee High School lost assistant football coach Dwayne Berry on January 18, 2021, after he was admitted to the hospital for symptoms related to COVID-19. He was 65, a veteran of the Air Force, and had coached former Alabama star Henry Ruggs III. Multi-sport coach DeCarlos Perkins of Montgomery's Park Crossing High School died two days later. He was 36. Robert E. Lee assistant principal Ennis McCorvey III and Robert E. Lee basketball coach Rodney Scott also died during the pandemic. When Ruggs scored touchdowns at Alabama—and he had 25 over three seasons before leaving school early for the 2020 NFL Draft—he would hold up a three-finger salute to Scott's son, Rod, who was Ruggs's best friend in high school and died in a car accident on March 4, 2016, of their senior year.

Would fewer educators have died in Alabama and around the Deep South during the pandemic with better leadership? It's a fair question that many families throughout the region will ask themselves long after anniversaries marking the COVID-19 pandemic are forgotten.

On July 7, 2020, the White House held a summit on education during the pandemic and UA System chancellor Finis "Fess" St. John IV (peach of a name) was on the task force. Trump asked St. John directly, "Will Alabama be playing some great football? What's going on with Alabama?"

"Mr. President, that's not the first time we've heard that question, I can promise you," said St. John, who was rewarded by the room with laughter. "We are planning to play the season at the University of Alabama. We understand that creates great difficulties and complexities and we're hoping for that. It's important to a lot of people. We'll do our best on that one."

By that point, the state of Alabama was already committed to its sophisticated testing scheme to get everyone back on campus and, in turn, help the SEC guarantee a season. Students were apparently doing their part, too. One week before that meeting in Washington, St. John and everyone else in the country was made aware of kids in Tuscaloosa throwing "COVID parties" to spread the disease. Tuscaloosa city councilor Sonya McKinstry said students were putting "money in a pot," and then trying to get COVID-19. That tall tale made national news because Tuscaloosa, due to the local college football team's national popularity, is always under the microscope.

"Whoever gets COVID first gets the pot," McKinstry said. "It makes no sense. They're intentionally doing it."

Those particular rumors proved to be either false or exaggerated, but of course students were getting together for parties during the summer. There wasn't anything else to do except drink and make TikToks while their parents went down dark-web spider holes of spent and wasted lives tricked into thinking their regret was righteous rebellion. It was just preliminary crapulence of the grossly selfish bacchanalia to come, and Alabama knew it was going to be a mess. The university had been carefully designing the festival of their own demise for decades.

Here's what St. John said in an interview with AL.com on August 3, 2020:

The worst result would be after all of this work and this system, which is so comprehensive, if faculty and students and staff don't do their part, then it will have been for nothing and we will not be successful. So, we are asking and imploring for everyone's participation, and everyone's support, and for everybody to do their part. And if that happens, it will be successful.

Yeah, shit was fucked from Day One because Day One on the college calendar is always Bid Day.

———

At Alabama, Bid Day is one of the most anticipated (and photographed) events on campus every year. That's the day freshmen race around learning which sorority wants them to be a part of their special society. (Talk about text chains from hell.) At its core, Bid Day is the culmination of a rigorous social experiment to figure out who's going to hold your hair like an angel when you're drunk and puking in a toilet in the Flora-Bama bathroom on spring break. It's also like a competition for friends, according to information acquired through extensive reporting on the subject (my sister).

As sorority girls squeal and run and dance and act like they've won the lottery, everyone else pretty much watches and enjoys the show. It's a curious custom, but one that is highly organized and celebrated with the seriousness of a wedding day.

Crazy thing about the sorority and fraternity scene at Alabama: Since the success of Saban's football teams, Greek life at the University of Alabama, according to the university's literature, "has held the coveted honor of being the largest fraternity and sorority community in the nation with regard to overall fraternity and sorority membership."

Alabama says over 10,000 students are members of 66 "social Greek-letter organizations." That's a lot of rum, in other words.

Smartly, the University of Alabama has spent over $200 million on upgrading its sorority mansions since 2013. The old Phi Mu house, for example, was completely demolished and replaced with a $13 million monument to gilded American swag. It's now 39,444 square feet of "this is what football pays for, fools." The white mega-mansion, which houses close to 70 Phi Mu sorority sisters, has a triple stack of rounded porticoes buttressed by four three-story Corinthian columns.

It's a "Greek-style revival," y'all, so don't call it antebellum. That's not the university's official language, but it's close. More accurately, it's a real-life fantasy dollhouse for kids who want to be close to the greatest football team in the country and the college dive bar one block over. The sorority mansion sits on the corner of Colonial Drive and Paul W. Bryant Drive, and out beyond the tri-level porches and across the street is the stadium where the college football team that has only lost one game since the new Phi Mu house opened in 2016 plays. That was the game Trump cursed with his attendance. In every other season since, Alabama has played for a national championship.

The Phi Mu house is one of many sorority mansions that have helped brand and market an ecosystem of national success for the University of Alabama. It's not all Saban and his players, in other words. Alabama's strategic panhellenic push deserves credit, too, and that's the foundation of generational wealth that will keep Alabama rolling long after Saban is gone. The children of those sorority girls and frat boys will also go to Alabama, and everyone will come back to Tuscaloosa time and again for Saturdays in the fall. Before their game days are all over, they'll donate large sums of cash to the university that shaped their lives.

Let's be real for a minute, though. The mansions are ridiculous. Like, right there on the edge of OMFG GTHO extra AF.

Fortress Phi Mu has white marble floors inside the white grand foyer, which, of course, featured a grand piano when it opened. High above the piano is a chandelier bought at auction that, according to the sorority, is from the Waldorf Astoria hotel in New York circa sometime in the 1930s. This author calls bullshit on that, but whatever. Author Kathryn Stockett, the Alabama graduate famous for the novel *The Help*, was a Phi Mu back in the day. She's from Mississippi, bless her heart, but in a twist only people in Alabama might fully appreciate because of a football game, actress Octavia Spencer, an Auburn grad, won an Oscar in 2012 for her role in the film adaption of Stockett's book. Spencer is from Montgomery, and graduated from a high school that the Montgomery County Board of Education defiantly named Jefferson Davis High School when it opened in 1968 because the federal government forced the new school's integration from its inception.

Oh, it's a nasty history, that one, but just another metaphorical middle finger from the Yellowhammers. Jefferson Davis, by the way, also ended up in Alabama by way of Mississippi. More than likely, he would have opposed federal aid for testing all Alabama college students so football could be played. He also was a noted coward who couldn't hold his rum, and that's a true story of American drunk history. Davis was fingered as a delinquent hoodlum for his role in the Grog Mutiny of Christmas 1826 on the campus of the U.S. Military Academy, but wasn't expelled like some of the other cadets who would later become principal Confederates in the American Civil War.

The Grog Mutiny, also known as the Eggnog Riot, was just a little sedition committed by some entitled shits who thought the rules didn't apply to them. Imagine: Twenty West Point cadets were court-martialed. Davis was not because, despite an already poor reputation at the academy and a role in the mutiny, he couldn't hold his liquor and apparently passed out before everything escalated and a faculty member was fired upon. Many of the participants in the Grog Mutiny, whether they were expelled or not, later led the Confederate States Army in the Civil War. This sidebar in drunk American history just goes to show the reckless and insane shit that college kids will do to drink rum.

And also it is an excuse to call Jefferson Davis a cunt.

———

On Bid Day 2020 for the University of Alabama, right at the very beginning of the fall semester when uncertainty was the hour, and fear of losing football was being measured out by the minute, hundreds and hundreds of sorority sisters lined up outside of Gallettes for Yellow Hammers despite bids being emailed. Gallettes even opened early on that day of days. It was so desperately important for everyone to be there, in fact, that pretty much everyone forgot to bring their pandemic masks. The debutantes risked spreading COVID-19 to all of their mansions and throughout campus for the most basic of reasons: good memories in bad times. They paid for their ticket, and no plague was going to spoil their fun. Gallettes had commemorative plastic cups made for Bid Day, and every freshman simply had to have one for a keepsake.

The standard Gallettes goblet for their signature drink is yellow with Roll Tide red script. It's like a boozy mustard-and-ketchup look, but an iconic color combination nonetheless for Alabama's All-Americans of all-nighters on The Strip. It's not uncommon for Alabama grads who later marry to use the motif for their own Yellow Hammer commemorative cups at receptions. It's also well understood around Tuscaloosa that cups from Gallettes are standard in all cabinets. For the kiddos, they're like fine china that displays street cred. When Alabama wins a national championship in football, Gallettes celebrates the achievement with a commemorative cup and Alabama grads throughout the country pay for them to be shipped.

On Bid Day 2020, the line of new sorority girls (and plenty of boys, too) for Gallettes was especially long because of social distancing guidelines. It carried down The Strip, and attracted a crowd of onlookers. At least one football player was there, but offensive lineman Chris Owens didn't want a cup. He just wanted to report a potential super-spreader event as any thoughtful double graduate in journalism and sports administration would. The majority of people weren't wearing masks, in violation of the statewide order, and Owens called them out on social media. A few months later, the redshirt senior would be Alabama's starting center for the 2021 College Football Playoff national championship game, and his team would allow Gallettes to sell thousands of new commemorative cups, but on Bid Day 2020 he was just thinking about saving the football season. Fall practice was scheduled to begin the very next day.

"How about we social distance and have more than a literal handful of people wear a mask?" Owens wrote on Twitter. "Is that too much to ask Tuscaloosa?"

The two primary institutions of college life at the country's preeminent university for pageantry and pride were squared off against each other on the first weekend of school. Owens's photograph of the blocks-long line set Tuscaloosa aflame. Everyone blamed the students and the beloved college dive bar, but were they really at fault? No. The bar was following the rules, and the students had all been told by social media that COVID-19 was a hoax that didn't affect young people. The tension in Tuscaloosa that day was higher than at any point during the pandemic, and that includes the fourth quarter against Florida in the SEC championship game. Alabama athletics director Greg Byrne took to Twitter in a plea for students to simply wear masks, and he used football as the motivation.

"Who wants college sports this fall? Obviously not these people," Byrne wrote. "We've got to do better than this for each other and our campus community. Please wear your masks."

Byrne would later contract the coronavirus during the football season, and called it "not a lot of fun." Behind the scenes, his leadership helped put the football and men's basketball teams in position to both win SEC championships during the pandemic and go 30–2 combined against conference opponents. More important, he oversaw the fevered completion of Alabama's renovated football stadium during the summer of 2020. That was a viral-loaded cluster perhaps worse than anything else the entire year, but those multimillion-dollar suites, pre-sold to corporations and the obscenely rich, had to be finished on time.

Byrne didn't have the toughest job in Tuscaloosa during the pandemic, though. Unquestionably, that was the mayor of the city, Walt Maddox (D), who was born and raised on the Crimson Tide, attended Central High, and then played college football up the road at UAB. More than anyone, Maddox was the guy responsible for protecting students from themselves, working with businesses that had to make money off of students, and, above all, doing whatever necessary to prevent the football team and its season from being compromised.

And all during an election year.

Maddox had the political cachet for the job after leading Tuscaloosa through its worst days. He was the young mayor during the monstrous April 2011 tornado that killed 65 people in Tuscaloosa and Birmingham. In 2018, he ran for governor against Kay Ivey (R), and lost in a landslide, but he was still a popular figure before the pandemic. In August 2019, he was promoted to senior fellow for the Program on Crisis Leadership at Harvard University's Kennedy School of Government. That's probably ponderous weighty stuff up there in Boston, but nothing prepares a politician for Bid Day during a pandemic when all the kids want to do is stand in line for rum drinks and get wrecked.

"Why?" Maddox asked rhetorically on Twitter in reply to the post by Alabama's athletics director.

Tuscaloosa's mayor had already declared a state of emergency for the city before students returned to campus. He used that authority to reduce the capacity of restaurants and bars to 50 percent, but that only put more students outside for the world to ridicule on social media.

"We are desperately trying to protect the city," Maddox said. "We are trying to have a college football season.

"Wearing a mask and social distancing is not much to ask for to protect yourself, your family, your friends, [DCH Regional Medical Center,] and the jobs of thousands of people."

It was an impassioned bit of political preparation for the inevitable. The time had come to start fining students and others in Tuscaloosa for not wearing masks. That night, police issued 12 citations, and arrested four, but none of that changed a thing. COVID-19 poured through campus, and especially the sorority and fraternity houses, over the next two weeks. There was only one thing left to do, and Nick Saban apparently had to be the guy to say it out loud: All of these piss-stained, rum-drunk mutineers must be stopped with martial law.

"I think democracy is great, and I think people who have all these freedoms, I think that's all great," Saban said. "But I think there's one thing that's probably a common denominator that really makes all that work, and that's that people have great moral integrity in the choices and decisions that they make.

"I'm not criticizing anybody here but a lot of people have asked that we wear masks when we're in public—when we're in crowds, when we're in large groups of people, that we keep social distanced. I don't think they're doing it just for the heck of it. I think there's a reason for it. We're trying to control the spread of this disease."

Saban, to his credit, appeared in several PSAs about wearing masks, including a cute skit with Alabama mascot Big Al. None of it helped. The University of Alabama reported over 1,000 new cases of COVID-19 on campus through the first two weeks of the fall semester. The students were back in Tuscaloosa, and no amount of levelheadedness from the olds was going to keep the frosh from their greenhorn grog. That was the prize all along for studying so thoroughly the SparkNotes of Macbeth for 12th-grade English. The university and the city had to have known all along that their plan was folly. "Was the hope drunk wherein you dressed yourself?" asked Lady Macbeth as she looked upon King Duncan as he slept. Come at the king, ya bes' not miss. Saban tried to play nice, but he wasn't going to let anything jeopardize a season for his players or the university. On August 24, Maddox shut down all the bars in Tuscaloosa for two weeks.

It's worth noting the thoughts of Gallettes co-owner Jeff Sirkin on Sunday night after Bid Day 2020 was all over. The distillation of Sirkin's 275-word post to Facebook: "Our industry is not the fall guy for any of this. 25,000–30,000 students showed up this weekend. Did you expect them to sit at home and read?"

Roll Tide.

And don't forget to tip your bartenders.

CHAPTER 3

FROM THE FLOOD

C hris Owens was the kid who just sat at home and read books. That's the most basic, elemental truth about all of 2020. There were the readers, and then there were the non-readers who did things like refer to journalists as the enemy of the state, and then refused to wear masks because they heard Tommy Tuberville say it was un-American. Both Americas were represented out on The Strip that mid-August day in 2020. There was the grog mutiny of the unread, and then there was Owens, the fifth-year backup center who took the photograph of the long line outside Gallettes in the hopes of saving his football season. He was only there at that crucial moment in time, putting his journalism degree to good use, after learning to read at three years old. That's how the story goes in the Owens house. If Chris Owens of two degrees and another coming in 2021 wasn't so smart so early, then who knows where he'd be? Back in New Orleans, he was reading books before anyone. This was before the big storm in 2005, and long before football was ever even introduced into his life.

But long damn lines of desperate people being where they are not supposed to be? Yeah, the Owens family, which is originally from the Lower Ninth Ward of pre-Katrina New Orleans, knows all about long damn lines on the news. All those old images of endless streams of cars fleeing New Orleans are burned into the Owens family tree like the scar from a lightning bolt. They left New Orleans the day of the hurricane with nothing, and they never went back because a little seven-year-old boy needed a school more than anything.

By second and third grades in Arlington, Texas, Chris Owens was so advanced for his age that his teachers had to give him busy work to keep him occupied because he finished all of his assignments in time to distract everyone else. He really never had homework either, according to his mom. He would finish it all before football practice, and was taking high school courses by middle school. That more than anything, says Sequin Owens, is what allowed her son to excel at football and gave him the opportunity to play at Alabama. It was all because Chris Owens read before anyone else, and by 11 years old he was falling asleep with his football team's playbooks. Not just the playbook for his assignments. No, he had the playbooks for every position on the offensive line, and he knew them all.

What makes the ultimate team during a pandemic? Smart players who know more than one position in case someone gets hurt or sick. Owens started the season as the backup center behind Landon Dickerson and backup left tackle behind Alex Leatherwood. He was recruited to Alabama as a guard. Senior DeVonta Smith started at receiver in 2020, but was also the backup return specialist to begin the season. In addition to that, he also practiced at defensive back in fall camp just in case. Sixth-year senior Josh McMillon was a backup linebacker and also platooned at fullback.

McMillon majored in mechanical engineering and then got an MBA. Owens had his bachelor's degree in journalism and creative media after three years, and earned his master's in sports administration after that. He made the dean's list all five years, served on the SEC leadership committee in 2020, and, probably for his skills as a journalist, was named to the All-SEC community service team, too. After returning for a sixth year of eligibility in 2021 due to the NCAA's COVID-19 eligibility waiver, he was scheduled to have his second master's degree, this one in marketing, before moving on to the NFL. He was a scout-team player or a backup for the large majority of five years. It's not like Owens wasn't any good. That's not how it is at Alabama, and that's why Alabama is different than any other team. The guy ahead of Owens in 2020 was an All-American, Rimington Trophy recipient for the best center in college football, black belt in karate, and an Eagle Scout. When Landon Dickerson injured his knee in the second half of the SEC championship game, it elevated Owens to permanent starter for the first time in his career. There were two more games left in his redshirt senior season.

Five years for two games? Some players who arrive as five-star prospects don't even get that. Redshirt senior linebacker Ben Davis of Gordo, Alabama, was a career backup. He committed to Alabama as the No. 1 inside linebacker prospect in the nation in 2016, and he's also the son of Alabama's all-time leading tackler. Wayne Davis, also of Gordo, had 327 tackles from 1983 to 1986. In 2020, Wayne's son, who was listed at 6-foot-4 and 250 pounds, was the second-string strong-side linebacker behind redshirt junior Christopher Allen of Baton Rouge, who waited four years to play.

Why would someone so good at their craft, with only a finite amount of time to perform it for free in the hopes of one day maybe cashing in, wait that long for the hope of an opportunity? The answer isn't complicated. It's a risk, sure, but after Saban's decade of dominance in college football, his players know that the percentage of their future success in the inherently risky business of pro football favors only starting one year at Alabama as opposed to three someplace else. In 2020, Alabama had 53 players on active NFL rosters after the final cuts of fall camp. Months earlier, nine Tide players were drafted from the team's failed 2019 season. Only LSU had more with 13. Failed, of course, is a relative term for Alabama. The Crimson Tide lost two games, and missed the College Football Playoff for the first time since its 2015 inception.

That's the raw, twisting irony of Alabama's empire of excess built upon the Crimson Tide. It takes remarkable young people of rare, inspiring courage and ability to keep the machine humming year after dominant year so that the party never ends, donations never stop, the future Hall of Fame coach keeps winning, and the out-of-state money of the affluent continues to pour into the bars after leaving the games early. It all relies on players like Owens, who are career backups waiting for something that's not guaranteed and might never arrive when all along they could transfer anywhere, like Tennessee, for example, and play immediately. That kind of desire takes ultra-competitive people who like to point out rather frequently that "Alabama isn't for everyone."

No, seriously, the players at Alabama say that shit all the time to build the mystique, and it's the first thing they all tell the five-star recruits who might never play. It's a brilliant bit of psychology, but Saban is always recruiting.

The players absolutely do not tell the recruits about Gallettes on Saturday nights after games, though. Saban hires other people to do that.

Is the success of Alabama football and the importance of the sport throughout higher education a sickness or part of the cure? For all of major college football's inherent corruption—and it runs the sport to the point of covering up criminality on all American college campuses—the entertainment enterprise that makes billions of dollars for everyone else while unpaid athletes trade hits for an education still breaks toward positive change and growth. Education still changes lives despite what cynical sportswriters might tell you on Twitter.

"Momma is a nerd," Sequin Owens said, "and I say that because I always focused on education, and to be honest I just knew he was born with three strikes. He was born Black, he was born a man, and he was born poor. To give my child a fighting chance in this world he was going to need an education. Sports is a 50/50 shot. Education is 100 percent as far as him having any kind of chance in this world at success."

It's a 50/50 chance that all competitive sports end before the 13th birthdays of little Jane and Johnny Narp,* but Sequin Owens makes a solid point nonetheless. Critical cognitive development for children begins a few weeks after birth. To make their infant son a quick phonetical learner, Sequin and husband Paul made a "conscious effort" to never use "baby talk" with Chris. In addition to reading to their son from birth, they also gave him a computer designed for small children to keep him entertained. The computer's only games were educational and helped teach him the alphabet. A New Orleans–based Head Start program at three years old challenged him to keep up with older kids. They were reading at four and five years old, and Chris was beginning to read at three.

"I truly believe this was and is the foundation as to why he majored in journalism," Sequin said.

So much else that Sequin couldn't control, however, put her son on a path to Alabama.

------

* Narp is an acronym for Non-Athletic Regular Person or Normal-Ass Regular Person commonly used by college athletes when referring to students or others who are not college athletes.

Chris Owens wasn't supposed to be a football player at all, the way his mother tells it, but football in Texas saved them when they didn't really have anything else.

How did Owens find his way inside the assembly line of Alabama football to position himself as one of the most important personalities and role players on Saban's team of teams? It started with a long car ride out of New Orleans on the day Hurricane Katrina hit the city. Not the day before. No, Momma was a nerd, but she wasn't a weather nerd like ol' Nick Saban. The Owens family left New Orleans the day Katrina swamped the city and turned it into one of the worst natural disasters the United States has ever seen. Chris Owens's personal success during a historic 2020 college football season defined by hardships was born from another historic national tragedy.

Fate, y'all. It's a dark snake of water that carries to the Gulf. It can be tamed by the hands of men, but sometimes the black-throated wind blows and the raindrops swell and the snake jumps and bends and changes the course of the river.

Following Alabama's 2020 national championship season, Chris Owens was presented with a ceremonial proclamation by the city council of Arlington, and mayor Jeff Williams naming February 9, 2021, as "Chris Owens Day." Arlington is where Owens ended up after the evacuation of New Orleans, and then in Arlington he stayed. One of those sprawling suburbs between Dallas and Fort Worth, it is the proud blue-collar municipality of the Dallas Cowboys and their monument to football, AT&T Stadium. Great place to watch a game. Alabama has the best winning percentage of any team that has ever played at Jerry World because Alabama has never lost there—5–0 all-time with a combined average margin of victory against Michigan, Wisconsin, Michigan State, Southern Cal, and Notre Dame of 29.2 points (197–51).

That last game, Alabama vs. Notre Dame, was a turn in the untamable river that pointed an unprecedented 2020 college football season toward something mythical for Alabama's backup center.

This is almost too unbelievable to be true, but the currents of courage and a life shaped by will to succeed converged in December 2020 when the always hopeful Owens was promoted to starting center for the first and only ever Rose Bowl played in Owens's adopted hometown. Because of COVID-19 restrictions in California, the College Football Playoff semifinal that was supposed to be played in Pasadena was, at the last possible moment, moved to AT&T Stadium. That meant that the displaced New Orleanian, after a spring and summer of upheaval and change, made his debut as Alabama's permanent starting center—physically, spiritually, and symbolically in the middle of it all—in the displaced Granddaddy of Them All, the Rose Bowl.

After all that he had been through, Owens was headed back to the place where it had all begun.

The city proclamation inspired by Alabama 31, Notre Dame 14 christened Owens as a hometown hero, but that sure as hell wasn't how he showed up in town late on the night of August 29, 2005.

The Owens family arrived in Arlington that day suddenly homeless and with nothing. Or was it early in the day on August 30? For Sequin Owens, the evacuation all runs together, and remains a blurry memory of trauma she had to bury away.

She remembers her father, James Price, making the late decision to board up his home in the Lower Ninth Ward. It didn't save the house, but maybe it saved their lives. They had to go, Dad said, and at that point the only place to go was north. According to estimates, between 80 and 90 percent of New Orleans evacuated the city before Hurricane Katrina made landfall. The Owens family was among those who got out, but Sequin says it was close. As a general rule, the people of New Orleans don't leave the city for storms. Instead, they usually do things like have parties and then hunker down. Sequin went out with a friend the night before Katrina, but when she got home she saw the "big red ball" on the television screen bearing down on her world. James Price had lived through Hurricane Betsy, a Category 4 storm that inundated the historic Lower Ninth Ward on the evening of September 9, 1965. He knew this one was different, and his wisdom might have saved his family. Most certainly, it set his grandson on a course for greatness.

But the river to get there was wild.

———

The Lower Ninth Ward started flooding around 10 a.m. on August 29. It didn't take long. Katrina was a Cat 5 storm, but the heavy winds were east of the city. At first, people thought New Orleans was spared the worst of it. It was, in fact, but a catastrophic storm surge in the Mississippi River–Gulf Outlet Canal caused 20 levee breaches, and then a cascading network of failures along canals, shipping channel levees, and floodwalls put most of New Orleans underwater. The Industrial Canal ruptured in two places along the Lower Ninth Ward, and rushing floodwaters picked up homes and threw them off their foundations. A barge—a whole big-ass river barge—was swept through one of the breaches and into the neighborhood. Some places were under 18 feet of water.

Sequin, Paul, and Chris Owens were in evacuation traffic for over 24 hours. They had to leave Sequin's Mitsubishi Eclipse in

New Orleans, and it was destroyed. Their getaway car was a silver Ford Taurus that inched up to I-20 in Mississippi, and then west.

"Eventually we pulled over at a rest stop," Sequin said. "Paul is exhausted and Chris is crying. It was somewhere before Canton. I remember Canton. People were sleeping on the floor. Tons of people. Just on the ground. I understand why they called us refugees, but I hated that term because I'm from this country."

Sequin remembers Canton, Texas, because that's where she broke down and cried. It wasn't because she was scared. Yes, she was frightened. They left New Orleans with nothing, thinking they were going to turn around after the hurricane and go home, and now, hours later, they were homeless. The tears weren't because of that, though. She doesn't tell this story often because it's too painful, but a stranger bought her family dinner in a packed diner there in Canton, and she sobbed because of the kindness. They also had finally reached Paul's sister on the phone, and learned where they were in Texas. Dallas wasn't too far from Canton. The worst day of their lives was almost over. When they finally arrived in Arlington, there were 14 people in a two-bedroom apartment.

"We had nothing," Sequin said. "I remember getting clothing for Christopher at the shelter downtown, and eating food at the mission."

The Lower Ninth Ward has never fully recovered from Hurricane Katrina, but most of the Owens family moved back to New Orleans in the weeks and months after the storm. For Sequin it wasn't that simple. There was no going back after that. Paul moved home and sent money, but Chris's education was too important. They weren't leaving Arlington, and so many thousands of children of New Orleans displaced by Hurricane Katrina never went back either. Rivers bend and break and move, but they don't reverse their course. Parents raised in New Orleans with so much love for that special city weren't about to lose anything else to the greedy snake of dirty water that forever flows out to the sea. Sequin found an apartment around the corner, and then Chris found football.

———

Alabama's offense to begin the 2020 college football season featured 11 starters from eight different states and a receiver from the Canadian province of Ontario who was born in Taiwan, lived in Ghana, and prepped in Maryland and New Jersey. Talent alone does not carry a person down that path. It takes something else, embedded and instinctive. Primal strength to succeed. Oddly enough, it would be the unteachable football instincts for someone who caught passes on Saban's "best team" to later make the most important tackle in the most difficult game. John Metchie, the international receiver of one very savage hit in the 2020 SEC championship game, got into football because his brothers enjoyed the sport, and then he moved around the United States to pursue playing the game at an elite level. The paths to Alabama are all different, in other words, but what keeps players there is a universal characteristic that forms unbreakable bonds. It's the competitive pursuit of excellence measured against the best in the country, and the sacrifice it takes to make everyone a better form of themselves.

"Coming to Alabama as a grad-transfer, it's a quick turn-around," said Landon Dickerson, who began his career at Florida State. "Luckily, I was surrounded by a phenomenal group of guys—a phenomenal team—and staff that embraced me ever since I got here, so I couldn't ask for much more. Really it's about coming in and competing, and it doesn't matter whether I was a grad-transfer, a freshman.

"Anybody that comes here, you're competing against some of

the best athletes in the country at the collegiate level, so I think that's the biggest thing. You just have to accept the competition and be ready for it."

That pressure forms uncommon leaders, and the greatest of all of them are guys like Chris Owens. He was not among those 11 starters in the beginning of the season, but he backed up two future All-Americans on the depth chart and could have played every position along the best offensive line in the country without it affecting anything at all except maybe making it better. His unwavering commitment to his teammates was the defining quality of the 2020 Alabama football Crimson Tide. Owens began playing football in Arlington as a form of therapy against depression after being displaced by Hurricane Katrina. He had the mental strength of a champion before he ever arrived at Alabama, but then his years in Tuscaloosa made him even stronger still. When starting center Landon Dickerson went down with his knee injury against Florida, Owens was ready to lead Alabama into the College Football Playoff, and it wasn't even a question. He had been leading from the back all season.

Here are Chris's prophetic words, which came not as a prelude to the College Football Playoff and Notre Dame, but on September 1, 2020, before the season even started. In the generation-defining summer of 2020, the first 24 hours of the ninth month was the day after Alabama's historic protest march for racial justice. For Alabama, that's when everything changed.

Said Owens:

We all want everyone to be successful. We're building depth, and depth is never a bad thing to have on a team. You want to have as many possible starters as you can on a team because you never know, especially in a year like this, if someone were to go down or get sick, we need as many bodies as we can.

I do believe over these last couple weeks we have come together, and we have more guys playing more positions than I've ever seen here, so as long as we continue to do that then I think we'll be just fine as a group up front.

Accurate.

Owens knew all those positions down cold, and could play every single one. The Texan was talking about players like redshirt junior Kendall Randolph of Madison, Alabama, who was a backup offensive lineman in 2020, and also a part-time starter at tight end. Really, though, Owens was talking about himself. Alabama returned four starters along the offensive line in 2020, and a brilliant mind backing them all up. Owens understands the game so completely that in 2019 he got in a little bit of trouble by his position coach for telling everyone the different mistakes they were making in practice. In the beginning, his mother didn't want him playing football, or any sports at all. But by the end, they all turn into their own individual versions of Nick Saban, perfectionists and disciples of a code that is gospel in the Mal Moore Athletic Facility and dictates even the smallest decisions: football above everything, and at all costs.

Get those damn masks up, Owens said to Tuscaloosa while the sorority girls waited in line for their yellow, rum-laced birthrights in a cup. Can anyone blame him for his passion on that infamous day outside Gallettes? Everything he had been given at birth had been washed away, and then, after he created a life for himself through school and football, he had already been waiting in his own line at Alabama for four years and preparing to do it for a fifth. In addition to that testament of perseverance, he also had already quarantined all spring back in Arlington without even knowing if Alabama would have a season. From the balcony of his mom's home, Chris could look out across the landscape of suburban North Texas and see AT&T Stadium. Months later, that very stadium was where he would make his heroic start for Landon Dickerson against Notre Dame.

"Landon is a hard guy to replace because of his leadership, his personality," Saban said before that last-minute Rose Bowl in Texas. "He's very inspirational in a lot of ways to all of his teammates. I don't know that you replace a guy like that, but we have confidence in Chris Owens."

———

This might be a little too inside baseball, but the Rose Bowl in Texas was so hurriedly thrown together that the Cotton Bowl folks who organized the game didn't have their press-box apparel for the game until the night before. The navy blue pullovers worn by the sports information staffers were one of a kind, with small logos of the Rose Bowl and Cotton Bowl side by side. They did an excellent job pulling everything together, and the limited-run commemorative merchandise from that game will no doubt be worth plenty in the years to come.

Someone definitely should send a couple posters and some merch to Chris Owens's mom. Of course she about cried all over everyone when her son took the field after everything they'd been through together.

When Dickerson went down against Florida in Atlanta's Mercedes-Benz Stadium, it was hard not to cry then, too. It was a freak injury, with his leg getting twisted underneath his big frame on a play that resulted in a 15-yard touchdown pass from quarterback Mac Jones to receiver DeVonta Smith. The score gave Alabama a 52–38 lead with 4:59 remaining in the game. Alabama won the *Dr Fucking Pepper* COVID-19 2020 SEC championship 52–46.

The final score was anticlimactic compared to the entire Alabama football team running onto the field to be by the side of their All-American center in what everyone thought at the time would be his final moments on a field in pads and a uniform for the Crimson Tide. The transfer from Florida State had given Alabama so much in his two years in Tuscaloosa, and he truly was a friend to all. Also, if we're being completely honest, Dickerson was the unofficial mechanic for all those shiny Dodge Chargers. Yeah, sorry for joking around during such a revered and sacred moment of Crimson Tide lore, but it's true. The Dodge Chargers driven by all the football players need oil from time to time. Anyway, Dickerson's knee injury was the most poignant moment of an emotional season, we can all agree, until the very last seconds of it all. That's when the Hollywood ending happened on the field of South Florida's Hard Rock Stadium.

Dickerson, being a general badass and a *literal* black belt in karate, was not going to go out on a cart. Daniel LaRusso was gonna fight, in other words. Dickerson, who refused to use crutches after his surgery, dressed for the national championship game in full pads and uniform against the advice of team trainers and doctors. He went through the warm-ups, too, serving as an extra shot of motivation for his brothers before kickoff. Chris Owens played the entire game, but at the very end of the final drive something special happened that no one in college football will ever forget. Dickerson asked Saban on the sideline for one play, and of course Mr. Miyagi said, "Hell fuck yeah get in there you crazy damn No. 69'd redneck."

Dickerson then gave Saban a bro-shake like he was about to go walking up into Gallettes on $1 beer night wearing cowboy boots and a straw hat he picked up at the Flora-Bama. Saban pointed to a referee and said, "Let this motherfucker in the game or I'll come over there and punch you in the throat. Landon Dickerson is a soldier of truth, aight?"

Maybe, or something like that. Print the legend. Gonna just have to assume everything Saban said on the 2020 sidelines in this here book. He was wearing a mask the entire time, so who's to say? We'll make do.

Dickerson bought himself two plays in Alabama's victory formation at the end of the national championship game. He jogged onto the field three weeks removed from surgery on his left anterior cruciate ligament, which, let's just also assume, had the doctors saying things through their masks, too. Chris Owens was the first player who realized Dickerson was on the field, and the former backup jumped into his buddy with a hug. They were so excited for each other. Owens slapped Dickerson on the helmet and then ran off the field. Next, redshirt senior tight end Miller Forristall strode through the pre-snap huddle, locked arms with Dickerson, and the two friends looked at each other like they agreed that the cowboy boots were a nice touch. Dickerson then gave guard Deonte Brown a hug with his right arm while simultaneously walking to left tackle Alex Leatherwood for an embrace. Guard Evan Neal was last on the love list, and then it was down in formation for the business of officially thanking *the* Ohio State University Buckeyes for making the trip to South Florida and helping Alabama complete a journey no other team will ever take again on the way to history.

Here's the real truth about the players of the Alabama football Crimson Tide in 2020, and their case for being the greatest football team of all time. When the sport and the country absolutely needed them most, they won that season before it ever started.

They came together over something so much more important, and they weren't losing after. Better by being different. Perfect by using all that to their advantage. Historic for capturing a flashpoint of American history in their fists, and then shaping it into art with the power that only young people with more love in their hearts than pain can create.

After the College Football Playoff was over, and Alabama was 13–0 following a college football odyssey that was a lens into America in so many important ways, Chris Owens went on Twitter to publicly thank Landon Dickerson for his role in making him a better football player. Their exchange should give us all hope.

"That's my brother, man," Owens wrote in reply to a video clip of Alabama's Cowboy Karate Kid running onto the field for the symbolic victory formations. "Landon has truly changed my life and I'm blessed to call him one of my best friends."

Dickerson's reply: "No sir, you have changed my life. I'm honored to be able to call you my Brother. Can't express how much I love and appreciate you big dog."

Words written as college football champions, but representing a friendship earned through the trust of something purer and perhaps harder to obtain, two lives changed through love. After the championship, and leading up to the 2021 NFL Draft, Landon Dickerson played the jester role when the time called for having fun, and people on the outside looking in loved him for that. There was something more there, though. His personality had a level of depth beyond the jokes and gags and the redneck-engineered truck bumper. The country-fried Carhartt overalls kid from Hickory, North Carolina, was willing to learn something when his "Brother" backing him up on the team said please listen. This is how change happens for the better.

Back on the penultimate day of May in 2020, with the country in flames after the murder of George Floyd by Minneapolis thug cop Derek Chauvin, Owens was hurting. He then made a promise that his teammates were going to help the journalism major keep. "Change is coming from this generation whether you like it or not," Owens cried out to the world on Twitter. "Enough is enough."

CHAPTER 4

THERE GOES SPRING

Almost every college kid in America went home for spring break in March 2020 and never went back to school. They then sat around on their couches and looked at their phones while the adults in the room went about the business of making an impossible problem so much worse. Major cities suffered first, and early tragedies at senior care facilities should have been enough to quarantine the entire country, but scoring political points seemed more important. Graduating high school seniors all got their degrees early, and then sat back and received a real American education.

The impact of the spreading coronavirus on sports happened suddenly. On Wednesday, March 11, 2020, French basketball player Rudy Gobert of the NBA's Utah Jazz tested positive for the coronavirus, and that news triggered the Great Canceling Event of American Sports. By the end of the next day, March 12, 2020, the games were officially done.

One thing remained, though. Spring football in the Southeastern Conference. Roll Tide.

Hashtag: It just means more.

Hashtag: Nick Saban was going to need it spelled out and put in writing because Alabama's first day of spring practice was scheduled for Friday, March 13, 2020, and Tennessee had already started on March 10, and if this coronavirus suspension—whatever in the hell that shit is—is going to fuck up spring ball for one team then it better be fucking up the spring for everyone, aight?

For the SEC, the men's basketball conference tournament imploded at Bridgestone Arena on March 12, and league commissioner Greg Sankey was there in Nashville dealing with it all. For the record, Arkansas 86, Vanderbilt 73 on Wednesday, March 11, was the final game of the winter sports season for the SEC. The next day, teams showed up to Bridgestone Arena, but there were never any games. Sankey finally made the call about an hour before the first game of the day. Alabama was set to play Tennessee at noon, but other teams were in the building as well. Kentucky was in the middle of a pre-tournament shootaround and players were told to stop practicing. Wildcats coach John Calipari didn't know what to do except phone his family from the court to see if everyone was safe. The walls of tunnels underneath the arena were decorated with life-sized graphics of players in the tournament, and as Alabama guard John Petty Jr. walked to the team bus he stopped to peel his own likeness off the wall as a keepsake.

A few minutes later, down the hall and next to the tournament's media center, Sankey held an emergency news conference and became the de facto voice of reason for college sports in America. He scribbled some notes onto a card and stepped onto the dais. From that moment until the start of football season, he was always a little more measured than any other commissioner or executive of college sports when it came to the disruption of football. Football for the SEC is too big to fail and shutting it down would have been a financial and cultural catastrophe. Months later, when NCAA president Mark Emmert released a statement saying it would be impossible to have college sports in the fall if students couldn't return to their campuses, SEC Network radio personality Paul Finebaum said Emmert was no more important to college football than Bozo the Clown and should be fired. If 2020 taught us anything about sports administration during a pandemic, it's that there were many clowns in the circus and they all had different tears painted on their faces. It's a tortured game of morality they perform on their stages, this theater of sincerely caring about athletes worth billions of dollars to leagues and universities whom everyone refuses to even consider paying because it will destroy their legalized form of human exploitation for a tax dodge.

That is to say, most of the people in charge of major, revenue-producing collegiate sports actually do have hearts and love their "student-athletes." Sankey is one of those people, and Saban is such a player's coach that he would probably just pay everyone at least $200,000 per season if he could. Alabama ain't lowballing, aight? Roll Tide.

It was heartbreaking, Sankey said inside Bridgestone Arena, that he had to end the dreams of the basketball players, and he meant those words. A former college athlete himself, he choked up and got emotional when recalling the 2008 SEC men's basketball tournament when a tornado hit the Georgia Dome during overtime of a game between Alabama and Mississippi State. Instead of canceling that event, Sankey managed to move the remainder of the tournament to nearby Georgia Tech. Improbably, the sixth-seeded University of Georgia went on to win the SEC tournament in their in-state rival's own gym, Alexander Memorial Coliseum. After the championship game, a jubilant Georgia player, trophy in hand and automatic bid to the NCAA Tournament secured, called it the greatest moment of his life. So Sankey cared about the athletes, and his recollection of that tornado tournament spoke to

something else important, too. Challenging times can push motivated young people to achieve things greater than themselves.

———

Pandemic Day One for the sports world was a tough one for many
college athletes whose careers were suddenly over. For business
leaders and administrators of college sports, Thursday, March 12,
2020, was like one catastrophe with many other even bigger problems fast approaching. Higher Ed's treasure galleon carrying all of
the tax-exempt, student-earned gold had been hit by one salvo, but
more cannonshot was already in the air. Football's total revenue
could not be lost. Sankey's tone altered course suddenly from sorrow to that droning lawyerese he has perfected so well when the
subject shifted to the real moneymaker. Representing the inter-
ests of belligerently devoted Southern folk who have built some of
the largest golden temples to the sporting gods the world has ever
seen will do that.

You canceled basketball, Greg, but what about spring football?
Incoming! Evasive maneuvers!

"I was on a conference call with one of our athletic departments where that was asked," Sankey said. "Our athletic director
talked about that afterwards. We've limited the size clearly of on
campus events, and campuses are doing that individually, but I
don't have a prescriptive list right now around what's going to happen with spring practice, spring football."

Completely cancel SEC spring football all higgledy-piggledy
just because a little international media hysteria over a pandemic
killed off basketball? Let's not get crazy here, aight? Greg Sankey,
who should probably be the national czar of collegiate athletics in
a perfect world devoid of pretense and bullshit bureaucracy, is, in

the end, just a highly paid roadie for the rock-and-roll band with a cult following of millions. Saban is the petulant golden god strutting onstage. The No. 1 rule of the help is that they are never allowed to look the talent in the eyes. Sankey instead put out a tweet the next day: "ALERT: The @SEC today announced that all organized team activities, including competitions, team and individual practices, meetings and other organized gatherings, will be suspended through Apr. 15. The SEC had previously announced all competition was suspended through Mar. 30." That Sankey had to clarify the SEC's verbiage at that critical hour of the pandemic speaks to the ultra-competitive nature of football in the league of the coach who never stops trying to gain an advantage.

If there is something that Nick Saban hates more than people wasting his time, then it is being surprised. He detests being caught off guard, which is not the same exact thing as failing to be prepared, but Saban makes little distinction. Everything in his world, down to the type of chewing gum he puts into his mouth, is highly organized, planned in advance, and orchestrated for maximum efficiency down to a logistical science. Swiss trains always run on time, and if the train is ever a couple minutes late then the government of Switzerland will give anyone who misses a connection free cups of Nescafé. Saban would fire the Swiss train operator, and then only travel via helicopter. This is the punctual aura that moves with him throughout his day-to-day, and it intimidates the hell out of the people who work for him or require his time. When Saban enters a room for an in-house media spot, everything must be ready hours before he walks through the door, and his handlers have been known to time sessions with stopwatches.

One of the hallmark traits of Alabama's coach is his willingness to adapt, but that does not mean he learns through trial and error. The team videographers who record practices cannot bring new technology onto the field unless it is pre-approved. Saban wouldn't allow drone cameras above his practices because he thought they would be a distraction. It took a videographer bringing a personal drone camera to Saban's lake house before he could be convinced that the tool would help his mission of conquering college football. In news conferences, a media assistant keeps a list of reporters who want to ask questions, and then they're called upon in order. There is a reason for this. It eliminates most pesky follow-up-question scenarios. As every reporter knows (or should know), a good interview isn't about the first question you ask, it's about the next one after that. There have been times on the Alabama beat when some reporters have been unofficially blackballed for asking the wrong questions. Too risky. Who knows what that guy is going to ask next? The process by which Saban wants his news conferences structured cuts down on the surprises.

The SEC announced in a tweet at 3 p.m. on Friday, March 13, 2020, that all organized team functions throughout the league were canceled because of the pandemic. At the Mal Moore Athletic Facility on the campus of the University of Alabama, Saban's first practice of the spring was scheduled to begin at 3:30 p.m. Those scoundrels. At that point in the offseason, it felt like the forces of the universe were conspiring to surprise him with one derailed train after another. First, his most loyal lieutenant, strength and conditioning coach Scott Cochran, deserted Alabama's players for Kirby Smart and Georgia during the middle of Saban's offseason workout sessions known as the "Fourth Quarter Program." Now this? What's next, no spring practice at all? For a neurotic man of structure, the beginning of the pandemic was like trying to gather confetti in the wind.

There were no confirmed cases of COVID-19 in Alabama that Thursday, March 12, but they were coming, and universities were preparing for a move to online classes and virtual learning. The University of Alabama released this convoluted message at 5:45 p.m.: "Student spring break is extended until March 30 as UA transitions to remote learning. After March 13, UA will extend spring break for students through March 29, to allow additional time for instructors to transition to alternative teaching resources." Huh? Auburn University had already made the decision to close its campus until April 10, but at that point Alabama's football coach still wanted his players back on campus by March 30.

It's easy to criticize Saban and his coaching brethren in hindsight, but remember this before getting all self-righteous *in your feels*. Who can really blame all of those obsessed football coaches in the SEC for hoping to salvage spring practice? After all, four SEC football coaches were fired during or after the 2019 season—Matt Luke (Ole Miss), Barry Odom (Missouri), Chad Morris (Arkansas), Joe Moorhead (Mississippi State)—and *four more* would be fired during or after the unprecedented season of 2020 despite it being played during a pandemic. Later that fall, the national media narrative going into the season was that all the coaches would be getting passes in 2020 because (a) pandemic, hello!, and (b) the financial calamity caused by said pandemic. Yeah, didn't happen. Criticize those coaches down in the SEC all you want, but it turns out they had reasons to be concerned about time lost for practice and training. Many of the wealthy football boosters who fund the SEC's nonstop hysteria, in the end, didn't care one bit about the unique challenges football during a pandemic presented to their schools' coaches. No spring football? So what. Recruiting via

Zoom? Deal with it. Somehow plan for fall camp on college campuses that are teeming with COVID-19? How hard is it to spell the word H-O-A-X, Coach? Lose projected starters to quarantine for two weeks at the beginning of preseason practice? Tough luck.

If boosters and fans in the SEC pretended to have patience before the season for the emergency exercise of playing football to save the bottom line, those silly attempts at logic were all forgotten after defending national champ LSU lost to Mississippi State in Week One. Auburn (Gus Malzahn), South Carolina (Will Muschamp), Vanderbilt (Derek Mason), and Tennessee (Jeremy Pruitt) all fired their coaches during or after the 2020 season, giving the SEC eight new coaches in two years for the 14-team league. Maybe from now on the sports agents of coaches should work clauses into contracts that make it impossible to fire their clients if they can't have spring practice due to things like nuclear war or, you know, acts of God like the plague. Would have made things easier back in March 2020.

With the country closing up shop the second week of that month, and spring looking more dire by the minute, Saban at least had that one final meeting to address his players scheduled for 3:30 p.m. on Friday, March 13. Then the SEC came over the top. Maybe it was Georgia coach Kirby Smart, Saban's former defensive coordinator turned fiercest league rival, who didn't want Saban to have the advantage of one spring meeting before the pandemic that Georgia was not going to be allowed. That's how competitive these coaches are in this glorious league of lunatics. Smart and his Bulldogs were on spring break when everything started shutting down, and they were scheduled to return to campus that next Monday, March 16, for a spring practice to begin the next day. Now Georgia was at a severe disadvantage to Alabama in the mind of an excellent coach who intimately understands the brain of the greatest coach of all time.

The SEC tries its best to manage its golden gods of college football immortality, but really it's an impossible task to fully govern the high-functioning madness of people driven to these extremes. Alabama was still going to have the meeting, aight? At the very least, Saban didn't want his players going down to the Flora-Bama and getting sick on this "extended spring break." The original plan for the 2020 spring practice schedule was to have one practice on the Friday before spring break. That would give Alabama's coaches the opportunity to emphasize the importance of accountability over the school holiday. The rationale behind that strategy was so players wouldn't backslide too much physically after the grueling Fourth Quarter Program. Now Saban didn't know how long his players would be gone. He was still certain of one unwavering truth, though. He was going to attack the situation as an opportunity and not as a handicap, and use the disruption to Alabama's advantage. And everyone knew it, too.

"We're going to be smart about this," was the meeting's conveyed message.

At that point, Saban didn't really have a working plan for the pandemic, but he had the right people for the job already surrounding him. In a stroke of luck, Saban had just hired two new strength and conditioning coordinators out of necessity, and one had a Ph.D. in sports science.

Meanwhile, Turncoat Cochran was off on Georgia's spring break somewhere screaming, "Yeah, yeah, yeah, yeah," and wasn't going to have a 15-day spring practice schedule to help with his transition to on-the-field coaching. The last remaining coach on Saban's original 2007 coaching staff at Alabama, Cochran had reached celebrity-coach status at Alabama despite being a glorified weight-room guy. That characterization isn't exactly fair to Cochran, who also served as a problem solver for Alabama behind the scenes and understood the personalities of players better than anyone in the Mal Moore Athletic Facility, but that's how he was later framed by fans when he finally decided to leave. And it's not like Saban didn't respect Cochran's judgment or intellect. Being the de facto head coach of the team in the offseason per NCAA rules, Cochran gained enough credibility with Saban through the years to evaluate which players had the psychological profile for Alabama's demanding level of accountability and which players were potential problems. By 2017, the New Orleans native and his raspy, Cajun-kissed sideline catchphrase of "Yeah, yeah, yeah, yeah" were marketable brands for Alabama. Cochran received more notoriety from a viral YouTube video of him destroying the 2017 College Football Playoff runners-up trophy in front of the team as a motivational ploy before the 2018 College Football Playoff national championship game in Atlanta. The opponent for the game, in a noteworthy plot point considering Cochran's future career path, was Georgia. Other universities would cherish and display a College Football Playoff national championship runners-up trophy, but Cochran called it a "consolation prize" and smashed it into the floor before the team left Tuscaloosa for the game. For good measure, he then bashed it to smithereens with a three-pound wooden-handled sledgehammer.

Cochran's video was leaked by a player on January 6, 2018, but now Alabama employs a team of six videographers and producers to capture every possible moment for Twitter and Instagram videos.

Did Saban OK the smashing of the trophy? asked AL.com's national award-winning beat reporter Michael Casagrande.

"Do you think I'm going to do something without him knowing?" Cochran said. "Do you not know who I work for? Come on."

Prophetic words for a coach who later hit Saban with a surprise move that not only caught Saban unprepared, but shocked the entire SEC. To take Cochran away from Alabama during Saban's Fourth Quarter Program, which Alabama football calls the most important month of preparation for every new season, was a declaration of war by Georgia coach Kirby Smart. It was a cold-blooded attempt at psychological assassination by Smart, and double-agent football treason by Cochran, who was making $595,000 as a strength coach. He took a pay cut of $45,000 to leave, per a records request by AL.com senior sports editor John Talty. Another Alabama beat reporter for AL.com, gumshoe newshound Matt Zenitz, broke the bombshell news this way: Scott Cochran, arguably the most important part of Alabama football beyond Nick Saban, will leave for an SEC rival to work for one of Nick Saban's protégés.

When the statewide news leader covers a strength coach leaving in the offseason with three beat reporters, a senior editor, a columnist, and video support, then you know you've found college football heaven. Make sure to stick around for Thanksgiving when things get really fun. Roll Tide.

Former Alabama assistant and college football's forever slouching genius, Lane Kiffin, who reportedly used the alias Joey Freshwater at Tuscaloosa bars to flirt with coeds, went from FAU to Ole Miss to begin the 2020 offseason, and pirate cosplaying football eccentric Mike Leach went to Mississippi State. Those two coaching moves in the effulgently moonstruck realm of the SEC West were not as fascinating for many people inside the coaching industry as Cochran's Benedict Arnold-ing Nick Saban on February 24, 2020. It was treated nationally as the biggest college football news of the 2020 offseason, and for good reason. The feeling in the SEC was that Cochran's defection from Alabama might actually be the beginning of the end of Saban's bulletproof dynasty.

The palace intrigue of college football is an SEC subgenre unto itself, and its impassioned cultivation is a quirky Southernism similar in a way to the constant tillage of tabloid gossip that enlivens interest in the royal family. People like to talk in the Deep South. Here's the difference, though. They aren't fetching a block for the Duke of Cambridge if he goes 7–5. In the Deep South, the public beheading of coaches is part of the culture, and executions are championed with the serious vigor of a coup d'état. Then everyone gathers 'round the radio for the radiant cultural bonfire that is *The Paul Finebaum Show*.

For good reason, Saban was angry like a startled badger when Cochran left Alabama for Athens, Georgia. He even issued an official statement on Cochran's departure, which was out of character for Alabama's coach and also dripping with contempt.

"Scott did a really good job for us here and was a big part of our success, but he was looking for a new career path," Saban said in a statement to AL.com. "He wanted to get on to the field coaching and would like one day, I think, to be a head coach. We didn't really have anything here to offer him along those lines, and Georgia did. I understand him wanting to take on that path.

"As good as Scott was for us here as our head strength coach, it's probably best for him and best for us if he's able to do there at Georgia what he wants to do now with his career."

He just wanted to be an assistant coach. That's it. After dealing with Saban since 2007, Saban's trusted ace, in the end, just wanted to keep on working with Saban after all those other guys left year after year after year. For reasons that should be obvious to any sane person not born in the SEC footprint, one can only scream "Yeah, yeah, yeah, yeah" for so long until one begins to question their self-worth. Under NCAA rules, teams can have 10 designated position coaches. Ten! If that sounds like a lot of assistants for a college team, that's because it is. Not one for Cochran, though? Saban collects assistant coaches like Lane Kiffin collects souvenirs from Gallettes. In Saban's final year with the Miami Dolphins, he had 16 on-field assistant coaches. Going into the 2020 spring practice, Alabama had—in addition to the 10 on-field assistants allowed by the NCAA—12 full-time "analysts," who are like assistants to the assistant coaches. Really, they're just football coaches by another name, and in 2020 included among them Charlie Strong, the former head coach of Texas; Major Applewhite, the former head coach of Houston; Dean Altobelli, a former equity partner of the multi-state, Michigan-based law firm Miller Canfield; Alex Mortensen, the son of ESPN NFL analyst Chris Mortensen; Gordon Steele, the son of former Auburn, Alabama, and Clemson defensive coordinator Kevin Steele; and Mike Stoops, the former head coach at Arizona.

That group of henchmen doesn't even count this list of invaluable shitdoers from 2020:

Daniel Bush, director of recruiting

Ellis Ponder, football chief operating officer (king of the shitdoers)

Butch Jones, special assistant to the head coach (former Tennessee head coach)

Cedric Burns, athletic relations coordinator (knows where all the bodies are buried)

Bob Welton, director of player personnel

Roger Bedford, assistant director of player personnel

Marc Votteler, assistant director of player personnel

Josh Chapman, director of player development
Denzel Devall, director of player development
Evan Van Nostrand, assistant director of player development
J. T. Summerford, director of football operations
Sam Petitto, director of personnel operations
Matt Clapp, assistant strength coach
Paul Constantine, assistant strength coach
Tyler Owens, assistant strength coach
Andy Kwon, graduate assistant
Jake Long, graduate assistant
Tino Sunseri, graduate assistant
Max Bullough, graduate assistant

And those are just the shitdoers in Miss Terry's utility shed next to the zip ties, orphaned triple-A batteries, and Channellock pliers.

Is it beginning to make sense how badly Alabama needed football to be played in 2020? We were never losing the season to the coronavirus, aight?

That long list of hardworking folks (who do important stuff, surely) doesn't even include the 49 other football staffers listed in the 2020 media guide. Among them are names like Jeff Allen, the associate athletics director of sports medicine. He's the guy who coordinated all of the daily testing for COVID-19. There are many other employees and contractors who work for the success of Alabama football but fail to make the yearly media guides. The millions and millions of dollars that Alabama pulls in every year as a "nonprofit organization" have to go somewhere, and we all know the players aren't getting their fair shares.

The Sabans spend liberally in the pursuit of America's best five-star recruits. In 2019, Alabama football reported $95.2

million in revenue, and spent $69.7 million. The compensation breakdown, according to information filed with the NCAA: $31.6 million for coaching salaries (Saban made $9,511,837), $32.1 million in salaries for support staffers, and $18.1 million for student aid. The catch: The accounting ledger that Alabama files every year with the NCAA does not require the bean counters to list the number of support staffers on the payroll. Also, sidebar, Saban is not above giving jobs to friends. He is an all-time Hall of Famer of giving jobs to old coaching buddies and fellow clients of college football super-agent Jimmy Sexton.

Saban wouldn't promote Scott Cochran, however, and that fact more than most anything is a picture of Saban's uncompromising ability to make ruthless decisions for Alabama football in the pursuit of unattainable perfection. Cochran was considered one of the best strength and conditioning coaches in the country, but he was pushed to leave in the way that smart bosses know how to freeze out employees who can't be fired. Cochran is well liked throughout college football, and there will be people rooting for him to succeed as an assistant in the hopes that he can one day be a head coach. Maybe Saban is even one of those people. After all, Cochran's only sin at Alabama was wanting to do that same thing that has always allowed Saban to thrive, grow professionally, and learn new things. Evolve, embrace change, and forever adapt: Those are some of Saban's greatest strengths as a coach and leader, and Cochran learned them from his longtime mentor. But when Cochran wanted to begin his metamorphosis, Saban wouldn't allow it. That's either a sign of the wise old coach's eye for talent, or an example of his paranoid abhorrence for the unplanned and the off-script and the gnawing hatred of the ill-prepared. A worrisome trend of major injuries to Alabama's best players haunted the program in 2018 and 2019, and people started questioning how the team was being trained. Ligament damage to knees and ankles is common in football, but Alabama lost both of its first-team inside linebackers, Dylan Moses and Joshua McMillon, before the first game in 2019. Those losses to the same knee injury might have cost Alabama a shot at the national championship before the season even started. Two freshmen, Christian Harris and Shane Lee, played in the middle of Saban's defense in 2019, and it was a learning experience. Alabama gave up 31 points to Ole Miss, 46 points to LSU, and 48 points to Auburn.

Despite all of Cochran's loyalty through the years—and he was with Saban at LSU for the 2003 national championship as well—Saban wouldn't budge, and then Saban wouldn't even allow Cochran to say goodbye to Alabama's players when he left for Georgia to be the special teams coordinator.

Hopefully he kept that three-pound sledgehammer, though.

"Scott Cochran might be the biggest hit to a Nick Saban Alabama staff we have seen," said SEC football analyst Cole Cubelic, a radio personality in Birmingham for WJOX and a sideline analyst for ESPN. "Massive loss. Goes much further than Strength & Conditioning."

It was only wishful thinking by the former Auburn offensive lineman turned talking head. 'Twas not the case. In fact, Cochran leaving for Georgia less than three weeks before the start of the pandemic shut everything down actually turned out to be a blessing in disguise for the Crimson Tide.

———

When it came time to find the first head strength and conditioning coach at Alabama since 2007, Saban wanted to make a forward-thinking hire because Alabama athletics had just completed a $16.1 expansion to the Mal Moore Athletic Facility for a new "sports science center." That's just a fancy way of marketing new training equipment and rehab stuff for recruits, but the people in the building leading the stretches and therapy sessions are truly invaluable to the success of Alabama's student-athletes. A cryotherapy chamber was one of the shiny new toys, but head nutritionist and dietician Amy Bragg also makes a mean smoothie. Alabama also employees a team psychiatrist, who is probably one of the more overlooked staffers in terms of importance to the performance of the team. The pressure that Alabama's football players are under can be crushing, and the psychological rewiring that some freshmen require after the sycophantic recruiting process takes real work and thoughtful guidance. Every scholarship player who arrives at Alabama is one of the best in the country at their position, and many are treated like royalty in their hometowns. When they get off the bus in Tuscaloosa, the initial experience is not unlike boot camp for the Army. Recruits are retaught how to think, how to measure success, and what is expected of them. Some players also require medication for previously undiagnosed disorders like ADHD. Psychiatry can accomplish a lot, and the ultimate endgame for Saban is developing committed teammates who stick around for four years (or five) and wait patiently on their turn to play after high school careers that made them, bizarrely enough, "All-Americans" of an annual high school all-star exhibition game sponsored by the U.S. Army.

The sports psychiatrist at Alabama hopefully will never make headlines, but the strength coach of the Crimson Tide football team is a highly visible, front-of-the-house position. When Cochran left Alabama, it was an all-time famous heel turn to rival Hulk Hogan saving his career by joining the New World Order (nWo) at the 1996 WCW Bash at the Beach.

"You fans can stick it, brother," Hogan said into the microphone as trash and full drinks rained down in Daytona Beach.

So it was with Cochran, who had grown stale, but was an enormous fan favorite. To replace him, Saban hired a couple of nerds. You know, "sports science" guys. Analytical data geeks. The type of dudes who attend Sloan and just say "Sloan," and get wood when the trailer drops for the next-generation Fitbit. New Age, plyometric-band-loving shamans of core strength and balance. The indispensable superheroes whom any coach would want by his side when the world goes sideways on the eve of spring football practice, in other words. Dr. Matt Rhea and David Ballou worked together at the Florida-based prep sports institute IMG Academy, and Alabama hired them away from Indiana University on March 3, 2020, to both replace Cochran. In between their partnerships at IMG and Indiana, Ballou was at Notre Dame for a year. Ballou's official title is director of sports performance and Dr. Rhea is director of sports science. They were new to Alabama, but their innovative collaborations were years in the making for that very important moment in their careers. A little bit of luck goes into every national championship run no matter how dominant the team, and maybe this is when Alabama tripped into a pile of pillows. The new strength and conditioning guys who built their reputations on tracking stats during every workout were hired 10 days before an international viral pestilence locked everyone out of the new $16.1 million "sports science center." By mid-April, long after the spring A-Day Game had been canceled, Saban was praising his new hires (and still throwing some shade at Cochran).

"Four or five years ago, these guys were at IMG, when actually some of our fourth- and fifth-year players were at IMG, and I heard a lot about some of the state-of-the-art sports science stuff that they were actually into and doing there, just when you'd visit in recruiting or whatever," Saban said during an interview with Eli Gold, the universally beloved play-by-play announcer, and longtime voice of the Alabama Crimson Tide. The topic of the new strength coaches came up during the athletic department's official *Spring Update Show* on the Crimson Tide Sports Network.

I never really thought much about it, and then when we had this opportunity come up, we researched these guys and they'd done a phenomenal job at Notre Dame of eliminating injuries by something like 50 percent, and even better at Indiana. So, when they came in and we interviewed them, there was no question that from a sports-science standpoint and from a conditioning standpoint they were, like, light-years in advance of what a lot of people have done in their programs for a long, long time, which we've done the same thing for a long, long time, too.

Here's the funny thing about that, though. Saban sent everyone home after that final team meeting on Friday, March 13, and then turned to his witch doctors and came up with a plan. But it didn't take a genius to remember that the old-timers used to work out at their homes in the summers before reporting to fall camp—just ask a 69-year-old head coach who could remember those days. Alabama would be fine.

Head trainer Jeff Allen, Ballou, and Dr. Rhea did have one of the pandemic's great ideas, though. When the NCAA ruled that schools could cover the cost of supplemental care packages for athletes, Alabama got everyone on the team to buy Apple Watches so the sports-science geeks could track all the data and monitor sleep patterns. Players slept with the watches during the pandemic, and then charged them in the morning. The Apple Watch idea was just another example of Saban's ability to solve problems and maybe find the slightest of edges against his rivals in the upper reaches of major college football. Opponents cried that Alabama was breaking the rules, and Clemson coach Dabo Swinney told ESPN that "we don't need an Apple Watch to know our guys are doing the right thing."

Swinney was just mad he didn't think of it first. And, yeah, the players at Alabama didn't need to be constantly tracked to make sure they were sweating off calories while they were away from campus, but, according to a player, one prominent linebacker did joke that he was going to strap his Apple Watch to his pet dog during workouts just to see if Big Brother Bama was actually watching.

A THEORY ON ALABAMA KICKERS

A native of Tooele, Utah, Dr. Matt Rhea was an excellent field goal kicker in high school. He was named to an all-state team twice, according to the twice-weekly *Tooele Transcript-Bulletin*, and also played soccer for three years. Dr. Rhea then kicked in college at UNLV and Southern Utah in Cedar City, which is a charming place if you're ever out that way. The point of all this backstory is that Alabama didn't just hire a revolutionary sports-science numbers nerd to replace Cochran. In a twist of fate only Saban and Alabama fans can truly appreciate, Dr. Rhea actually had more fucking special-teams experience than the guy he was replacing who left for Georgia to be the special-teams coordinator. Now, this is significant for two reasons.

Reason One: Alabama kickers under Saban were notoriously snakebit before 2020 when sophomore Will Reichard of Hoover came along and was perfect on the season. He was 14 of 14 on field goals and 84 of 84 on extra points. For many Alabama fans, who really shouldn't have the right to complain about jack shit, poor kicking has always either been a running joke or a point of vengeful anger (all forms of frustration, of course, are contingent on said fan's stage of insanity and current blood sugar levels). A former kicker who played under Saban (who will go nameless) has a theory why Saban's kickers always sucked so badly, and this theory was actually relayed to me in 2019, long before the 2020 season. It's because the kickers, before Dr. Rhea and Ballou came along, were all required to do the same workouts as the other football players. This ruined their flexibility and upset their ability to accurately kick an oblong ball through metal piping. Kicking a field goal is more like a delicate art, the kicker explained, like making a putt in golf. Auburn had this right years ago.

Reason Two: The guy who messed up all those Alabama kickers is now the special-teams coordinator at Georgia.

CHAPTER 5

CENSUS MAN

They just wanted Alabama football YouTube star Jermaine "FunnyMaine" Johnson to talk about the 2020 Census.

That fact cannot be lost in the telling of this story of how the most prominent and divisive Confederate statue in the state of Alabama came down in Birmingham one day before the University of Alabama football Crimson Tide was scheduled to report back in Tuscaloosa. Saban sent everyone home for spring break on March 13, 2020, and players began returning to campus around the final weekend of May. At that confluence in the river of our summer of WTF, for the first time in many of those players' lives, football was not the preeminent thing on their minds, and they were all alone together in the socially conscious incubator of a college campus shaped by football, a pandemic, and now racial injustice.

George Floyd was killed on May 25 in Minneapolis, and the civil demonstrations, marches, and riots that followed his death carried through the entire summer. What Alabama's players witnessed that weekend less than an hour away from campus in the state's largest city sent ripples of energy through the country. On Sunday, May 31, 2020, Alabama football superfan Jermaine Johnson, who goes by the stage name FunnyMaine, shocked everyone to attention at a protest rally for racial injustice in Birmingham's famous Kelly Ingram Park, and gave young people in Alabama something to think about.

The cult of personality that is the Alabama football Crimson Tide, and its worldly sphere of influence upon the Yellowhammer State and things beyond, cannot be fully appreciated without understanding the people who make it all so, the fans. Their devotion to a higher power shapes the consciousness of an entire state, and brings people together in commonality the way nothing else can. It is that imputable fan-ology found in the SEC, and especially in Alabama, that people describe as something close to a religion. The religion organically creates clergymen, and Jermaine "FunnyMaine" Johnson is Alabama's high priest. For the humans outside the fishbowl, breathing this Tide water probably seems a little odd. It's not so much that Alabama and Auburn fans are crazy. Most of them are not. They were just raised that way inside a crazy world.

Birmingham native Warren St. John, a former feature writer for the *New York Times*, dipped his toe inside the fishbowl when he wrote a book exploring sports fanaticism in America by profiling a segment of Alabama football diehards. It's a glorious text about Alabama's 1999 college football season as St. John traveled around the SEC for a season with Alabama's lovable RV cavalry of hell-raising fans. Through that lens, and the one created by *The Paul Finebaum Show* to prod, celebrate, and maybe sometimes mock that passion, and other caricatures like Forrest Gump, there is a lingering attitude outside the Deep South that Alabama football stands as some kind of monolith to redneckery. This is grossly incorrect, but maintaining stereotypes reinforces perceptions and is good for business. Be wise not to conflate old Southern whiteness with the new theology.

When Nick Saban was hired away from the Miami Dolphins in 2007, Alabama fans had an impromptu pep rally at the Tuscaloosa airport for their modern savior. Hundreds of people went to the glorified airstrip and waited all day for the private jet carrying the Sabans. Media began arriving at 8 a.m. Students and fans partied in the parking lot, reported the *Tuscaloosa News*, like it was a scene outside Bryant-Denny Stadium on game day. When he stepped onto the tarmac, Saban was engulfed by a level of fawning hysteria reserved for boy bands and wartime liberators. In a classic scene that made her SEC-famous, Alabama superfan Alana Colette Collins rushed Saban, wrapped her arms around his neck, and gave him a kiss. Alana, who was 43 when she passed away in 2014, knew in her heart, just like all the other Alabama fans around the state, and SEC fans watching from afar, that the Crimson Tide was back.

"We love him!" Collins shouted into the camera of a WBRC Birmingham Fox 6 reporter before unleashing a guttural scream of unbridled, sloppy-drunk ecstasy. "Yeah, we ball'n, baby! We ball'n!"

It was a liberation of sorts for the Sabans, too. The NFL experiment with Dolphins owner Wayne Huizenga was over. The power couple college football dream team was back in that warm water of the SEC. "Mr. Huizenga didn't want to let us go," Terry Saban said to reporters that day at the airport. "It took us a long time to get out of there, but we're glad to be here."

FunnyMaine, then 26 years old, remembers that day well: "It caused traffic jams in Tuscaloosa."

He was a part-time student at Alabama then while also working full-time at nearby Stillman College as an admissions officer. Stillman is Tuscaloosa's HBCU, and that's where FunnyMaine went to school after graduating from Jackson-Olin High School on the west side of Birmingham. Located on Avenue F in Ensley, Jackson-Olin is a proud Birmingham City School with famous alums like Eddie Kendricks of the Temptations and bobsledder Vonetta Flowers, who ran track at UAB and then became the first Black athlete in history to win a gold medal in the Winter Olympics. Barbara Humphrey, one of the track coaches credited with Flowers's success, is also a highly influential J-O grad. She currently serves on the UA System Board of Trustees and is the wife of former Alabama running back Bobby Humphrey and the mother of NFL star cornerback and former Alabama national champion Marlon Humphrey. Mike Anderson, the current men's basketball coach at St. John's, who has had stints along the way at UAB, Missouri, and Arkansas, is also a J-O grad, and so is former Alabama and NBA basketball star Reggie King. For Alabama football fans, J-O is most famous for one thing and one thing only, and that is producing the great David Palmer, who was a running back, receiver, quarterback, and return specialist for Alabama from 1991 to 1993. "The Deuce," a former first-team All-American and Heisman Trophy finalist, is one of the most singularly gifted athletes to ever play football at Alabama, but if you want to launch into a spirited debate with a longtime Alabama fan, then try taking the position that Palmer (the Tide's first-ever 1,000-yard receiver) wouldn't have been good enough to start at receiver for Saban's offense in 2019.

At the wrong time of night, there's a chance that conversation could end with stitches.

For FunnyMaine, because of his loyalty and allegiance to J-O, Palmer is his favorite Alabama football player of all time. His favorite player of the Saban era, he says, would have to be Mark Ingram because he was Alabama's first Heisman Trophy winner and then went on to star with the New Orleans Saints. Like most college football fans in Alabama, no matter which side of the church they choose to represent, FunnyMaine says he can't remember a time when he wasn't a fan. He does remember being broke, though. FunnyMaine had a huge heart and a small bank account for most of his adult life, and if we're all being honest with ourselves, that's really the story of an entire state. The same year that Saban arrived in Alabama, FunnyMaine had his first taste of working at a radio station. He was at Birmingham's FM 95.7 Jamz for three months, and by that time he was already hooked on the business of trying to make people laugh. Tough hustle, that, but he honed his craft as a stand-up comic and public speaker in those early years while Saban built Alabama into the most powerful force in college football.

FunnyMaine was back at Jamz in 2012, and by 2015 he was part of one of the most popular radio shows in Alabama. Birmingham is one of the most predominantly Black cities in America (72 percent), and Jamz is an institution there as the city's "No. 1 Hip-Hop and R&B Station."

Humorist Roy Wood Jr., a Birmingham native who went to Ramsay High School, got his start at Jamz by volunteering to make prank phone calls. He later had his own No. 1–rated show for the station before leaving in 2012 for the TBS sitcom *Sullivan and Son*. His big break came in 2014 as a correspondent for Comedy Central's *The Daily Show*.

FunnyMaine wanted to make his own path through Birmingham's radio industry. On January 21, 2016, he posted a heartfelt promotional video to YouTube starring himself and the city of Birmingham. There is a scene near the end that's like a motivational speech for his career. In it, he embraces Wood Jr. before his voice is dubbed over another video clip of Birmingham: "It's going to happen for me, man. Like, I have no doubt in my mind it's going to happen. Until then, I'm just working, writing, and performing, and not sitting back waiting on no handouts. It's real to me. This is my passion. Yeah, I'm patient, but I'm still hungry, too."

At 40 years old in 2021, FunnyMaine grinded a long time in the Birmingham-based entertainment business until he sat down in front of a camera in his home following the Crimson Tide's 2016 season opener and hit the record button. Alabama destroyed USC that Saturday night by a score of 52–6 at the Dallas Cowboys' AT&T Stadium in Arlington. It was supposed to be the day's marquee game. It was not. Meanwhile, other teams around the SEC struggled in Week One. Here's the thing about college football fans in Alabama. They don't just watch their team. People in the state sit in front of multiple TVs all day, beginning with *ESPN College GameDay* in the morning, and watch every game all the way through to the late-night stuff out west. If they're at a tailgate, it's the same setup only on campus and surrounded by thousands of fans. And everyone does this every Saturday. And it's just the way of life for most of the state.

This is why Birmingham is the No.1 market for college football year after year, why the local sports radio station in Birmingham, 94.5 Jox-FM, is one of the most successful in the country, why the state news website, AL.com, was saved during the difficult transition from print-first to online-first, and why Birmingham is the nation's capital for the game. Love of college football binds the state together even while other forces have forever ripped it apart from the inside out. That universal love creates its own pronounced divisions, though. More than maybe seeing their own team win, Alabama fans love to watch the other teams lose. Sadistic? Maybe, but Auburn is into that same kind of game-day kink. The whole SEC-solidarity myth only applies to a degree, and that's during bowl season. Alabama fans want to see Auburn and LSU suffer embarrassing losses, and on September 3, 2016, both of those things happened. The Bayou Tigers lost to Wisconsin 16–14, and the Plainsmen lost at Clemson 19–13. FunnyMaine made a YouTube video called "How Bama Fans Watched the Week One SEC Games," and it instantly went viral. Finally, FunnyMaine of Birmingham's Pratt City had solved the formula of comedic alchemy and created his own nugget of gold.

"Thank God for radio," FunnyMaine said. "It prepared me."

He made a video every week, and by the Iron Bowl he was a statewide celebrity. Just an assumption, but there probably weren't too many Black comics who hit it big with a conservative white audience during the 2016 presidential campaign. FunnyMaine did that using Crimson Tide football, and suddenly he had a very rare opportunity as a Black man in Alabama to reach across the color line in what was, by that Thanksgiving Iron Bowl weekend, Trump's white America.

———

Being hugely popular with Black Alabama and white Alabama between the years represented by Trump's time in office might be the single greatest accomplishment in comedy history. As a host for the most popular radio station in Birmingham, FunnyMaine still MC'd a constant schedule of community events for 95.7 Jamz from 2016 to 2019. At the same time, he was touring the state as a stand-up comic, and selling out shows to racially mixed audiences of Alabama fans. Something else happened leading up to the week of the 2016 Iron Bowl that projected his rising star even higher. FunnyMaine was featured on Comedy Central's *Kevin Hart Presents: Hart of the City*. It was the debut season of the show, and Hart filmed an episode in Birmingham. It dropped on November 20, and FunnyMaine had his first four major stand-up gigs lined up that week at Birmingham's StarDome Comedy Club. Hart featured FunnyMaine in his show, and it legitimized him.

"Oh, he's a real stand-up comedian," FunnyMaine said, looking back and poking fun at himself.

He sold out every show, and never stopped gaining fans throughout the South until the pandemic hit. Among his biggest fans: Holly and Gordon Jones, who are the parents of Alabama quarterback Mac Jones. Galu and Diane Tagovailoa, Tua's parents, also counted themselves as friends of FunnyMaine during their time in Alabama. Everyone loved FunnyMaine all over the state and beyond, and his dream had come true. He was able to engage Trump supporters on Twitter because of his comedy, and even have some meaningful conversations with them from time to time about race in America. That's the power of the Alabama football Crimson Tide.

How does FunnyMaine explain the importance of college football in the state? A comic, out of necessity, must understand the pulse of people better than any reporter or anthropologist.

"I tell them they have to be here to understand," FunnyMaine said. "We can explain it, you can watch docs, but until you're here, you can never really understand. Once you're here, even the transplants get it then. It's like . . . it's like you got to pick a side. I've seen divorces over this. I've seen fights. All around this football we take very seriously every day. Using logic is not acceptable. I tried to be a non-hater at first in my career. I thought basketball was a safe space. Oh, hell no."

FunnyMaine learned quickly that Alabama fans loved his jokes, but all that love was far outweighed by hate for even the slightest compliment given to Auburn. The Auburn men's basketball team went to the Final Four in 2019, and it was a sensational, All-American-Everything run through the bracket. To reach Minneapolis, coach Bruce Pearl's team knocked off Kansas,

North Carolina, and then SEC rival Kentucky in a row. Those three teams have the most victories in NCAA Tournament history. It was a miraculous ride, and Auburn, which had fewer trips to the NCAA Tournament (10) than Kentucky had appearances in Final Fours (17), was the gritty Cinderella that the country adored. Auburn's best player, Chuma Okeke, even tore the anterior cruciate ligament of his knee in the win against North Carolina, and Auburn still managed to upset Kentucky to become the first men's basketball team in Alabama state history to reach the semifinals of an NCAA Tournament. Maybe even a few diehard Alabama fans were secretly rooting for Auburn there in the end against eventual champ Virginia. They had to keep that bipartisan joy locked away down deep, though. Appreciation for the enemy cannot be expressed aloud, and FunnyMaine learned real quick that complimenting Auburn was off-limits for a stand-up comedian who had built his brand as an Alabama fan. The No. 1 commandment of SEC fandom is not "Love thy team above all others." It is "Thou shall always hate thine rival even more."

"I caught all the heat," FunnyMaine said.

On May 31, 2020, it was his turn to give it.

The young entertainer who had grinded for so long loved his new fanbase, and he was proud beyond measure that his comedy was able to cut through the hell-storm of division in America created by President Trump's racist rhetoric, and he felt blessed by God that he could actually pay all his damn bills making people laugh about football in the only place in the country where that's even possible. But when it came to using his new platform to speak out about racial injustice following the death of George Floyd, the funny man who loved Birmingham and the Crimson Tide with every detail of his countenance wasn't about to flinch and be anyone's Uncle Tom.

The SEC-crazy thing about all that, though, and what really illuminates the depth of the inner strength of the proud Jackson-Olin grad who became a generation's new image of the Alabama superfan, is that the city leaders that day in Birmingham's historic Kelly Ingram Park just wanted FunnyMaine to talk about the importance of participating in the 2020 Census. They asked him on the spur of the moment, too. FunnyMaine wasn't originally scheduled to speak, and he was under no pressure to say or do anything controversial. The city-sponsored rally "for peace and hope" was, according to the city's news release the previous day, officially called "Birmingham, the World is Watching." There were dozens and dozens of rallies and protests happening all over the country after George Floyd's death in Minneapolis, and Birmingham was just doing its part to promote peaceful demonstrations. It's different in Birmingham, though. It's always different in Birmingham because of the people there who helped to start the revolution. They toppled the walls of a city government girded by laws of oppression, backed by a state constitution of white supremacy, and reinforced by the police department and the Ku Klux Klan.

Here's the thing about the freedom fighters of Birmingham in the 1950s and 1960s, though. Among them was one of the toughest dudes in American history. His name was Fred Shuttlesworth, and he was a man of God, but if he had five good minutes in the matador's circle of life, it'd only take him about two to fool the bull and bleed it dead. Answer this question about what little civil rights history you learned in school: Why does America celebrate the "nonviolent protests" of the civil rights era when there wasn't a damn thing nonviolent about them? Is the distorted premise taught that way to absolve whites of guilt, or to teach children, Black and white, a myth built on a lie? There is great shame in that modern framing of America, and maybe that pacifist bullshit has done more harm than good. The civil rights era was a war by another name in the American South, but the only weapon Blacks had was the racist hate in the souls of whites. Gains were made in the name of civil rights, but hate didn't go home. That's the horrific truth. A quiet so loud persisted and the echoing heartbeats of cowards can still be heard today.

"Nonviolent protest" is a warped worldview that allowed oppression to fester. Do fathers teach their boys to punch back against bullies on the playground, or to crawl into a ball and take a beating like a coward? Fred Shuttlesworth, pastor of Bethel Baptist Church in Collegeville, was enjoying Christmas Day with his family in 1956 when a bomb built by terrorist Klansmen exploded outside his bedroom. He was beaten by men with ties to the Klan while attempting to register his children for high school in September 1957. There were more attacks against him for organizing the Alabama Christian Movement for Human Rights after courts in Montgomery banned the NAACP from Alabama. If you know anything of civil rights history, then you know Shuttlesworth came up swinging every time with fire in his belly and saintly courage in his heart. He helped lead the revolution, but here is what people need to know, too. Terrible damage had already been done to the city because Jim Crow laws and the Klan forced so many Black residents to leave the South.

On Christmas Day 1956, the people of Collegeville and Douglasville were frightened from their homes and into the streets by the bombing in their neighborhood. A short walk from the explosion, a young girl of 14, Jerrel Lamar Sanders Jackson, was inside her packed three-bedroom home celebrating the holiday. The Sanders clan of Collegeville lived at 3477 33rd Avenue North in those days. Jerrel was the second-to-youngest of 16 children brought into this world by Theodore and Elizabeth Washington Sanders. The son of a sharecropper, Theodore came to Birmingham in 1922 by way of rural Bullock County in Alabama's earth-rich Black Belt. Also of the Black Belt, Elizabeth Washington moved to Birmingham in 1920 from Fort Deposit, in Lowndes County.

"I know they picked cotton," said Jackson in April 2021, then 79 years old, a longtime resident of Irondale and a mother of four, grandmother of nine, and great-grandmother of 13.

Sanders's Bullock County and Washington's Lowndes County are separated by Montgomery County, home of Alabama's state capital and the former capital of the Confederacy. When his father died suddenly in rural Bullock County, Theodore Sanders could not migrate to Birmingham until his father's sharecropping debt was paid off by his surviving family to the plantation owner. Theodore and Elizabeth met at a local Birmingham Industrial League baseball game, married on Thanksgiving Day 1925, and started a family in Collegeville.

Despite being removed from 1956 by almost 65 years, Jerrel Sanders Jackson vividly remembers the concussive blast of the Christmas Day bombing. The walls shook and the windows wobbled, she recalled for family members.

"I will never forget it," Jackson said. "I was laying on the bed—oh-ee—it sounded like the world was coming to an end."

The Sanders family walked through their neighborhood to see what happened.

"The top of the house was just on the ground," said Jackson, who was a freshman at Parker High School at the time. "He didn't get hurt at all. He climbed from under there and got out. That was real bad, y'all."

Jackson was at Parker from 1956 to 1959, and did not

appreciate having to walk almost two hours to and from school during the on-again, off-again Birmingham bus boycotts, but she did it because "they'd beat your ass if you got on that bus."

She didn't mean the whites.

Jackson was at Alabama A&M in Huntsville in September 1963 when the 16th Street Baptist Church was bombed, "and cried and cried and cried. All you could do was cry. I wanted to go home."

While in high school and during college breaks she attended community meetings at "packed churches" in Collegeville— Bethel, Oak Street Baptist, and others, including her church, Douglasville Methodist.

"We weren't scared," Jackson said. "I don't know why, but I know now I would be scared. But I know I wasn't scared. They would have the meetings changed up every month. The churches would be full—I mean packed. They could have just thrown a bomb in there and killed us all because the police wasn't going to do nothing. We all would have died together."

This is how soldiers think when they look back at war.

One of Jackson's daughters, Patrina Jackson Lee, served in the Army for 24 years and retired a first sergeant in charge of 230 soldiers. She had two tours each in Operation Iraqi Freedom and Operation Enduring Freedom.

"What Mom is describing is what we call selfless service in the military," Lee said. "It is the inherent value of people who are dedicated to a particular cause. It gets instilled in you, and you don't even realize it is instilled in you."

Selfless service. Soldiers in a "nonviolent" war. Monuments of freedom.

The integration of buses and the boycotting of businesses were the actions, but the point of it all for Jerrel Sanders Jackson, aside from fighting for common civil rights, was the lack of jobs for Black residents. There weren't any, and Birmingham's iron- and steel-making age was beginning to end. Theodore Sanders worked at Sloss Furnace and then L&N Railroad as a "railman." Segregation and racial terror wasn't just about schools and department stores. It was also about whites not wanting to compete with Blacks for jobs.

"The only thing men could do was be an elevator operator or clean the floors in the white businesses," said Jackson, whose first job was as a waitress in the cafeteria of the six-story, all-brick Crittenden Building on 3rd Avenue North, which at the time was the location of department store Burger-Phillips. She was 16 and a junior in high school. The year was 1958. The song on the radio was "Johnny B. Goode" by Chuck Berry, and Jerrel Lamar Sanders Jackson of Irondale by way of Collegeville can still sing every gunny-sacking word.

She fell in love and remained in the Birmingham area, moving to the segregated Scott's Bend neighborhood in "old Irondale." Soon, the family grew and Jerrel Sanders Jackson wanted to move to "new Irondale." There was a planned community down a dirt road, Beacon Drive, but the neighborhood's sales team made up excuses to avoid Jerrel Sanders Jackson for weeks. She was resolute. They did not know Irondale's new Queen was about to take her throne. Finally, she contacted the housing authority and Jerrel had her first cousin, Juanita Johnson, "fake the voice of a white woman" to get an appointment. This was 1975. Irondale, Alabama. The subdivision on the hill would later be called "Holiday Gardens." They were the second Black family in the neighborhood after the Roberts family across the street. The Klan burned a cross in the vacant lot next door as a welcoming gift. Husband Tom Jackson ripped one of many harassers off a motorcycle while he was driving through the Jacksons' backyard.

"But the people were very nice," Jackson said. "Very nice. Good folks."

Always are.

Family reunions hosted by Jerrel Sanders Jackson, the greatest smoker of fine meats and hot links in Holiday Gardens history, brought home to Alabama around 300 people from across the country. Two of her siblings remained in Birmingham. All others moved away while the city's white supremacists were destroying the potential of a town. The Family Sanders diaspora: twin David Sanders (Birmingham, Daisy died at five of pneumonia), Walter Sanders (Philadelphia), twins Eddie Sanders (Detroit after serving in the Air Force in the Korean War) and Freddie Sanders (Birmingham after serving in the Army during the Korean War), twin Louise Sanders Brown (Detroit, twin was stillborn), Howard Sanders (Buffalo, New York), Theodore Sanders Jr. (died age five), Johnnie Robert Sanders (Buffalo), Loveless Sanders (Detroit), twins Evelyn Sanders (Philadelphia) and Elbert Sanders (Philadelphia), and twins Chauncey Sanders (Detroit) and James Sanders (Detroit after serving in the Army).

Five sets of twins. There is not a big enough Presidential Medal of Freedom, y'all. Like, Birmingham should throw a Valentine's Day parade every year for Theodore and Elizabeth Washington Sanders.

A career employee of the U.S. Postal Service, Jerrel Sanders Jackson gave her youngest child a familiar middle name in Alabama, but Kevin Bryant Jackson was not named for the famous coach. The postal worker named her baby boy after a famous, revolutionary man of American letters, William Cullen Bryant. He was a romantic poet, journalist, and longtime editor of the *New York Evening Post*.

Kevin Bryant Jackson is a proud graduate of the University of

Alabama, though, and was college roommates with former Birmingham mayor William A. Bell's son. Growing up, Kevin played front-yard football in the same era of Holiday Gardens that would later send Irondale's Saleem Rasheed to Alabama. He was the first true freshman at middle linebacker to start a season opener in Alabama football history. As for his love of the Alabama football Crimson Tide, Kevin Bryant Jackson will tell anyone who wants to know that it should have been Jalen Hurts in the 2019 season's national championship game against Clemson and not Tua Tagovailoa. Roll Tide.

History always remembers the leaders, but it was the Black residents in the homes, those everyday people of courage and resilience, who changed the world, too.

Younger people who have repopulated Birmingham's urban core in recent years wear that spirit, or at least cover themselves in that pride. Like many urban cores around the Deep South, Birmingham has experienced a rebirth even if the city might physically still look like a place stuck in time. "It's nice to have you in Birmingham," as they say. Downtown is a retroville brickscape of buildings once abandoned, but now endearingly hopeful and hip. It's a still-scarred city, but it now celebrates its place in civil rights history after generations there walked over the mountain and away from it. Give it a visit and order a Sex Panther at the Atomic Lounge, which has a back room named after Birmingham native and political activist Angela Davis. Atomic is one of the funkiest saloons in America. Its 1960s and '70s motif is like a commentary on a town that's finally crawling out of its bomb shelter, but with the energy of Birmingham native and experimental jazz mystic Sun Ra in everyone's first drink. Quasars and comet dust by the glass. For a scoop on the city's latest dirt, head over to the unofficial journo lounge Lou's Pub and Package in the Lakeview

District and buy a top-shelf Bushwacker. When local columnist John Archibald won the 2018 Pulitzer Prize for Commentary, Lou's is where he threw down. A 1986 graduate of the University of Alabama, Archibald lives and dies with his Crimson Tide. Without having to think, he will tell anyone who wants to know that quarterback Richard Todd was his favorite Alabama football player until Najee Harris came along.

The son and grandson of Methodist preachers in Alabama, Archibald wrote a beautiful memoir in 2021 titled *Shaking the Gates of Hell.* The book comes to terms with his father's silence from the pulpit during the civil rights era, and the narrative is framed against King's "Letter from Birmingham Jail," which was a clap-back at white clergy in Birmingham. Eight of them had written "A Call for Unity," published by the *Birmingham News*, the day of King's arrest.

"The point" of King's letter, wrote Archibald, "was, in many ways, the rebuke…For retreat, in the name of peace. For obedience, in the name of law. For silence, in the voice of God."

Archibald continued: "The point of this letter was not a message to Black people who lived the struggle and knew the barriers and blockades. It was a message to cautious and careful white people, like those eight clergy members—the Waitful Eight, some call them—to whom King addressed the letter."

Roll Tide.

Archibald's call for whites to speak out against racism, and the much-needed pub crawl through Birmingham, and the postmodern history and social context of the town, is important to understand for this one, singular truth. Everyone there—young, old, Black, white, Alabama and Auburn—all enjoyed seeing the Confederate monument come down in Linn Park. It stood at the northern terminus of 20th Street, which is downtown's main north–south artery. With Angela Davis as his spirit guide, and Sun Ra as his creative muse, and a Civil War history that never had anything to do with Birmingham still holding his city back like a shackle around the leg, FunnyMaine agreed to talk about the Census as a spokesperson for the mayor's office that day in the park, but things changed. The sacred earth there in Kelly Ingram Park will do that to people.

"Birmingham as a city and a community has always been a blueprint for a nation ailing from racism," said Birmingham mayor Randall Woodfin leading up to his rally.

Woodfin attended Jefferson County's Shades Valley High School in Jerrel Sanders Jackson's nearby Irondale, which, as a modern-day suburb of Birmingham, has strong connections to Alabama football and Nick Saban. Shades Valley High School is located on Old Leeds Road. Left out of the parking lot of the school points in the general direction of Charles Barkley's adjacent hometown (Leeds). Take a right out of Shades Valley and Nick Saban's Birmingham-area Mercedes-Benz car dealership is about two minutes away. Irondale was originally a mining community founded in 1887, and later the hometown of author Fannie Flagg. Her novel *Fried Green Tomatoes* is based loosely on the town and locally famous Irondale Cafe. Jerrel Sanders Jackson's husband, Tom, always refused to eat there because he could remember the day when the Black residents of Irondale had to go around the back of the Southern diner for meat-and-threes to go.

"Good food, though," Jerrel Sanders Jackson said.

NFL defensive tackle Daron Payne, Alabama's wrecking-ball star of the 2017 College Football Playoff, is from the same Irondale neighborhood (Holiday Gardens) as Jerrel Sanders Jackson and her family. He grew up on Fulmar Drive, or two stop signs away from 541 La Salle Lane.

After graduating from Shades Valley, Birmingham mayor Randall Woodfin began his political career with an election to the Birmingham school board in 2013. He then upset longtime Birmingham city councilor and two-term mayoral incumbent William Bell in 2017. Identified early in his mayorship as a potential future star for the national Democratic Party, Woodfin was the fourth consecutive Black mayor to be elected in Birmingham, beginning with Richard Arrington Jr. in 1979. Woodfin's an Alabama football fan, too. The Birmingham mayor's professed fandom is noteworthy because in Alabama that always matters. Birmingham is the capital of college football in the country, and there isn't a close second. For the last 20 years, an entire generation, the city has been ESPN's top-rated television market for college football. The SEC is headquartered in Birmingham, it's where the Iron Bowl between Alabama and Auburn was born and grew into the nation's greatest rivalry, and Birmingham is where, on the first day of school, teachers ask students who they're for and everyone has to pick a side. Those are the rules. Birmingham is one of the greatest sports towns in America, and the local pro teams are Alabama and Auburn. Choose carefully. Woodfin certainly did.

Birmingham's mayor has interacted publicly and privately on occasion with Alabama coach Nick Saban, and even been invited to a practice or two. That detail speaks volumes about Woodfin's appeal and reputation. Saban, historically, loathes involving himself with politicians, with the lone exception, of course, being his childhood friend West Virginia senator Joe Manchin (D). Saban famously once declined a lunch with President George W. Bush (R) while coaching the Miami Dolphins, but it's doubtful that had much to do with Bush's political affiliation. Former Alabama senator Doug Jones (D) said he was once "snubbed" by Saban at the Birmingham Civil Rights Institute. As U.S. attorney for the Northern District of Alabama, Jones prosecuted two of the Klansmen responsible for the 1963 bombing of Birmingham's 16th Street Baptist Church. They placed 19 sticks of dynamite along the wall of the church basement and committed murder. The act of domestic terrorism killed Addie Mae Collins, 14; Cynthia Wesley, 14; Carole Robertson, 14; and Carol Denise McNair, 11, and wounded many others, including Addie Mae's younger sister, Sarah Collins, who was blinded by shrapnel in one of her eyes. Two of the victims were decapitated by the blast, which was one of about 50 recorded dynamite bombings in Birmingham from 1947 to 1965 as Birmingham's Black residents continually committed the mortal sin of attempting to live among the whites in their Yellowhammer State.

The 16th Street Baptist Church, designated a National Historic Landmark in 2006, catty-corners Kelly Ingram Park, and is across the street from the south-facing Birmingham Civil Rights Institute. The larger Birmingham Civil Rights District includes the historic A.G. Gaston Motel, which is where Martin Luther King Jr. and Ralph David Abernathy stayed in Birmingham when Birmingham civil rights leader Fred Shuttlesworth invited King and Abernathy's civil rights organization, the Southern Christian Leadership Conference, to town to plan the 1963 Birmingham Campaign. "As goes Birmingham, so goes the Nation," Shuttlesworth wrote to his fellow pastors.

It was at the A.G. Gaston Motel where King and Abernathy planned to surrender themselves to Birmingham police by defying a court order and parading without a permit. Friends since both served as young ministers in Montgomery, King and Abernathy were booked into the Birmingham Jail on April 12, 1963. It was there, while alone in solitary confinement, that King wrote not just a "clap-back" but one of the most profound texts in American history. His "Letter from Birmingham Jail" criticized white moderates for their silent complicity of police brutality and domestic terrorism. The white clergy's "A Call for Unity" referred to King, Abernathy, and the SCLC as "outsiders" and framed the silence of everyone as the means to peace. That misguided cultural sentiment remains prevalent in Southern culture even today. "If you don't have anything good to say, then don't say anything at all." White church leaders penned a similar letter to Black citizens of Alabama in January 1963 when segregationist George Wallace was elected governor. Priests have brokered for peace before wars throughout history. Violence comes to those who do not submit, and the white clergy knew it. They encouraged Birmingham's Black residents to refrain from joining King and Abernathy in their protests of Birmingham's "racial problems."

King's response to that letter resonated loudly in the summer of 2020. Long before that, however, San Francisco 49ers quarterback Colin Kaepernick was blackballed by the NFL in 2016 for taking a knee during the national anthem. Kaepernick was trying to raise awareness for that same ongoing and systemic problem in America, police brutality and racial injustice. Instead of listening to his pleas, America distorted his message, and Donald Trump then villainized Kaepernick for the benefit of his presidential campaign. A year later, Trump referred to anyone who joined Kaepernick's protest as a "son of a bitch" during a political rally in Huntsville.

"I love Alabama," Trump said at the event. "It's special."

Indeed, but for reasons beyond his capacity for thought. Even then, Trump was pushing a country toward its brittle ledge.

From Kaepernick's news conference on September 1, 2016, following the San Francisco 49ers' final preseason game:

The message is we have a lot of issues in this country that we need to deal with. We have a lot of people that are oppressed. We have a lot of people that aren't treated equal, given equal opportunities. Police brutality is a huge thing that needs to be addressed. There are a lot of issues that need to be talked about, to be brought to life, and we need to fix those.

On February 9, 2018, former ESPN reporters Cari Champion and Jamele Hill, along with Kevin Merida, the former editor in chief of ESPN's website *The Undefeated* and a former managing editor of the *Washington Post*, hosted a television special at Birmingham's Sixth Avenue Baptist Church to celebrate Black History Month that year, and commemorate the 50th anniversary of King's assassination. The program tied together King's "Letter from Birmingham Jail" and Kaepernick's peaceful protest against police brutality. The topics centered around the role Black athletes play in shaping America.

Before the taping of the show, Champion established urgency for the live audience. "This is an extremely important time. If you don't speak, you are in agreement." The loudest cheers that day were for Hill, who had famously called President Trump a white supremacist surrounded by white supremacists in September 2017.

"Now is not the time to be silent," Hill said inside the church.

In 2016, there was something worse than silence, though. There was Roger Goodell.

When the commissioner of the NFL criticized Kaepernick for kneeling during the national anthem, it was a disastrous and consequential mistake by an appointed national leader of great influence. Goodell was protecting the system and the shield and sacrificing a player of courage. He should have had Kaepernick's back, but he sided with the bottom line. Worse still, an argument can be made that Goodell was contributing to the "racial problems" of the day. Clemson coach Dabo Swinney, who played at Alabama and is from the white-flight Birmingham suburb of Pelham, responded to Kaepernick's peaceful protest by vilifying him in the most sick and twisted way possible. Swinney bastardized King's message and then turned it into a commentary on the right-wing myth that Christians in America are politically persecuted.

"With Martin Luther King," Swinney said, "I don't know that there's ever been a better man or better leader. To me, he changed the world. He changed the world through love in the face of hate. He changed the world through peace in the face of violence. He changed the world through education in the face of ignorance. And he changed the world through Jesus. Boy, that's politically incorrect. That's what he did. It's amazing when we don't learn from our past how you can repeat your mistakes."

Which is to say, how could Dabo Swinney, a child of post–civil rights era Birmingham, be so devastatingly wrong about world history that happened in his own backyard? Dabo, the Birmingham Civil Rights Institute was *right there*. Once the heir apparent to Nick Saban at Alabama, the former Crimson Tide receiver might want to brush up on his talking points before ever thinking about returning home to his Yellowhammer State. Then again, the opportunity might now never come. Swinney's job is to convince young men to play football for him for free so he can collect a multimillion-dollar salary, and he is on record saying he'll quit that job if the players are ever paid.*

Swinney's ignorance begs another important question: Just what the hell kind of history did they teach at Pelham High School? When it came to the civil rights history of Alabama and America, the answer was the same for all students in the state—little to none at all. Swinney's hometown Birmingham-area suburb, 20 miles removed from Jones Valley, exists in its present form because whites didn't want their children going to school with Black girls and boys. Modern-day Metro Birmingham, still fighting against itself but somehow a place with so much potential, is the undeniable legacy of white people who never learned from their own history after they were forced to integrate the schools. Instead, they drafted alternative forms of facts, and established opposing municipalities, and now seven-county "Greater Birmingham" is one of the most segregated places in America, with 46 separate governments in Jefferson and Shelby counties alone. There is even one Birmingham suburb, Mountain Brook, whose residents refer to it as "The Tiny Kingdom," and whose many high school graduates convince themselves their most important goal in life is to move away and never return. Mountain Brook's neighboring Birmingham suburb, Vestavia Hills, was incorporated in 1950 with an official city motto of "A Place Apart." Vestavia Hills High School, formed in 1970 in defiance of forced integration by the federal courts, is still the home of the Rebels, and their football uniforms look like Confederate salutes to the stars and bars circa Ole Miss's unis 1963.

A sculpture of Collins, Wesley, Robertson, and McNair, the four girls murdered that year by Klansmen terrorists, now rests in

---

* A new NCAA rule allowing college students to earn money for endorsements went into effect on July 1, 2021. Time to hang up that whistle, Dabo.

Kelly Ingram Park, and in the center of the public square a statue of Martin Luther King Jr. faces the place of Christian worship where those children's lives were taken up to heaven and away from this hateful world at 10:22 a.m. on Sunday, September 15, 1963. At the foot of the sculpture is the name of the sermon for a Sunday morning service that never happened: "A Love That Forgives."

Birmingham celebrates and cherishes its important role in the civil rights movement of the 1960s, and Kelly Ingram Park is the lodestone that still magnetizes the hearts of people there in that city formed from Blacks and whites both turning iron into steel during its industrial boom. Kelly Ingram Park is where Woodfin wanted to have his hurriedly scheduled "Birmingham, the World is Watching" rally on May 31, 2020. Less than a month after King's jailing in 1963, the park was the staging ground for the series of children's protests in the ongoing Birmingham Campaign that finally did force the world to take notice. The demonstrations were first met with mass arrests, and then by the high-pressure fire hoses and attack dogs of Bull Connor's army of government thugs posing as firemen and police officers. Theophilus Eugene "Bull" Connor was Birmingham's longtime "commissioner of public safety," and is now the eternal godfather of American police brutality. Was he racist, or did he just want law and order in the defense of states' rights? Those tired, stale words of Confederate contrivance never changed. They just shifted and moved through the years like guilty eyes that always refused to see. Sometimes, though, it's impossible to look away.

In some of the images from those notorious scenes of the Birmingham's Children's Crusade, it took four grown men to control and aim one fire hose, and the weapon of water that was blasted out carried for 100 feet. In addition to ordering violence against Black children, Connor also deputized pretty much every buddy he knew who was in the Klan. If you know where to look in some of the houses out in the Birmingham suburbs, it's not hard to find old guns and badges that Connor gave out like Klan rally door prizes. It has always been easy to enlist foot soldiers for the war when they have been taught that they're under siege by people who do not look and think like them. Maybe those people all along just wanted their lives to matter, too. In a populist social phenomenon that still continues today with voices like Clay Travis, Bull Connor gained notoriety in Birmingham first as a sports personality on the radio.

The 2020 First-Team All-Grift MVP of capitalizing off of the Lost Cause myth of Southern white man victimhood was Clay Travis, who was named a radio successor to Rush Limbaugh following the conservative firebrand's death from lung cancer. A television and radio personality in SEC country and a resident of Nashville, Travis leveraged the division of America during Trump's years in office to build his media brand. It was a lucrative hustle before the pandemic, but Travis really went to work on his craft when Trump began politicizing the coronavirus pandemic. Copying Trump's successful pattern of delegitimizing the work of journalists by labeling it as "fake news," Travis ascribed the term "corona-bro" to any media member in the sports world who was worried that the COVID-19 pandemic was going to disrupt sports or threaten the health of athletes. He then started pushing the populist myth, created by Trump, that the coronavirus was less of a risk to public health than the seasonal flu. No doubt it was good business telling people what they wanted to hear during a pandemic. Did anyone actually listen to the two-bit pettifoggery of this crusty limp-penciled rich boy? We can only hope not. In Alabama, deaths from COVID-19 in one year surpassed the state's total of deaths attributed to the flu in a decade. Proportionally, the Black community suffered the most, but the Black community is probably not the target audience of a person who has argued, in some kind of bizarre defense of Confederate monuments and statues, that allowing slavery to continue in America would have benefited Blacks more in the long run.

A passage from Clay Travis's popular blog on his website from August 18, 2018:

The removal of Confederate statues isn't about making things better, it's about attacking people. If you told me that removing Confederate statues would end racism, I'd be all for it. But that's not what this is about. This is about attacking people who the left wing disagrees with politically. The left wing in this country looks down on white Southerners and considers their opinions unworthy of respect.

Shameful words from someone in a position of influence who should have known better.

On June 17, 2015, a radicalized, homicidal Southern white man walked into a Bible study at another house of Christian worship, Emanuel African Methodist Episcopal Church in Charleston, South Carolina, and murdered nine Black parishioners. They were Clementa C. Pinckney (age 41), Cynthia Marie Graham Hurd (54), Susie Jackson (87), Ethel Lee Lance (70), Depayne Middleton-Doctor (49), Tywanza Sanders (26), Daniel L. Simmons (74), Sharonda Coleman-Singleton (45), and Myra Thompson (59). God's children all, robbed of life in a massacre just for being Black.

When pictures started circulating online of the 26-year-old domestic terrorist celebrating with symbols of white supremacy and the Confederate battle flag, public leaders around the Deep South decided it was probably a good time to take down the stuff celebrating the Confederacy. In Montgomery, Republican governor Robert Bentley, who was a physician for Paul Bryant, quietly ordered the removal of four Confederate flags around the enormous Confederate monument outside the Capitol building. After Richmond, Montgomery was the capital of the Confederacy during the Civil War, and former CSA president Jefferson Davis later laid the cornerstone of the monument in 1880. When asked why the flags were taken down, Bentley said it was the right thing to do. In New Orleans, mayor Mitch Landrieu told the city council their town's Confederate war stuff had to go.

Two years later, but after Trump had been elected, the city of Charlottesville, Virginia, decided to take down a public statue of Confederate general Robert E. Lee, and it was like all of a sudden every blistered-handed, mule-faced, always-picked-last-in-everything white supremacist whom no one had ever heard of before all decided it was time to climb out of their sex-gimp coffins and parade around the streets while singing Nazi show tunes. They called it a "Unite the Right" rally, but it was not that. It was a coming-out party for the normalization of hate in the name of preserving a long-dead, Lost Cause hero insurrectionist. A day later, another radicalized, murderous troll then committed murder by driving his car through a crowded street of protesters in a homicidal rage. He killed 32-year-old Heather Heyer of Charlottesville, and injured 19 others.

Always remember what sells in the Deep South: "White Southern men" are the real victims of history, no one is racist except the "outsiders," it's always the wrong time to protest, and the opinions of Black people aren't even worth counting because their lives don't matter, but the real truth is they're just being used to divide everyone politically. Quick: Someone cue up the clip of Charles Barkley saying he doesn't care about Confederate statues. That'll own libs.

When New Orleans decided to take down its four Confederate monuments, Mayor Mitch Landrieu offered into the American literary catalogue one of the most brilliant speeches on race in modern-day America. Google it.

Said Landrieu:

These statues are not just stone and metal. They're not just innocent remembrances of a benign history. These monuments celebrate a fictional, sanitized Confederacy; ignoring the death, ignoring the enslavement, ignoring the terror that it actually stood for. And after the Civil War, these monuments were part of that terrorism as much as burning a cross on someone's lawn. They were erected purposefully to send a strong message to all who walked in their shadows about who was still in charge in this city.

Landrieu went on to remind people that, yep, the Civil War was about "maintaining slavery and white supremacy" by pointing to the infamous words of Alexander Stephens. A very victimized Southern white man (and not just because he was a Georgia grad), Stephens was the vice president of the Confederate States, and he gave a speech in Savannah, Georgia, two weeks before the Civil War began that said Blacks are slaves because their lives just don't count for anything other than servitude, and this new country the South is building is God's plan. The "corner-stone" of the Confederacy "rests," Stephens said, "upon the great truth, that the negro is not equal to the white man; that slavery—subordination to a superior race—is his natural and his normal condition. This, our new government, is the first, in the history of the world, based upon this great physical, philosophical, and moral truth. This truth has been slow in the process of its development, like all other truths in the various departments of science."

A Southern politician talking science? That's a harbinger of doom every time. About 620,000 soldiers died in the American Civil War.

The post-Reconstruction government that Stephens helped establish in Georgia has its problems, but the Peach State ain't got noth'n on Alabama when it comes to the legacy of white supremacy as government policy.

Around the same time that New Orleans started planning the removal of its Confederate monuments, the city of Birmingham wanted to do the same thing to the 52-foot Confederate Soldiers and Sailors Monument in Linn Park. The Birmingham Park Board voted unanimously in favor of removing it, but a group of Alabama's victim class called "Save Our South" sued to keep it up. From the "Save Our South" Facebook page: "We are a not for profit organization and our goal is to preserve history and provide a voice for Southerners. Heritage. Hope. Unity. Hear our voice!"

The lawsuit did a crucial thing for the forever Lost Cause narrative of white Southern victimhood. It gave the state government down in Montgomery, a Republican supermajority, some good political ammunition to make strawman enemies out of the people in Black and blue-dot Birmingham. When governor Robert Bentley unceremoniously gave the order to take down the Confederate flags outside the Capitol building in 2015, he simply told reporters, while walking to his car that morning, that it was the right thing to do. Now, amid Trump's America, it was all an attack by the "left wingers" against *the very foundations of freedom this country was built upon* and blah, blah, blah. All horseshit, but Alabama governor Kay Ivey—and may this stroke of her pen live in the infamy it deserves—signed the Alabama Memorial Preservation Act into law on May 25, 2017.

For an unelected Republican, strengthening the myth of the Lost Cause of the Confederacy was just smart politics. Kay Ivey was sworn in as governor in April 2017 after Robert Bentley resigned in disgrace because of an extramarital affair. She announced her campaign for the 2018 election in September 2017.

In Alabama, the cult of the Lost Cause is rooted in a white supremacy of historical fact that was established into state law in 1901 with a new constitution. White supremacists needed a governing document after post–Civil War Reconstruction to legally win back power over the Black population. With the help of Klan terror in the Black Belt, an election for a new constitution carried the state in a general vote. From the Anniston newspaper the *Hot Blast* on the eve of the statewide vote to create a constitutional convention:

> It is good for the white man and better for the negro that the basis of suffrage be fixed now while it may be done peacefully and with an eye to the best interests of both races...If you favor the rule of the white man and want to see once more honest election methods in Alabama, you will go to the polls and vote for the convention...It took two thousand years to prepare the white race for freedom and the exercise of the ballot. The negro was given the ballot without a day of preparation. What has he done to be so favored among the races?..."Blood is thicker than water." We stand by our race in this fight.

Southern white man, always the victim.

The president of the constitutional convention, John B. Knox of Anniston, reportedly said before the drafting of the new document that "just as long as 180,000 negroes have as much right to vote as you and I, there is standing a constant menace to all of us. The great object we have undertaken is to maintain white supremacy—not by force but by law."

"The new constitution eliminates the ignorant negro vote," Knox later said after the new constitution was established, "and places the control of our government where God Almighty intended it should be—with the Anglo-Saxon race."

Four years later, they erected the 52-foot Confederate Obelisk of Hate in Birmingham's Linn Park as a salute to the Alabama Yellowhammers who fought in the Civil War. But here's the kicker on that: Birmingham wasn't even a city during the Civil War. It was founded six years after the war ended, in 1871, when it became apparent that the area had huge deposits of iron ore up in the surrounding Appalachian foothills.

And that's why the country's best damn college football rivalry game, which made Birmingham the craziest city for the sport in the world, came to be called the Iron Bowl. The rivalry between Alabama and Auburn has a clenched grip on the heart of the city at all times, and that cultural gravity allows for unexpected things.

FunnyMaine didn't know what he was going to say in Kelly Ingram Park on May 31, 2020, when one of the mayor's strategists asked him to speak, but the comedian knew with absolute certainty that he wasn't going to talk about the Census. Kelly Ingram Park is three blocks west of Linn Park in downtown Birmingham. That's all FunnyMaine was thinking about that day.

Was he worried about his career? He would later say, after everyone wanted to blame him for causing a riot, that he wasn't "scared" if speaking up meant the end of his dream, "but I thought that would be it.

"But I was ready for it to be it," FunnyMaine added. "If this was it, then it was a good run, and we had some great times, but I was ready for it to be over for this cause. I'll let it be it. I'm fine with that. We had some good smiles."

The transcript of his impromptu speech:

They call me comedian FunnyMaine, but my name is Jermaine Johnson.

I'm from Pratt City. I'm Black as hell and I'm proud of it.

Too many times we say Black lives matter. They say all lives matter.

We say, hold the police accountable. They say, all police ain't bad.

Dammit, it ain't all about all. Sometimes it's about enough. We got enough bad police. We got enough white people upholding white supremacy.

You don't have to score all the points in sports to win, dammit. You just got to score enough.

So now we need enough white people to march with us. We need enough Black people to come back to Birmingham. Come back to the city school systems. Come back to our neighborhoods. Come back to West End. Come back to Ensley. Come back to Norwood where I live.

Come back.

Come back to Black churches.

So, they're telling me to say something, but there is so much I can't say.

So, let me tell y'all what I can't say.

I'll give y'all a little history about the city of Birmingham that I love.

Birmingham was founded 1871. That's six years—six years—after the Civil War ended. For some reason, this land that was known as Elyton or Frog Level, it served no purpose in the Civil War. They didn't fight here. They didn't march here. They didn't do nothing on this land in the Civil War. Yet for some reason, three blocks over at Linn Park, we got a Confederate statue sitting in the middle of our city to remind us to stay in your damn place.

So this is what I'm not going to say.

We got a lot of cities around the country. They're tearing down Target. They're tearing down they city hall. We can't do that.

We got to protect our city.

We can't tear down 16th Street Baptist Church. We can't tear down the Civil Rights Museum. We can't tear down Carver. We can't tear down A.G. Gaston Plaza. But what I'm not telling you to do is walk to Linn Park. I'm not telling you to walk to Linn Park after this rally. I'm not telling you to tear something down in Linn Park.

That's what I'm not telling you to do.

I'm not telling you that I'm going to be over there after this rally.

That's what I'm not telling you to do because the law says I can't tell you to do that.

I cannot tell the police to look away. We don't see you.

I cannot tell the police to march us over there. I can't tell you that, so I'm not telling you to meet me at Linn Park at 7:30 p.m. central tonight. I'm not telling you that.

But while the whole world is on national TV tearing stuff down, we need to tear something tonight. They need to see Birmingham, the home of the civil rights movement, tear some shit down tonight.

But I'm not telling you that.

And now that I'm on all your cameras. Now that I'm on all your Facebook Lives. Now that I'm on the back of your pictures because some of y'all just out here to take selfies. Now that they see me. If they come for me. Don't hashtag me. Don't hashtag me. Because I love the Second Amendment, too.

And if they come for me, you tell them Jermaine Johnson said kiss my ass.

Protestors tried to tear the 115-year-old statue down that night, but in an attempt to send everyone home the mayor promised it would be removed. It was time, but Mayor Woodfin waited another day. Birmingham took down the 52-foot symbol of white supremacy in the middle of Alabama's proud Black town on June 1, 2020, which was an official state holiday in Alabama honoring Jefferson Davis's birthday.

After that, statues throughout the country and the world started to come down in the summer of 2020. Fred Shuttlesworth had it right back in his letter to Dr. King: "As goes Birmingham, so goes the Nation." About 45 minutes down the road, a group of young men were alone on the campus of the University of Alabama and watching that history at a powerful moment in all of their lives. Soon, they would be the agents of change and hope.

Jermaine "FunnyMaine" Johnson, the new face of Alabama football superfandom, should be remembered for his historic words on a profound day for the city of Birmingham, the state of Alabama, and the United States of America. He didn't talk about the 2020 Census, but he sure as hell took an accounting of the country.

CHAPTER 6

RESURRECTIONS

There are no perfect heroes, and especially not in America. At the University of Alabama, there is Paul Bryant Jr., the shadow-master savior of the Alabama football Crimson Tide.

Nick Saban is not the only power broker in Tuscaloosa whose leadership is the reason the Alabama football team is so successful year after year. The considerable business acumen of Paul Bryant Jr., son of the "Bear," has played a key role in the Crimson Tide's historic run, and the overall explosive growth of his university, but the private nature of his puppetry has gone largely unnoticed. That's a considerable statement considering he served on the University of Alabama System Board of Trustees from 2000 to 2015. President pro tempore of the UA Board from 2011 to 2014, Bryant Jr. is among the wealthiest people in Alabama. For much of his adult life he was probably the most powerful, too, and being the son of the famous coach certainly helped along the way. It gave him connections in the Alabama legislature beginning in the 1980s that helped him establish an empire in dog-track racing, but Bryant Jr. played his life's most valuable trump card when his relationship with former Alabama governor Don Siegelman helped put him on the UA Board despite his reportedly making obscenely racist, and morally horrific, unforgivable statements about exploiting poor Black people in Alabama.

Paul Bryant Jr. was Alabama-famous on the day he was born, which, illustrating the guarded nature of his life, is incorrect on his Wikipedia page. It says 1945 and doesn't give a day, but Bryant Jr. was born on December 19, 1944. A war baby, he was born with Paul Bryant Sr. away finishing his service in the Navy. Paul Bryant Sr., a tough-as-sin football player for Alabama from 1933 to 1935, famously played with a partially broken leg against Tennessee in 1935. His head coaching career was just starting (University of Maryland in 1945) when Bryant Jr. arrived. Here's how sports editor Zipp Newman of the *Birmingham News*, "The South's Greatest Newspaper," announced the news in his notes column on Thursday, December 21, 1944: "Capt. Charles Boswell, wounded in action on the German front, is now in a Belgium hospital...A long-shot All-American end: Paul Bryant, Jr., 1964. Hank Crisp Jr. should be a junior when Paul Jr. is playing freshman football. Congrats to Mary Harmon and Paul."

Bryant Jr. was supposed to play football from the day he was born. He couldn't anymore after the seventh grade. Everyone's hellish year at home that was 2020 was not the first trip around the sun stuck indoors for Paul Bryant Jr. He was quarantined to his home for about a year after falling ill with hepatitis in the eighth grade. When he emerged from isolation, his father was the new king of Alabama football Crimson Tide, returned home to his alma mater from Texas A&M to save Tuscaloosa from Jennings Bryan "Ears" Whitworth.

Whitworth went 2–7–1 in 1956 and was fired. Alabama's offensive line coach that season attempted to resign out of shame when Whitworth was canned, but Paul Bryant Sr. wouldn't let Hank Crisp Sr. do it. In a display of loyalty and love for Alabama that would later be the strongest characteristic of his son's conflicted moral code, Bryant Sr. gave the order from College Station, Texas, to put Hank Crisp in charge of recruiting while the Bear and Heisman winner John David Crow finished up their time together in the Gator Bowl. On Crow, Bryant Sr. said, "If John David Crow doesn't win the Heisman Trophy, they ought to stop giving it."

He did win it.

Paul Bryant Jr. played a little basketball growing up in Tuscaloosa, but his natural gifts in life were his intellect and his ability as a leader. After graduating from Alabama, he used them both to make an enormous fortune, taking smart risks with shrewd genius and limitless ambition. Some would call that ruthless. Others would just call it the stuff that made America. Bryant Jr. amassed wealth in a wolfishly diverse array of businesses: dog tracks, casinos, concrete, banking, and reinsurance, among other ventures. What the hell is reinsurance? In short, it's insurance that an insurance company buys from another insurance company. It's also how smart business moguls with a bunch of money can make money at a percentage with little risk.

Greene Group, Inc., is one of Bryant Jr.'s umbrella organizations, and under that parent company was Alabama Reassurance, which was in the business of insuring insurance companies until 2007. That's when its outstanding liabilities were assumed by a newly formed Greene Group, Inc., company called Alabama Life Reinsurance Company with a transfer of $43 million in assets. According to an examination by the State of Alabama Department of Insurance dated December 31, 2009, the new shell company "does not write or have any direct business; it does not have any agents or brokers; and the business it does assume, is in run-off. Once the run-off is completed, the company intends to exit the life insurance business."

Gotta know when to fold 'em.

Here's a fun hustle. As noted in a 2013 profile of Bryant Jr. by Bloomberg titled "Alabama Football Dominance Powered by Greyhound Fortune," Alabama Reassurance "paid Bryant and his two partners a total of $46 million in dividends from 2002 to 2006...At the time, it had just two employees." Moving around large sums of money sometimes rubs people the wrong way, though. As one former Mississippi regulator put it bluntly to Bloomberg, "They were propping up broke companies for a fee. Companies knew they could call on Alabama Re because Alabama Re had to offset dog track profits."

By the late 1990s, Bryant Jr. had secured his fortune, and it was time to dedicate his talents, money, and bear-claw ambition to the greatest love of his life outside of family—the University of Alabama. The last Democrat to serve as governor in Alabama (1999–2003), Don Siegelman (Alabama grad and former president of the student government association) was only in office for one term, but he lobbied for Bryant Jr. to be put on the UA Board, and in 2000 a spot opened up. (Ironically, Siegelman, who later went to federal prison for an unrelated bribery conviction, doesn't get enough credit for his role in saving Alabama football.) The political maneuvering to put Bryant on the UA Board was not universally loved by all in Montgomery, and in order for the University of Alabama to avoid an even more embarrassing controversy than it already was, UA Board member Frank Bromberg resigned his position on April 22, 2000, so Bryant Jr. could begin his reign on the most powerful privately appointed government entity in the state. The UA System Board of Trustees, which governs the campuses in Tuscaloosa, Birmingham, and Huntsville, is a self-perpetuating insiders' club that wields enormous influence. Said Bromberg to the Associated Press upon his resignation,

"Things were getting very complicated, and it seemed like the thing to do."

Roll Tide.

It wasn't complicated, though. The Southern political shenanigans were all for the Crimson Tide. Never forget the most important thing: football at all costs. Protecting that was Paul Bryant Jr.'s birthright, but finding him a seat at the table was, at the very least, a compromise of the very necessary ethical standards needed for a flagship university of a state in the Deep South. It was all a lot of effort to give one person amazing power in Alabama despite the publication of comments made by Bryant Jr. in 1989 that would later cast doubt on the entire mission of the University of Alabama System Board of Trustees. In probably the biggest misstep of his calculated and private life, Bryant Jr. agreed to an interview for the September 1989 edition of *Esquire* magazine. The profile by William M. Adler, titled "The Bear Trap," was about the cutthroat nature of a businessman who was also the son of the famous coach.

A side note: There is nothing more that writers with dicks enjoy doing, present company included, than explaining how dudes are always the inevitable psychological consequence of their fathers. "By virtue of his name alone," wrote Adler, "doors to the interlocking worlds of sports and business and politics have flown open to him. But part of his father's legacy is also the overwhelming pressure to succeed, to somehow measure up to his haunting presence."

Maybe so, but Bryant Jr. was his own man, too. His father wanted him to attend law school, but Bryant Jr. became a young baseball executive instead. In other accounts of his life, he would say that his dad never pressured him to do anything other than work hard at what he enjoyed. Good advice. Bryant Sr. should have warned his son about making racist comments to the national media, though. In Adler's profile about Bryant Jr. and his questionable character as the owner of dog tracks, Bryant Jr. offered these thoughts of the clientele at his gambling dive in Greene County: "Greenetrack's so successful because everyone in Greene County brings their last two dollars and thinks they're gonna win a million... The crowd is rough here, it's a low-class, low-income crowd. Down here, it's generally your lower class of blacks. Your welfare blacks. You want them to have enough room to get in and out, but at the same time you want to get as many in as possible."

Bryant Jr. denied the comments and apparently wanted a retraction. Despite those terrible words, and what they represent when applied to the history of the state, the UA Board wanted Bear's son to be a trustee of higher education for the people of Alabama. His friends would say he was misquoted, but the Alabama Legislative Black Caucus had it right. The 27-member body passed a resolution voicing their concern of the appointment. In a story by the Associated Press in the April 7, 2000, edition of the *Selma Times-Journal*, the caucus pleaded that what Bryant Jr. was quoted as saying "'totally insults the integrity of all blacks,' and 'does not give the impression of sensitivity towards blacks.'" That's putting it nicely.

"He hasn't said, 'I'm sorry. I apologize,'" said Representative John Rogers (D) of Birmingham to the Associated Press. "From what I heard, he still feels that way." The AP story in the *Anniston Star* that day went on to report that Rogers would "withdraw his opposition to Bryant if he takes it back and says 'I apologize.'"

It is never too late to ask for forgiveness. Even the deepest of wounds can heal.

It seems like Bryant Jr. should have known better, too. After all, he was a student of history from a very young age. Throughout his life, he served and worked with various historical societies:

the Alabama Heritage Foundation (director), the Museum of the Confederacy in Richmond, Virginia (trustee), and the Civil War Preservation Trust in Washington, D.C. (chairman).

When Bryant started on the UA Board in June 2000, he went to work immediately on reshaping Alabama athletics and the finances of college football at the University of Alabama. His keen mind and cunning business sense have helped create a financial apparatus that gives the best coach in college since Bryant Sr. all the money he can spend. At the very beginning, Bryant Jr. donated $10 million to restructure the debt of the athletics department, and then started a capital building campaign called the Crimson Tradition to raise many more millions of dollars. He threw $10 million more into the coffers that reportedly went for the north end zone stadium expansion (where the damn kids leave early to go to Gallettes!), and that snowballed so successfully that the Crimson Tide Foundation was established in 2005. Bryant Jr. was the first and longtime chairman.

More important to the University of Alabama than all of those things, though, is the simple fact that Bryant Jr. helped bring Nick Saban to Alabama by trusting and supporting his good friend, athletics director Mal Moore.

Moore was under heavy fire from Alabama fans after coach Mike Shula, the son of Miami Dolphins legend Don Shula, was fired on November 27, 2006, and Moore went searching for Alabama's fourth coach in six years. Bryant Jr. supported Moore during the extended coaching search, which included, famously, West Virginia coach Rich Rodriguez turning down the Tide. For context of how thoroughly Alabama, Auburn, and the SEC is covered by Alabama's statewide news website, AL.com, senior sports editor John Talty wrote a lengthy 10-year anniversary piece on December 8, 2016, about the domino effect of Rodriguez's decision. "Rodriguez's decision to stay in Morgantown considerably changed the futures of at least three college football programs. It has become the source of one of college football's greatest what-if questions especially given Alabama's success in the last decade," Talty wrote.

Moore and Bryant Jr. finally landed the Sabans at the beginning of January in 2007. Moore and Bryant Jr. were extremely close, and Moore always represented the ultimate teammate to many older Alabama fans. He played as a backup quarterback his entire career for Bryant Sr. (1958–62).

Saban, Moore, and Bryant Jr. are the triumvirate responsible for the modern-day success at Alabama. It's just a shame Moore didn't get to see the university complex he helped build. He passed away on March 30, 2013. The Mal Moore Athletic Facility is like the mothership for Alabama football, and Saban has been a good steward. Like Saban and Bryant Sr., Bryant Jr.'s exacting attention to details have set up the University of Alabama for generations of future success in both athletics and academics.

And he's apparently as clever as he is ruthless.

In a stroke of competitive, the-SEC-is-so-gloriously-crazy-y'all accounting, Bryant Jr.'s brainchild that is the Crimson Tide Foundation said, "You know, what? We're just going to quit counting our money." Paraphrasing here, but the Crimson Tide Foundation stopped filing its IRS 990s so no one could see who was donating what, and where exactly all the money was going. The given reason for Alabama's secrecy, in the words of Pulitzer Prize–winning columnist John Archibald of AL.com: "When Deborah M. Lane—assistant to the president and associate VP for University Relations—finally explained that decision this week she said the group believes it does not have to file the form because it is affiliated with a government entity: The UA Board of Trustees."

That excerpt of Archibald's reporting came in a column titled "Paul Bryant Jr.'s bank is the tie that binds UA trustees." Archibald went on to note that some of the board members in the Crimson Tide Foundation and the UA System Board of Trustees were employed together at Bryant Bank, which Bryant Jr. founded in 2005 when he started the Crimson Tide Foundation. Also a vice president for the bank: Bobby Humphrey, the famous Alabama running back, who is married to UA trustee Barbara Humphrey and is the father of Marlon Humphrey.

At what point does typical Southern political cronyism make the leap to distorted Southern gothic fairy tale? In this case it was probably when the football team in Birmingham was killed off by its own president with an OK from the UA System Board of Trustees, and then rose from the dead like some reanimated zombie dragon complete with a brand-new stadium in downtown Birmingham built by a partnership, perhaps the first of its kind in Alabama history, between the city, county, state, UAB, and private, really pissed-off businesses. A mythic thing, that, but the story of UAB football is the subject of another book. The tale of the Alabama football Crimson Tide is a parable for the nation.

Would an insurance wizard get wealthy Alabama alums to take out massive policies so that when they go to the great Iron Bowl in the sky, all that coin rolls into the Iron Bank? [Lawyerspeak: This is *totally* a use of sarcasm as a literary device, and not an actual assumption because that would be crazy.] But, hey, when no one can see the records, then the imaginations tend to wander like the private jets. The Crimson Tide Foundation aviation wizards actually did have the tail number of the jet registered to the Crimson Tide Foundation blacked out from flight-tracking websites. Why the need to hide everything and be so secretive? Recruiting, the lifeblood of college football, is the reason. With Saban, it's always about recruiting. Paint that on the bridge in Tuscaloosa that flies across McFarland Boulevard and down Paul W. Bryant Drive and then on into the heart of the underfunded Black Belt region of Alabama.

Through a Freedom of Information Act request, here's what Alabama reporting wizard Michael Casagrande of AL.com wrote in 2014 about the final two months of Alabama's recruiting push: "The aircraft—an 1125 Westwind Astra built by Israel Aircraft Industries in 1990—made 66 trips marked 'football recruiting' on the logs. Saban was on board for 53. The plane touched down in 15 states from coast to coast."

The 2014 recruiting class was ranked No. 1 in the nation by recruiting website 247sports.com, and featured players from 14 different states, including J. K. Scott of Denver. Saban took a private jet to recruit the punter? Nah, not even Alabama is that nuts. An important year in college football, 2014 was the first for the College Football Playoff. Future seniors of that 2014 recruiting class participated in the first College Football Playoff (42–35 loss to Ohio State) and then the next three, winning two. An inside baseball sidebar: Scott's No. 1 fan in the Alabama press corps was special-teams-loving, FOIA-filing Casagrande, who made video recordings of Scott's punts and kickoffs from the press box his senior season, and of course was well aware that Scott broke Alabama's all-time punting record with an average of 45.6 yards per kick. Scott's recruiting class won national championships in 2015 and 2017, but of course the one during Scott's career that everyone remembers most is the loss in the 2016 national championship game wedged between the wins. That's the one when cornerback Marlon Humphrey, the son of the UA System Board member and former Alabama running back Bobby Humphrey, was the victim of the most famous goal-line pick play in college football history and Alabama lost at the gun 35–31 at Tampa's Raymond James Stadium. With Alabama, everyone remembers the losses more, and especially when they're to Clemson and Pelham, Alabama, native Dabo Swinney.

Between 2015 and 2018, the College Football Playoff was like an invitational tournament for Alabama and Clemson. They met every year, with the teams splitting the four games, and Alabama's loss for the 2018 national championship was the absolute stunner. Alabama was a 5.5-point favorite, but Saban's guys were pantsed on national television 44–16 at Levi's Stadium in San Jose. Alabama quarterback Tua Tagovailoa was still injured, and, looking back, people have to wonder if backup senior Jalen Hurts would have been a better option. After all, it was Hurts who led the fourth quarter against Georgia in that season's epic SEC championship. Swinney, playing his "little ol' Clemson angle perfectly," showed his team *Rocky III* the night before playing Alabama for the third time in a championship game in four years. He turned Alabama into Clubber Lang, in other words, a soft-bellied bully. "We Want Bama" had jumped the shark, but, hey, whatever works.

When Saban and Swinney meet in the College Football Play-off, it always makes for grand theater in the spirit of Don King, and that heavyweight prizefight of coaches draws the limelight away from everyone else. Take care, however, not to forget the breakout star from the first meeting between Alabama and Clemson in the College Football Playoff. The path that NFL and Crimson Tide tight end O. J. Howard took from Autauga County, Alabama, to Offensive MVP of the 2015 national championship game is a gen-erational journey of heroism in the face of tragedy.

———

The road that winds down into the middle of Alabama from Tusca-loosa to Howard's Autauga County is U.S. 82. That drive through the Deep South is a pretty one, and it skirts the geographic area in the state known historically as the Black Belt. It's a reference to the rich soil, which made that region perfect for growing cotton. The rich culture of the Black Belt is like a muse for Southern writers. All the imagery, y'all. All the ghosts of the Southern pines. All the quilting and the singing and the Friday night football. It's a treasure of a place because of the Black Alabamians there who have persevered, and are mostly happy for their daily blessings, despite the long history of neglect by the state and the sons of the sons of the sons of the sons of their white neighbors. The spirit of the people in that region of the world is inspiring, and soul cleansing, to all who go there either in person, in thought, or in soul. To find the heart of America, just step into a diner in Marengo, Washington, or Wilcox counties. It's cooked right in the greens along with, probably, way too much bacon. Children's novelist Rita Williams-Garcia of Queens, New York, set her spiritual celebration of the American Black family, *Gone Crazy in Alabama*, in O. J. Howard's Autauga County. The people who award the book prize named for Coretta Scott King, made a widow by the assassination of her husband, then told everyone to go out and read it. The award's description: for the most distinguished portrayal of African American experience in literature for children or teens.

The term "Black Belt" in modern-day Southern America is also a reference to the social and political region that extends from Louisiana and Mississippi, through southern Alabama's Black Belt, and all the way into Georgia and then South Carolina. SEC football country, in other words. Where Saban flies around and brings home to Tuscaloosa all the best recruits. Alabama's portion of the Black Belt is populated by the descendants of slaves, who suffered horrific racial terror before and after Reconstruction, and then were left for dead after the new constitution in 1901. The Alabama Blacks of Alabama's Black Belt did not die, but places like Autauga County, home of O'Terrius Jabari Howard, still have their demons.

———

Autauga County is a geographical transition in the state between the Black Belt below and to the west and central Alabama above. To the east of Autauga County is the Black Belt also, and it extends into another region of the state known as the Wiregrass. If the physical shape of the state of Alabama were a human head, then Autauga County would be that place right below the nose where everyone pulled down their pandemic masks. Autaugaville, the little town of Howard's very large extended family, is located on Alabama State Road 14 about 24 miles east of Selma, and about 24 miles west of Montgomery. The civil rights history of Autaugaville's corner of the world is rich like the soil, and the people who worked for voting rights there in 1965 were of the same resilience as the stands of beautiful wildflowers that grow freely in the roadside ditches, creek beds, and forest floors.

One of America's great champions of civil rights was a seed of strength for Selma in 1965 when that quality was needed most. Amelia Boynton Robinson was a "home demonstration agent" for the U.S. Department of Agriculture in rural Dallas County before becoming a leader in Selma's fight for the voting rights of Black residents. A graduate of the Tuskegee Institute, she was an educator in subsistence living, but between 1963 and 1965 she was a lead local organizer for Selma's voting campaign. Robinson, 52 years old in 1965, was one of the few Black residents who could vote in Selma at the time. The city's population was 50 percent Black then, but only 1 percent were registered voters, according to *The*

Jim Crow Encyclopedia. To raise awareness of the discrimination following the passage of the Civil Rights Act of 1964, Robinson and other key civil rights leaders, including Hosea Williams and James Bevel of the Southern Christian Leadership Conference, organized a protest walk from Selma to Montgomery for March 7, 1965. The day would later be called "Bloody Sunday." Robinson was knocked unconscious and that image of oppression went around the world. Other leaders of the first Selma-to-Montgomery march were beaten as well when they were met by Alabama state troopers on the Edmund Pettus Bridge, named for a former officer of the Confederate States Army who would later become a grand dragon in the Ku Klux Klan. Among the victims of police brutality was young John Lewis of Pike County, Alabama, who had been helping to organize demonstrations for civil rights since 1961. The violence against protestors in Selma, the passage of the Voting Rights Act of 1965, and the history of Alabama's eternal struggles for equality remain connected to the present-day country roads that run through the Black Belt.

O. J. Howard grew up on an unpaved road—just like one of his best friends, Derrick Henry—and the dirt track's name, Burns Lane, should have a special meaning to fans of Alabama football. Burns Lane wasn't named after the best, and wisest, assistant coach during Nick Saban's unmatched run of dominance, but Burton Burns, the mystical New Orleans sage of running backs, and the pride of St. Augustine High School in the Seventh Ward, did bring Henry from pine-tree-rich Yulee, Florida, to Tuscaloosa to join Howard in the Tide's No. 1–ranked recruiting class of 2013.

Part of Autauga County sits on a limestone aquifer, and cold, clear, refreshing water just bubbles up out of the earth in random places all over. O. J. Howard grew up drinking that water out of an artisan fountain across the street from his grandmother's restaurant. Lauretta Parker-Tyus bought the place after working there as a waitress, and Laura's Country Kitchen was the only restaurant in Autaugaville for many years. O.J. loved working in the family business with his grandmother, and they could turn it out. The biscuits were made fresh every morning, and O.J. helped bake them in the summers. Lauretta's sweet potato pies, still a family legacy, were the perfect blend of love and sugar, and everyone in Autauga County knew it (and most ordered at least one for the holidays). Hamburger steak was the special on Monday night, and the community came together at Laura's on Tuesdays for fried pork chops, mac and cheese, and cabbage. Not a Cracker Barrel, in other words. Roll Tide. Laura's County Kitchen thrived on the real spirit of the South, y'all, and that means kindness, service, and love. Mac and cheese, greens, and fried green tomatoes will save us all, eventually, if the Iron Bowl doesn't kill us first.

Lauretta Parker-Tyus died suddenly in 2006 from a blood disease, but O. J. Howard and his mother, Lamesa, carried on his grandmother's love for cooking. When 2020 NFL Offensive Player of the Year and Alabama Heisman Trophy–winning running back Derrick Henry, raised in the rich cultural foundation of rural northeast Florida, came to visit Howard's family in Autauga County, they had a Southern feast and ate everything, including one of Derrick Henry's favorites, pigs' feet. In his Heisman Trophy season, Henry rushed for 2,219 yards and 28 touchdowns, and those totals are both single-season rushing records at Alabama. In 2020, Najee Harris would rush for 26, but in one less game (although it was actually *two more* games against SEC opponents). The crafty onside kick call by Nick Saban in the 2015 season's national championship game cemented the performances of Henry and Howard as the stuff of Alabama football Crimson Tide lore. Henry rushed for 158 yards on 36 carries for three touchdowns in the 45–40 victory against Clemson, and Howard turned out to be the secret weapon for offensive coordinator Lane Kiffin. The pride of Autauga County had 208 yards receiving on five receptions and two touchdowns.

The people of Autaugaville threw a parade for Howard after his heroic performance, and the city celebrated him like a champion. In the end, his tiny high school even changed the name of an access road out front to O. J. Howard Lane. It was a happy conclusion, and a healing moment for an insular and mysterious little place in Alabama that had to go through so much suffering to get there. O. J. Howard went to high school at Autauga Academy, and when he made plans to bring his white girlfriend to the prom all hell broke loose when the school's old racists on the board told him he couldn't. True story. And this happened in 2011.

To be completely accurate, what happened at Autauga Academy in 2011 is that the cowards on the board didn't have the courage to deliver their message of racial discrimination against Howard themselves, so they made the "headmaster" do it. Now, understand, by Howard's junior year when this happened, he was already committed to play football at the University of Alabama. At 6-foot-5½ and 221 pounds, Howard was an athletic phenomenon in little ol' Autauga County, and could have been drafted into Major League Baseball if he didn't choose to go the way of football. Just let that marinate for a minute. Howard mattered a whole heckuva lot when he was on the football and baseball fields for Autauga Academy, but the future star player of Alabama football's first kicking in of the teeth of Dabo Swinney could not, according to the leaders of Autauga Academy, live his life under the same protection of "unalienable" constitutional rights as the white children in his school. Some, if not all, of Alabama's football coaches knew about the discrimination against Howard at the time, too, and were absolutely furious, but O.J.'s mom told Saban's men in so many words that she could handle that business herself. Oh, Lamesa Howard, daughter of Lauretta Parker-Tyus, cooked those racists on the fiery coals of justice. All the heat, y'all. After the board was told to go to hell during a meeting, O. J. Howard and his girlfriend went to the prom together, and their parents walked into the formal as mixed couples, too.

In 2016, after the school had already named the road outside after O. J. Howard, there was still a portrait of a Confederate general hanging in the front entrance of the main building. It was such a sad and pathetic piece of art, though, it was hard to tell if the painting was of Klan grand wizard Nathan Bedford Forrest or some other insurrectionist made into a hero by the Lost Cause descendants of the Civil War. Autauga Academy grew from the traumatic experience, but the ingrained systemic racism that created the school is the real problem in the Deep South, and it's going to take the hard work of politicians and community leaders many decades to correct it. Autauga Academy, a necessary antagonist here to understand a greater historical paradigm, was created in response to the 1964 Civil Rights Act that made illegal "separate but equal" Jim Crow laws in the South. Like foul and toxic sludge oozing from a new lake of boiling hell, "segregation academies" just started burping up out of the ground all over. When the whites in Jefferson County were forming Vestavia Hills High School ("A City Apart"), and Dabo Swinney's Pelham in Shelby County was preparing for its population boom from all the white flight out of Birmingham, and the school board in Montgomery was defiantly naming its new high school after Jefferson Davis, many of the whites in rural Alabama started their own schools so their children didn't have to learn alongside Black children and maybe—oh, the horror—even date each other and go to the prom.

You're probably asking why Howard went to Autauga Academy at all, and why he didn't just leave the school after the discrimination. He stayed because the Howards are some pretty amazing people, and even though the school's board was racist, most of the people at Autauga Academy rallied around the Howards, supported them, and wanted them to stay. O.J. attended Autauga Academy because educational options in Autauga County are limited. He was originally at Prattville High School, but the Howards didn't feel like it was the right fit for their child. Unfortunately, Autauga Academy was the only other viable option, in the Howards' opinion, because Autaugaville High School was grossly underfunded through no fault of its own. It was designed to be depressed by government-sponsored white supremacy. After the state voted for a new constitution in 1901, this was the screaming front page, in wartime-sized font, of the *Montgomery Advertiser* (November 11, 1901):

THE CITIZENS OF ALABAMA DECLARE FOR WHITE SUPREMACY AND THE PURITY OF BALLOT

The Putrid Sore of Negro Suffrage Is Severed From the Body Politic of the Commonwealth.

NEW CONSTITUTION CARRIES BY MAJORITY WHICH IS OVERWHELMING

Harangues of Disappointed Office Seekers Fail to Swerve the Electors from Their Duty to Themselves and Their Posterity===The Bulk of the Anti-Ratification Vote Cast by the Negroes, but the White Men Were Aroused and Worked Hard for the Adoption of the New Instrument.

That last bit was no doubt a nod of the ol' Klan hood to the members of the KKK who organized voter intimidation through violence to win the election. According to historians, statewide voter fraud, but especially in the Black Belt where the population was two-thirds Black, helped determine the outcome of the 1901 constitution. And that tome of bewilderment is so long. It is longer than the Coastal Southern accents of hungover, fourth-generation Mobileans in two-days-past-tired Mardi Gras tuxedos on the third morning after Joe Cain Day in a Waffle House on Government Street. "Juss give us suum eeeh-ggs, cheese griss, and toh-ss, huun."

With each individual county requiring a statewide vote for local amendments, the 1901 Alabama constitution grows and grows. From Ballotpedia.org: "The Alabama Constitution has been amended more than 800 times since 1901 and is the longest constitution in the world." Alabama's 1901 state constitution of white supremacy has more amendments than Joe Namath had passing yards his junior (765) and senior seasons (756), and Alabama was awarded national championship designation that last time. While we're counting things, Alabama lost to Texas 21–17 in the Orange Bowl following the 1964 season, but that year still counts as national title No. 12 in Alabama's grand total of 18 (through 2020). Why? They used to give out national championships like Mardi Gras throws back then. Arkansas went undefeated that year, and knocked off No. 1 Texas 14–13 at Texas Memorial Stadium, but the Hogs didn't catch their doubloon until after the bowl season.

Cool story, bro, but Alabama ain't giv'n back natties no matter what, aight? Roll Tide.

Definitely someone should light that 1901 constitution on fire, though. Lord knows there were plenty of fires to make sure it passed. It's a legacy of murder, racial terrorism, and complete destruction of any chance vulnerable and abused people of scarred humanity had at making it out of Reconstruction as freed slaves of American potential. The Pharoah won, y'all, and Moses's children have been wandering in the fallow wasteland of a barren sea asking permission to cry for over 400 years. Don't matter what your Facebook friends say. In the name of Jesus, make this right.

Even then, in the November 11, 1901, edition of the *Montgomery Advertiser*, it was reported that voter fraud was likely. Still, the chairman of the Democratic Campaign Committee, O. W. Underwood, reportedly said in Birmingham, "I claim the State for the new Constitution by 27,800 majority."

And just like that, Blacks in Alabama couldn't vote, and most of Alabama's Black children didn't have anywhere to go to school.

━━━

Between 1877 and 1950, 360 individuals were lynched in Alabama, according to research by LynchingInAmerica.org. The region of the state where Autauga County is located was one of the villainous capitals of it all. Between the counties of Autauga, Dallas, Lowndes, Montgomery Elmore, and Chilton, there were 77 reported lynchings. Most assuredly there were more that went unreported. Nationwide there were over 4,000 racial-terror lynchings, per LynchingInAmerica.org. Opened in April 2018, the National Memorial for Peace and Justice in Montgomery is anchored by a memorial to Black victims of lynching in the United States. Go there. Seek it out. Do not turn away. Stand among the installation's 805 pieces of long steel hanging from above like a suspended forest of death and terror. Each piece of cold metal represents a county in the United States where someone was lynched and the murder was documented.

The whites of Alabama rigged the state government to keep Blacks in Alabama poor, undereducated, without political representation or even a chance to determine home rule for themselves. After the Civil Right Act of 1964 and subsequent court orders to integrate schools, Autauga Academy was founded in the spirit of racial cleansing inscribed into law by the state of Alabama in 1969, or 68 years after the conscience-absolving laws of the 1901 state constitution. "States' rights" in Alabama have been used since before the Civil War not just as moral licenses to sin without guilt, but rhetorical tools to bend the minds of men into thinking the dehumanization of people is a birthright and righteous responsibility to defend. Just ask Greene County welfare Blacks with their last $2 in their pockets. Some 50,000 white students left public schools in the mid-1960s and early 1970s, and private schools increased by nearly 100 during that decade.

Of course the segregationist academies, still the schools of choice for many whites in rural Alabama, mythologized the Confederacy and the Civil War. Even the public schools did. That's how minds are won, and people are convinced that others with different opinions are inferior and unworthy of compassion. It's a seductive drug, and it's OK when it comes to hating Alabama or Auburn or LSU, but it's grossly dangerous when used against people for political power. In September 2016, when Colin Kaepernick's protest against police brutality was gaining momentum on football fields throughout the country, an incident occurred in the Black Belt town of McKenzie, Alabama, that should have given everyone pause. That didn't happen, of course, and the hate speech got much worse until it successfully turned a country against itself over the simplest of things like wearing masks during a pandemic. Before the playing of "The Star-Spangled Banner" at a football game between McKenzie High School and Houston County

High School, the McKenzie public-address announcer screamed to the crowd, "If you don't want to stand for the national anthem, you can line up over there by the fence and let our military personnel take a few shots at you since they're taking shots for you." The crowd erupted into cheers. The announcer, Allen Joyner, was the pastor of Sweet Home Baptist Church in McKenzie. This is the same psychology that allowed whites in Alabama to lynch Blacks under the moral authority of God and with the civic persuasion of the state government. If the Blacks wanted to vote, then the Blacks deserved to die. If Americans support Kaepernick, then cheer for them to be executed. Black lives don't matter. All lives matter. If the protesters stand in the street, then run them over.

It's a fundamental, republic-rotting manifestation of social decay to see an American walking around with a T-shirt that reads, "Rope. Tree. Journalist. Some assembly required," but that was pretty much the average day-to-day in 2020 with the nation's highest elected official, and commander in chief of the military, labeling reporters as the enemy of the people. The statues of actual enemies of the state deserved protection, though. Heroes and myths can never die, after all. They just turn into yellow-crested birds and fly away. The Autauga Academy football team was first called the Confederate Volunteers, until they figured out how dumb that sounded and changed it to Confederate Generals. Now, as a private school in the Deep South of Alabama, what do you think was taught at that school?

Even recently, Autauga Academy has produced at least one graduate of political ambition who appeals to the ideological myth-building of white supremacy. Will Dusmukes, a 31-year-old graduate of the school, made headlines in 2020 as a Prattville-area state congressman when he attended a "birthday celebration" (picnic with the Klan) for Confederate general Nathan Bedford

Forrest in Selma, Alabama. He gave the invocation, too. It was the same June weekend that Alabama celebrated the life of civil rights leader Congressman John Lewis, who was born and raised in rural Pike County, and was beaten by Alabama state troopers on Bloody Sunday as he walked over Selma's Edmund Pettus Bridge.

The decision to send O. J. Howard to Dusmukes's Autauga Academy was difficult for the Howards, and then school leaders stripped away his humanity without pause for dating a white girl. One of Nick Saban's recruits. From Alabama.

The country celebrated the end of slavery on Juneteenth, and then President Trump followed with a political rally on June 20 in Tulsa, Oklahoma. That city is synonymous with the history of racial violence in America after arming its white residents for a race riot against Tulsans living in the wealthiest Black community in the country. The 1921 Tulsa race massacre of the Greenwood District, known at the time as "Black Wall Street," put 800 people into the hospital, and anywhere from 75 to 300 people were murdered. It was hard to get an accurate number as white Tulsa residents firebombed 35 blocks from airplanes and reduced it to ash.

With the Black Lives Matter movement growing, the rally served as Trump's answer to Confederate monuments coming down across the country. "The unhinged left-wing mob is trying to vandalize our history, desecrating our monuments, our beautiful monuments, tear down our statues and punish, cancel, and persecute anyone who does not conform to their demands for absolute and total control," Trump blasted out. "We're not conforming."

Persecuted victims of Confederate white supremacy emboldened by the moral truth.

Except not in Mississippi.

One tweet made by Mississippi State running back Kylin

Hill showed the new power of college football players in a changing Deep South that relies on them, many of whom are Black, to shoulder an entire industry of profit by higher education. "Either change the flag or I won't be representing this State anymore ["100%" emoji] & I meant that... I'm tired," wrote Hill on June 22. Let's just say that made them squirm in their very pleated pants. The SEC understood the ramifications of that smoldering threat, and suddenly had nightmares of clutching its last $2.

SEC commissioner Greg Sankey was not going to wait around and see if Hill's viral tweet turned into a movement of SEC football players leaving Ole Miss and Mississippi State. He told the state of Mississippi to change the flag or the state wouldn't be hosting any more league championships. An overreach by Sankey? More like an executive business decision made in the name of financial preservation. He said some pretty words in a statement. Hill's tweet did the damn deed. Seventeen words and an emoji, which later put him on the cover of *Sports Illustrated* with a feature story by sports writer Ross Dellinger, who suddenly had the honor to chronicle the revolutionary role of sports in the shaping of his native state. Mississippi refused for years to even seriously consider removing the Confederate battle flag from its official standard. Hill made it disappear with a tweet that didn't even bother observing the respectful conformities of correct punctuation.

Imagine, for the enjoyment of the thought, explaining this sudden cascade of events caused by Hill's tweet to, say, then–college student James Bevel of Itta Bena, Mississippi, as he walked out of one of the first workshops for nonviolent activism organized by the Nashville Christian Leadership Council. Led by activist and counselor James Lawson, those meetings in March 1958 were attended by future leaders of the civil rights movement like John Lewis, Marion Barry, Bernard Lafayette, Diane Nash (married to

Bevel from 1961 to 1968), and C. T. Vivian. They helped to spawn the Nashville sit-ins of 1960, and then Nash, Lewis, Lafayette, and Bevel went on to participate in the Freedom Rides of 1961.

> **You, a time traveler:** Hey, James, let me get that door for you. So, listen, there's this thing called the internet... and the kid was just sitting alone on his bed.
> **James Bevel:** Hell, at State?!

A powerful instrument for change (especially if you run a Russian bot farm), social media was the flowing river of thought that pumped into the turbines of 2020 and electrified students in the Deep South. Amazing now to consider, but social media was not involved in illuminating the case of school-sponsored discrimination against O. J. Howard his junior year at Autauga Academy. In the digital age, Howard's incident of racial abuse never got out while he was in high school. It was never on Twitter. It was never leaked on Facebook to later mushroom into important conversations about racial equality in Alabama's Black Belt. It was never reported by the local newspaper. Not a single coach at Alabama texted a writer on the beat or nationally to use the power of journalism as a check against racial intimidation. Nothing left tiny little Autauga Academy to hold that school responsible for what it did. The family couldn't afford for that to happen. Not for O.J., necessarily, but for his younger sibling who still had important years of education ahead. Silence in the name of preservation. It took Howard being named the Offensive MVP of a championship and then returning to Tuscaloosa for his senior season for a reporter to get in his car and drive from Birmingham to Autauga County and then sit and listen in astonishment as an unprompted tale of civil rights abuse came bubbling up out of the buried psyche of a mother like the cleansing waters of Autauga County's many freshwater springs.

Older generations of white Southerners, trained since childhood to ignore the uncomfortable topics of race, and whisper the word "Black" because they grew up in a world where the word was a slur, might have the initial reflexive reaction to Howard's story as something that should have never been told. What's more damaging than even that, though, is the common Southern truth that making people feel uncomfortable is the greatest sin of all.

Howard's is a painful story, and it's difficult to even think about, but it is representative of a state history built upon civil rights abuses celebrated as moral heroism through myth-building by the cult of the Lost Cause. They had a birthday picnic in Selma for Nathan Bedford Forrest, the first grand wizard of the KKK, on the *same* weekend that Alabama celebrated the life of John Lewis. Y'all know how many times the cops tried to beat the courage out of John Lewis during the civil rights movement? No, you do not. And that's the problem.

No one is born racist, but all people are raised in this world built upon the social structures of racial abuse. The cruel trick in 2020 was making people think they were political victims through someone else's pain. Like, let's be honest here, how dumb is it that the people who were offended by Kaepernick kneeling for the American national anthem in a protest against police brutality were the same people who later felt persecuted by the removal of Confederate statues? Those statues are celebrating insurrectionists made into heroes that helped absolve the white South of racial violence, and created a justice system that spawns overpolicing of the Black community and the acceptance of police brutality to this day.

So, yeah, super, super dumb, y'all, or maybe just people looking for a reason to hate a messenger instead of reflecting on the
actual thing Kaepernick was trying to tell people.

College football players in the SEC recognized the value in
their platforms from the very beginning of the summer of 2020,
and they set about trying to help a divided South understand the
perspectives of young Black men. On May 31, while Alabama
superfan Jermaine "FunnyMaine" Johnson was busy in Kelly
Ingram Park, Alabama coach Nick Saban released a statement saying he was "shocked and angered" by the police killings of Floyd
and Breonna Taylor, and the modern-day lynching of Ahmaud
Arbery by private citizens. As a good coach, Saban was just echoing the voices of his players. Four days before that, and only two
days after Floyd's death, Alabama fifth-year senior center and
journalism major Chris Owens, the New Orleans–born, dean's
list Texan who commanded respect from every person in the Mal
Moore Athletic Facility, wrote on Twitter, "It's murder. It's an
abuse of a badge. It's the people designed to protect us once again
being our biggest enemy and failing us. It's absolutely sickening."

When Kylin Hill was lying in his pandemic bed in Starkville, Mississippi, and tweeting about that state's flag, Owens's close friend,
senior offensive lineman Alex Leatherwood of the Alabama football Crimson Tide, was laying down words, too. The month of
June after the death of George Floyd started with nationwide
protest marches and the Confederate statue coming down in Birmingham. College athletes walked in solidarity together on campuses all over the Deep South and the SEC that month. Still, it
was like people refused to listen, or, much worse, were now using

the frustration and sorrow of young people as political leverage to further divide the country.

There are no perfect heroes in America, and the University of Alabama and its larger-than-life football team cannot be considered such, because that would ignore an uncomfortable truth that must be acknowledged in an effort to understand the bigger picture and maybe help spur lasting progress. The legacy of state-sponsored racial terror, well-designed political isolation, and forced educational abandonment helped build the football empire $2 at a time. They made laws to take away the schools, and then told Blacks they couldn't vote if they couldn't read. When the welfare checks came, they tried to take those away, too, and then had the police and the prosecutors put people in prison for nonviolent drug crimes. It destroyed the bonds of families for generations.

That's why the story of O. J. Howard is so important and must be fully understood when attempting to grasp the importance of the Alabama football team's decision to use their voices for the hope of a greater good. The Howards represented a family that made painful sacrifices for education in the depressed Black Belt. They were community leaders who only ever loved the people of Autaugaville. It still didn't matter. The white board members of Autauga Academy thought it was O. J. Howard who was committing racial terror against them.

If Alabama football was a metaphor for the country in 2020, then this is true, too. There are no absolute villains either, just ruthless, cunning businessmen taught from an early age that the pursuit of wealth and power at all costs is the American Dream. They teach that in every business school in America, and it's a pop culture anthem, too. Get rich or die trying.

The spirit of American capitalism wasn't the problem in the summer of 2020, though. It was a White House that seemed hell-bent on dividing the country along the fault lines of every weakness, and the sports world was not off-limits.

Alex Leatherwood had heard enough, though. He wrote an essay on race in America that Alabama's well-funded and, of course, amazingly staffed video editing department cut into something that felt like spoken-word poetry when heard for the first time. Leatherwood's essay, entitled "All Lives Can't Matter Unless Black Lives Matter," was like a declaration of the players' value to the country, and why 2020 was about to be so important beyond the field. It made this book possible and inspired its completion, and these are painful conversations, but at least now we're having them.

In 2020, a nation witnessed a shift in the evolution of power for college football from the system to the individual, and then the Alabama football Crimson Tide took that new power and formed one of the greatest teams of all time through sacrifice for each other. And they didn't even have to play the season. And they had to stay isolated in their apartments and sit through the COVID-19 pandemic to do it. No Gallettes ever, in other words.

Here are the list of players who participated in the telling of American football's most important piece of literature in 2020: Leatherwood, quarterback Mac Jones, offensive lineman Emil Ekiyor Jr., offensive tackle Evan Neal, receiver Slade Bolden, cornerback Patrick Surtain II, receiver DeVonta Smith, long snapper Thomas Fletcher, tight end Cam Latu, tight end Major Tennison, tight end/linebacker Josh McMillon, defensive lineman Stephon Wynn Jr., receiver Jaylen Waddle, linebacker Jarez Parks, defensive tackle D. J. Dale, linebacker Ale Kaho, and linebacker Dylan Moses.

Nick Saban tagged along, too, because he loved his players like children. (And recruiting, y'all. Never forget!)

Said Leatherwood after the completion of the 2020 football season, "Everything was heavy on my mind and on my heart. It was just like a couple days' process to write it, and I wanted it to be a message that would be effective, but attention-grabbing at the same time. I wanted to get at the hearts and the minds because I knew the platform that we had and knew it would reach a wide audience. As young Black men, we wanted our voices heard."

"ALL LIVES CAN'T MATTER UNTIL BLACK LIVES MATTER"

By Alex Leatherwood
June 25, 2020
Tuscaloosa, Alabama

Alex Leatherwood: We are a team, black, white, brown.

Mac Jones: Together, we are a family, we are brothers.

Emil Ekiyor Jr.: We represent ourselves, our families.

Evan Neal: Our hometowns.

Slade Bolden: Our university.

Patrick Surtain II: And our country.

DeVonta Smith: We stand on the shoulders of giants.

Thomas Fletcher: Our grandparents and parents.

Cam Latu: Our ancestors, our heroes, Alabama alumni.

Major Tennison: And former players who have changed the world.

Mac Jones: Beginning on our historic campus, we speak as one.

Patrick Surtain II: Acknowledging our history.

Josh McMillon: Honoring their legacy and building a better, more just future.

Stephon Wynn Jr.: On the field, we are relentless.

Evan Neal: We are strong, we are conquerors.

Jaylen Waddle: But we are human beings first.

Nick Saban: And in this moment in history, we can't be silent. We must speak up for our brothers and sisters, for our sons and daughters.

Jarez Parks: We speak for justice, for fairness.

DeVonta Smith: For equality, for greater understanding.

Mac Jones: We stand together against racism.

Emil Ekiyor Jr.: Against brutality.

Patrick Surtain II: Against violence.

D. J. Dale: For a better world.

Ale Kaho: When we see our families, our neighbors, our classmates subjected to violence, we recognize the fear in their eyes.

Dylan Moses: And when we experience racism, it hurts.

Cam Latu: In the game, we are one team.

Nick Saban: One heartbeat, one mission.

Stephon Wynn Jr.: Yet we are diverse.

Jaylen Waddle: We don't always agree.

Jarez Parks: But we learn so much from each other.

Thomas Fletcher: And we are so much better together.

Nick Saban: Until I listen with an open heart and mind, I can't understand his experience and his pain.

DeVonta Smith: The virus has shown us how much we benefit from being together.

Evan Neal: And how much we need each other.

Dylan Moses: We believe the solutions to our challenges are within us.

Jarez Parks: We choose to listen.

Mac Jones: We choose to hear.

Evan Neal: And understand others' perspectives.

Mac Jones: Let's listen.

Emil Ekiyor Jr.: Let's unite.

Jaylen Waddle: Because all lives can't matter until Black lives matter.

D. J. Dale: Until Black lives matter.

Ale Kaho: Until Black lives matter.

Mac Jones: Until Black lives matter.

DeVonta Smith: Because all lives can't matter until Black lives matter.

Roll Tide.

CHAPTER 7

GIVE 'EM HELL, ALABAMA

When Nick Saban agreed to make a video with Black football players that explained to America "all lives can't matter until Black lives matter," and then signed off on the final edit using a clip of himself framing the urgency of "this moment in history," guess who didn't say a word?

Behold, America, the awesome power of Nicholas Lou Saban Jr. and the Alabama football Crimson Tide. The only thing strong enough to silence racism's mouthpiece of hate in our burning summer of hell. Love don't win all the time, y'all, but Alabama does.

Roll Tide. Roll Tide. Praise Our Almighty and Ever-Living Touchdown Jesus, Roll Tide.

Go in peace to love the Iron Bowl, and serve many various meat snacks at your tailgates.

Hey, Don-ald!

Hey, Don-ald!

Hey, Don-ald!

WE JUST BEAT THE HELL OUT OF YOU

Rammer Jammer Yellowhammer

Give 'em hell, Alabama

Now, whether you loved Donald Trump while he was in the

White House, or hated him an awful, awful lot-a-ly, there should be one thing America all agrees upon. No one felt comfortable with the "most powerful man in the free world" having his fat, stumpy finger on the send button. In one of life's little victories, Trump dared not tweet about the Tide.

So, yeah, it's a great song. Who's got the rum?

The University of Alabama considered banning "Rammer Jammer" in 2005, but the students voted hell-to-the-naw by a margin of 98 percent to keep it. Good decision, that. Pour a cup of bittersweet sunshine out for the 2 percent of students who grew up Auburn fans but followed their girlfriends to Alabama. "Rammer Jammer" is one of the most iconic songs in American sports, and now it's easy to understand why. Dunking on fools is damn fun. The yellowhammer is a bird of striking savagery, and *that* song-bird can sing.

"We must speak up for our brothers and sisters, for our sons and daughters," Alabama senior Alex Leatherwood wrote for Nick Saban to read. "One heartbeat, one mission…Until I listen with an open heart and mind, I can't understand his experience and his pain."

They were cathartic words spoken by the greatest college football coach of all time. We're not in the business of myth-building here, though, aight? The year that was Twenty Twenty sent us on the search for a more perfect truth through a season that was going to happen no matter what out of financial necessity. That burden then put young people on the stage, and they had something to say. The players had all the power because they shouldered the entire system. There were no heroes there in 2020, but the moment did find constantly evolving imperfect leaders who ate enough of history's burning, biting sin until, at last, they realized by choice or through force that it was time to sing a new song of the South. The young people of Alabama football in the SEC, collected from all over the country, were clutching the power, and in their desperate moment of urgency one of the greatest living leaders in America got that much better by following the people he was paid to lead. Saban is the college football G.O.A.T. because he knew that would be the path to victory.

The champions of the hour, and maybe the entire year, were the words of Alex Leatherwood. Poetry and grace they were, but then disliked more times on YouTube than given the ol' thumbs-up. Everyone hates the writers, so get used to it, *ya click-bait hack. I mean, this is why your precious newspapers are all gone. Journalism is dead. Stick to sports and make my sheltered world great again.* Roll... Snide?

See? The victim bit is not a hard one to play.

In a former world, in a different time, with healthier brains devoid of social media, the essay written by Alabama offensive tackle Alex Leatherwood of Pensacola, Florida, might have earned him a formal commendation from the president of the United States of America, or maybe a nomination for a Pulitzer Prize, or, instinctively, an immediate ticker-tape victory parade down New York's Canyon of Heroes with FunnyMaine riding shotgun. The destructive barrage of media has muted humanity's heightened senses, however, and the hurricane resets by the hour to denude every fucking last sacred tree of knowledge in the forest. Leatherwood's essay "went viral" for a fleeting moment, and then it was universally weaponized for the melee in our constant fog of war. Look on the bright side, though. Maybe it all needed to happen, and freed a few attention-sick, catatonic, scrolling basement bats from their bondage of the mind. The Old Testament spoke of only one contagious pestilence to free God's children, but the iPhone-thumbed hellstorms of locusts and frogs and hail and wild beasts and bugs covered the earth, too, in 2020. The year of boils on everyone's backsides was a couch-ride freakshow through digital thralldom, and we had all the plagues, y'all. It hurt bigly, in other words, and then Tennessee sacrificed another coach to make it all official.

Pass the rum again, and drink to this: Maybe one day the bluebird of Twitter will be invited into the college dive bar by the drunk but happy yellowhammer, and then taught how to sing of glee together before the blackbird's last call.

At the very least, everyone should be of agreement that we need to chisel into marble Alex Leatherwood's prayer of hope and display it permanently in the Birmingham Institute for Civil Rights and the College Football Hall of Fame in Atlanta, and erect it in monument form on the Quad at the University of Alabama. Behold, America, the awesome power of education in the face of hardship and fear. When Leatherwood saw people on TV hurting, he sat down and helped in the highest, most advanced form of angelic creation our evolved species allows, and that is through art. The summer of change was just beginning for Leatherwood and his offensive line, but it had already been a spring like no other. Leatherwood worked out in Orlando with a friend, and his backup, who would also double as Alabama's backup center, trained in Texas.

When Chris Owens returned home to Arlington on March 15, 2020, everyone on Alabama's football team was still hoping to return to campus after the hastily announced "extended spring break." That changed quickly, and within days it was pretty clear to everyone that "extended spring break" might stretch on for months. Sequin Owens was thankful to have her child home during the pandemic, but it was a challenge. This was the way of America after the Ides of March. For the football players of Alabama, days quickly turned into a never-ending scheduled routine of Zoom calls with coaches, and workouts with Apple Watches, and, like everyone else, wondering just what the hell was wrong with those crazy Netflix Tiger people in Florida. Owens worked out locally at a park near Nichols Junior High School, and also was fortunate to have access to some dumbbells and other equipment from a nearby rehab facility. In Birmingham, players who returned home worked out together wherever they could. Eventually, players began training outdoors with friends from their old high schools.

"It's amazing what Alabama did for everyone, the team itself, in order to get everyone ready for a season they didn't even know they were going to have," Sequin Owens said. "From down to the watches. People have no idea what that team went through to stay in shape and hold people accountable."

Alabama was able to review everyone's sleeping patterns in the morning, and one player said he actually appreciated that structure. The trainers had minimum requirements for calories burned and sustained heart rates each day. Spring football by Orangetheory, in other words. In the end, though, Alabama's staffers could only do so much from afar. Accountability came down to the individual players and their families. The Owenses' small family unit was dedicated to keeping everyone healthy and free of COVID-19 in the spring of 2020, which should go without saying for just about every family in America, but that challenge was exponentially more difficult and stressful for those who were cohabiting and hunkered down with frontline health care workers. Sequin Owens worked in the ICU of Methodist Hospital in downtown Dallas during the entire pandemic of 2020 and 2021.

Back when little Chris was molding himself into a future dean's list scholar, Mom was putting herself through nursing school. The struggle made them stronger. Turns out, growing up in a home that required sacrifice and perseverance for survival and a better life turned into mental shields of strength during the pandemic. The glass iPhone and TV screens told the story while refracting everyone's perception. Some Americans were made of the right stuff in 2020, and some were not. The NCAA lifted its nationwide moratorium on May 31, and Alabama's players were on campus that day, the same day FunnyMaine stepped to a microphone in Kelly Ingram Park. The first day to report back to the Mal Moore Athletic Facility was June 2, so it's not hard to guess what happened next.

Players started giving COVID-19 to each other.

Looking back, this shouldn't really shock anyone, says Sequin Owens, considering the virulence of severe acute respiratory syndrome coronavirus 2.

"It was kind of hard not to get it considering players worked out so closely," she said.

When Sequin Owens makes a point, she does it in the type of *hello!* voice mothers with little tolerance for nonsense are known to project. It is the tone of *what did you think was going to happen?* Another parent of a player on the team said they "lost count" of Alabama's COVID-19 cases over the summer. At the time, the national rumor was that Alabama wanted its players to gain herd immunity before the season. Alabama athletics didn't share medical information of the football team publicly during the pandemic, so that fueled the speculation, too. Herd immunity doesn't seem likely, though. Alabama had players who tested positive during the season, and there was an outbreak among assistant coaches. Major outbreaks among players during the season were avoided, however, and that was an advantage for Alabama in several of its games. Missouri had to quarantine 12 players less than two weeks before the season. That number dropped to seven on game week after it was determined one of the tests was faulty, but missed practice before playing Alabama isn't where any team wants to be. The Tigers lost assistant secondary coach Charlie Harbison before the game. Good luck! Alabama won in a rout 38–19.

Missouri coach Eli Drinkwitz, after making his coaching debut for the Tigers, complained to ESPN later in the week about the lack of fairness in the league because Mizzou was being transparent about its COVID-19 cases, but Alabama was not. Welcome to the SEC, Drink. The Sun Belt Conference it is not. To quote the late great Lady Vols basketball coach Pat Summitt's iconic and forever greatest SEC advice: "Toughen up, buttercup."

Ah, the plight of a first-year football coach at a university known for its journalism school. The problem, as Drinkwitz saw it, was that Alabama didn't have to tell Missouri if it had any players out with COVID-19.

"It's kind of a free-for-all," Drinkwitz said.

Well, actually it kinda wasn't.

Every team was reporting results to SEC headquarters in Birmingham, but Drinkwitz wanted SEC commissioner Greg Sankey to run out of the front doors there in Uptown and gallop down Richard Arrington Jr. Boulevard with his shoes off screaming to everyone how many players at Alabama had COVID-19 over the summer.

Well, that just wasn't going to happen. Auburn coach Gus Malzahn took the opportunity to throw some shade over at his in-state rival: "For me, transparency is really good. So I'd be all for that."

Bullshit. Gus Malzahn, who was fired after the 2020 season

despite a winning record (6–4), wouldn't admit that his throwback Auburn sweater was on fire if it went up in a blaze during a post-game news conference.

Now at UCF, Malzahn was the type of SEC coach who never got enough credit, or a fair shake from fans, because he was guarded and standoffish. It's a conference that runs on secrets, though. The SEC might as well have stood for "Shouldn't Everyone Cornteen?" during the summer, but who's counting? Uh, everyone if that means money. Malzahn had a good run at Auburn before finally getting to walk straight the heck outta town with enough money to start a bank and without even stopping at the Waffle House to say it was all scattered, covered, smothered, and diced.* Giving Malzahn grief is fair, but he deserves credit, too. One, he was Auburn's coach for one of the most electrifying moments in college football history (Kick Six), and, two, he honored the late Auburn and SEC coaching legend Patrick Fain Dye in the Tigers' 2020 season opener. Dye played at Georgia and was a respected assistant for Paul Bryant's Alabama before stealing away a kid from McAdory High School named Bo Jackson and building the Iron Bowl into the greatest rivalry in college sports. Dye was the beating heart of the SEC. It was win at all costs, rules be damned, and he was a good man for it. He once had a starting quarterback (Jeff Burger) who got busted for plagiarism. Auburn's vice president of academic affairs let the player off the hook.

Dye later joked, "They said they got Burger for plagiarism. I said, 'What kind of disease is that?'"

The SEC ordered independent third-party screeners for all 14 football teams in August, and that was a problem for transparency-loving Malzahn. He suddenly had someone outside of the department monitoring all the players. So many positive cases in September

---

* Gus Malzahn would eat at the Waffle House in Auburn after home victories.

were recorded and contact-traced that they had to cancel three practices. Disorganization was the daily routine, according to the parents of players. Malzahn knew his team was going to struggle in 2020 before it even started. His inexperienced offensive line featured only one returning starter (center Nick Brahms), and then the unit didn't practice together as a complete group for the first three weeks of September. In the SEC, where the best defensive linemen in the country play football, continuity along the offensive line is Rule No. 1.

Rule No. 2 is the SEC office schedules an off week for Alabama around Nick Saban's birthday.

Rule No. 3: There are no other rules.

Three players at Auburn opted out of the 2020 college football season before September cases wrecked practice schedules. Linebacker Josh Marsh said on August 21 that he was struggling with symptoms of COVID-19. For anyone who would listen, it was proof that college football players in the SEC, thought to be invincible, were not.

"As a result of contracting Covid-19 and its continued, current complications, I have made the decision to opt out of the 2020 football season," Marsh posted on social media. "This is a tough decision, but one that was made with prayer and consideration. I appreciate the support, understanding and guidance my coaches have shown me while working through this decision. I wish my teammates the very best this year and am believing for a great season. I am extremely thankful to be a part of the Auburn family and look forward to coming back next year stronger and better than ever. War Eagle."

Auburn's offensive line caught the bug during fall camp, and that set the team back for the entire season. By the end of fall camp some of the best players, or some of the most critical to their teams' seasons, would opt out: Georgia projected starting quarterback

Jamie Newman, LSU wide receiver Ja'Marr Chase, LSU defensive lineman Tyler Shelvin, LSU defensive back Kary Vincent Jr., Texas A&M wide receiver Jhamon Ausbon, Texas A&M linebacker Anthony Hines, Texas A&M cornerback Elijah Blades, Ole Miss center Eli Johnson. Everyone at Mississippi State was like, "Mike Leach? Yo, I'm out." The SEC West, the most competitive division of athletics in the world, was hit especially hard by players making the choice, for whatever reason, not to play in 2020.

Alabama had a clear path to a perfect season from the beginning if it could navigate the pandemic, and with Saban in charge it seemed like they had a good chance of that, too. Saban is wired to be so maddeningly precise and efficient that he insists on chewing Dentyne spearmint gum that's in the shape of squares instead of sticks. *Gotta fold the sticks, aight?!*

Just beat whoever comes out of the SEC East, and natty No. 18 would be on ice waiting for them next to the black-cherry-flavored cans of White Claw.

The other critical advantage was this: Alabama was projected to have the best offensive line in college football in 2020, and when Chris Owens of Arlington, Texas, returned to campus for the beginning of June's workouts he almost immediately got COVID-19.

Chris Owens's bout with COVID was not a particularly easy one either.

"He had all the symptoms," Sequin Owens said.

After an initial wave of COVID swept through the team, Saban beefed up the testing. No one in the SEC office had to tell Alabama how to be logistically prepared for frequent testing. Alabama head trainer Jeff Allen organized schedules. Everyone, and that means everyone, was tested every morning at 7 a.m. in the end zones of the indoor practice field.

"There were lots of players and staff who got COVID," Sequin Owens said, but "Alabama did an amazing job with testing and quarantining."

Players were diligent, too, and the leaders of the team did their jobs to hold their teammates accountable. Journalism major Chris Owens sounded the alarm on Bid Day, August 16, and eventually the power of Alabama football helped to protect Tuscaloosa during the pandemic by having the whole Strip shut down. The timing of Owens's concern, echoed by athletics director Greg Byrne, framed the fear of losing the season in that moment. Five days earlier, the Big Ten and Pac-12 made the announcement that they were canceling all fall sports.

Players in the ACC, Big 12, and SEC were going to do their parts to save their seasons.

"The health, safety, and well-being of our student-athletes and all those connected to Pac-12 sports has been our number one priority since the start of this current crisis," Pac-12 commissioner Larry Scott said in a statement on August 11. "Our student-athletes, fans, staff, and all those who love college sports would like to have seen the season played this calendar year as originally planned, and we know how disappointing this is."

Out as the Pac-12 commissioner in June 2021, Scott and Big Ten commissioner Kevin Warren canceled fall sports, on behalf of their conferences' presidents and senior administrators, after evolving research into the new respiratory disease linked it to myocarditis. A rare but dangerous symptom of viral diseases, myocarditis causes inflammation of the heart. The Big Ten was deeply concerned about the health of their athletes during the pandemic after the mother of Indiana lineman Brady Freeney published a message on her Facebook page at the beginning of August that explained her son's situation. After reporting for summer workouts, he had been admitted to the emergency room after struggling to breathe. She called it "14 days of hell" and wrote that blood work was showing "additional problems and possible heart issues."

"Even if your sons' schools do everything right to protect them, they CAN'T PROTECT THEM!!" Debbie Rucker wrote. "I pray my son recovers from this horrible virus and can lead a healthy normal life!! Football does not really matter when your child's health is in jeopardy!!"

Those frightening words of a mother, as well as other evidence pointing to potential myocarditis, were the reasons the Big Ten and Pac-12 canceled their seasons, and no one can blame them for doing it.

Now, the reason those conferences then later brought it back is open for interpretation. Several factors were involved, including SEC commissioner Greg Sankey and the commissioners from the other Power 5 conferences taking measured and cautious approaches. They had time to think things through, after all, and hopefully come up with plans for testing procedures to protect their athletes. If thorough testing, strict guidelines, and third-party reporting policies could give college football at least some of the season, then that would save hundreds if not thousands of jobs at universities, in addition to entire non-revenue-producing varsity sports. The financial apocalypse of not having college football would have reached far beyond the campuses, though. Most everyone has a stake in college football in small college towns throughout the Southeast, and the very reasoned perspective of athletes being safer on campus than out in communities had to be considered, too. In Alabama, keep in mind, the Alabama High School Athletic Association just went ahead with fall high school sports without required testing by the state. High school football is big business in small towns, too. The other significant factor that brought Big Ten and Pac-12 football back were the athletes. They wanted to play. On August 16, Ohio State quarterback Justin Fields shared a petition on social media with the hashtagged phrase #LetUsPlay! It was Fields who crafted the message.

"We want to play. We believe that safety protocols have been established and can be maintained to mitigate concerns of exposure to Covid 19," Fields wrote. "We believe that we should have the right to make decisions about what is best for our health and our future. Don't let our hard work and sacrifice be in vain. #LetUsPlay!"

There is also this perspective, though, on why the Big Ten and Pac-12 reversed course and went forward with an abbreviated season that required three weeks of contact tracing (compared to two weeks for the SEC). President Trump inserted himself into the debate in an attempt, it seemed, to gain political leverage and votes in key Midwestern swing states in a presidential election year. To do this, he began putting public pressure on Warren, the Big Ten's first-year commissioner, to make it seem like the White House was going to be the savior of college football for the league. After first canceling fall sports, the Big Ten announced a return of football on September 16 with a projected starting day for the season of October 24. The SEC had already announced plans for its unique and immediately beloved schedule back on August 17. It would be a 10-game, league-only schedule beginning on September 26. Fans thought they might lose everything, and then Sankey gifted them a fantasy all-SEC season to be celebrated for eternity.*

The SEC's approach was controversial, and it had its critics. Certainly, it sent a mixed message on the importance of football at

---

* The joyride continued in 2021 when Sankey, a cold-blooded gangster, helped design a proposal for an expanded, 12-team playoff while also preparing to steal Texas and Oklahoma away from the Big Twelve.

all costs. But Sankey's leadership also helped facilitate the important messages of all the leagues' athletes when they marched in protest for racial equality, social justice, and ways to make the country better for everyone. The SEC commissioner delivered the schedule and championed his athletes' voices during a difficult time for the country. That's a pretty good year for the chief executive of the Deep South's most powerful cultural influencer, and former SEC commissioner Mike Slive, who built the league into an instrument of social change as a media giant, had to be looking down with pride.

And nice work with the social media reporting, Chris Owens. Student journalism, in the end, maybe saved the season.

Owens is close friends with Alabama athletics director Greg Byrne. Going into his sixth year with the football team, the Crimson Tide's persistent offensive lineman was expected to be one of Alabama's four permanent captains. It's a prestigious honor, and permanent captains have their handprints preserved in concrete at the base of Denny Chimes on Alabama's campus Quad every spring A-Day Game following the season of their captaincy. If Owens is running a pro or college team or a league in 15 years, then that'll be just one more Alabama alum with a journalism or PR degree out there in the world making it all run. He played a small but significant role in making sure the most important season of SEC football in the league's history was won by his team.

With its players all committed to the season and no one opting out, Alabama was on a path to potentially having a perfect record in the season when maturity, togetherness, trust, and friendship probably meant more to success than the recruiting rankings.

There was definitely one guy rooting for them to fail, though, and that was the president of the United States of America.

Donald Trump pretended to be an Alabama fan when it was bene-
fiting his agenda, but that changed after Alex Leatherwood's video.
Forty-Five started trash-talking Alabama about the Iron Bowl in
mid-July while endorsing the Alabama GOP's candidate for U.S.
Senate. This gets even more SEC-gothic than that, though. The
Republican challenger to Alabama senator Doug Jones (D) in
the summer of 2020 was former Auburn football coach Tommy
Tuberville. Doug Jones is the former Alabama prosecutor who
saved the state from electing Roy Moore (R), the controversial and
embarrassing former Alabama Supreme Court chief justice. Jones
and Moore squared off for U.S. Senate in the 2017 special election to replace Trump's appointment to attorney general, Jefferson
Beauregard Sessions III.

Twice removed from the Alabama Supreme Court, Moore was
a big "states' rights" guy, too. Lost Cause pro-Confederate-victim
groups like the "League of the South" held rallies outside Moore's
"Foundation of Moral Law" in 2009 and 2010. In the run-up to the
2017 special election for Alabama's vacant U.S. Senate seat, Moore
was accused by several women of sexual misconduct and abuse when
he was in his 30s and they were in their teens. He was defeated nar-
rowly by Jones thanks to an enormous turnout by Black voters across
the state (and also the whites in Shelby County just not voting for
anyone that time out of protest). Jones, a middle-of-the-road Democrat for whatever that means anymore, was the prosecutor, don't forget, who sent the Klansmen to prison for the murder of those four
girls inside the 16th Street Baptist Church. Any used flat tire on the
side of I-65 was going to defeat Jones in 2020, but Trump was going
to make sure that it rolled over the Tide for what they did to him.

In a phone conference with reporters to endorse Tuberville, Trump tried his best to take some shots at Alabama and Nick Saban while whistling Dixie. Before defeating Jones for the Senate by a margin of 61 percent to 39.7, Tuberville was most famous for helping Auburn defeat Alabama six times in a row from 2002 to 2007. "Fear the thumb" was the catchphrase after victory No. 5. While a coach at Ole Miss, Tuberville lobbied to have Confederate flags banned from Vaught-Hemingway Stadium because it was hurting recruiting, but he didn't have to take much of a stand on anything to be senator of a one-party state that runs a political race to the right every primary season. Tuberville isn't a bad guy. He just didn't have anything to do with his life after coaching except count all his cash from coaching buyouts, and Alabama's big timberland political mules knew they could use him.

"Really successful coach," Trump said of Tuberville on the conference call. "Beat Alabama, like, six in a row, but we won't even mention that."

A dip of the tiny virgin toe as far as Iron Bowl jabs go, but Trump was just warming up. He wasn't finished with Alabama, but it was time to go after Saban.

"As he said...because of that, maybe we got 'em Lou Saban," Trump went on. "...And he's great, Lou Saban, what a great job he's done."

Trump called Nick Saban by his middle name on the conference call, and then, to make sure everyone knew he didn't misspeak, he hissed it again and placed it awkwardly inside a backhanded compliment.

Think what you want to think about Trump, but let's all agree on one thing. Keep him away from SEC football, please. Ronald "the Clockwork Orange Clown, King of the Tiny Hands" McChump ruined everything he ever touched, and the Yankee best not come 'round this way or he'll ruin the one thing we all love. Have faith, though. The Black football players with all the power will make sure that never happens.

Now, that's how someone raised on Southern football and baptized in the crucible of a molten Iron Bowl talks shit. And if you didn't know before they stood in front of the schoolhouse door, then now you know, dammit.

CHAPTER 8

SCHOOL IS COOL

O ne heartbeat, one mission," Nick Saban said during the recital of Alex Leatherwood's essay on unity. That was the message of America's athletes from the very beginning of the summer, and its spirit emanated strongest of all from the One True King. The sports world had leaders of leaders in 2020, and then it had LeBron James leading all. Naturally, Chris Owens of Alabama football grew up an enormous fan.

A reflection on the activism of athletes in 2020 would be incomplete without highlighting the role of LeBron Raymone James of the Los Angeles Lakers. He was one of the top pro athletes in American history before 2020, but then he took his place on the all-time Mount Rushmore of his country's most culturally influential sports figures in a year when America needed him most. With the country's young people stuck at home during the spring, LeBron used his voice to champion the importance of education. Later in the summer, his influence on American culture helped unify athletes for a common purpose.

LeBron's growth as a leader of civil rights began to take shape when he played alongside Dwyane Wade, Chris Bosh, Udonis Haslem, Shane Battier, James Jones, and others with the Miami

Heat from 2011 to 2014. At the time, "the Heatles" were the biggest story in American sports. The team used that platform to mourn the killing of 17-year-old Trayvon Martin on February 26, 2012, and the Heat's hooded tribute to Martin on social media became an international story that helped strengthen the Black Lives Matter movement. LeBron and Wade continued their activism after the Heatles split up and LeBron returned home to Cleveland. In December 2014, he and some of his teammates with the Cavaliers were among the NBA players who wore "I Can't Breathe" T-shirts during pregame warm-ups in a tribute started by Derrick Rose of the Chicago Bulls. Rose first wore the T-shirt before a game on December 8, 2014, to raise awareness of police brutality following news that the police officer who choked to death Eric Garner of Staten Island, New York, would not face criminal charges. Wade would later wear a pair of special edition "Black Lives Matter" basketball shoes in February 2015. LeBron noted at the time that the "I Can't Breathe" T-shirts were "more of a shoutout" to the Garner family "more than anything," and Kobe Bryant of the Los Angeles Lakers said the shirts spoke to people "really questioning the justice system. They're questioning the process of the legal system and those who have authority, and whether or not they're abusing authority, and what's the threshold to use that force."

At the time, NBA commissioner Adam Silver said he supported the players' messages on the shirts, but added in a statement that "my preference would be for players to abide by our oncourt attire rules." Summing up the NBA players' collective shift to social activism, ESPN columnist J. A. Adande wrote on December 10, 2014, "It is about lost lives, the sorrow of the families, the public policies that need to be addressed."

The point is this: Positive conversations for necessary criminal justice reforms had been building for years among NBA players before Republican presidential candidate Donald Trump took aim at Colin Kaepernick's protest of police violence in September 2016. Trump was considered a fringe political outsider before U.S. senator Jeff Sessions (R) of Alabama organized a well-attended and boisterous rally for Trump in Mobile in August 2015. At the time, Trump's biggest talking points were building a wall along the U.S.-Mexico border and ending "birthright citizenship" because, as he said at Mobile's Ladd-Peebles Stadium, "you have 300,000 babies a year that you have to take care of."

By 2018, the country's rhetoric had spiraled down into Trump's spider hole. Here's how far the country fell in two years. After years as a social activist, LeBron was told to "shut up and dribble" by a Fox News host in 2018 after a racial slur had been spray-painted on the gate of his Los Angeles home. Hate speech had been aimed at the star of the Lakers in the proudest NBA town of all, and Fox News intimated that it was LeBron's own fault. The player's great sin? In an interview with Cari Champion of ESPN after the incident, LeBron was asked about President Donald Trump's role in America and LeBron said the president didn't understand "the people" and that many of Trump's comments were "scary."

Long before COVID-19 brought the country to a halt and gave "the people" time to sit at home and think—and scroll— America's athletes had been watching a White House and its various mouthpieces use the sports world for political ammunition like everything else. As a response to the dog-whistling "shut up and dribble" line, LeBron responded with the positive message of "#MoreThanAnAthlete" on social media and then went on a "More Than An Athlete" world tour in the summer of 2018 to Shanghai, Paris, Berlin, and New York. The King had never been one to back down from a challenge or, as a savvy influencer, pass up an opportunity to craft his own message and dictate the conversation. In the spring of 2020, he immersed himself in a worthy project for every high schooler in America who was robbed of a senior graduation.

The schedules and lives of college students and professional athletes were impacted by the COVID-19 pandemic, but let's keep things in perspective. Compared to others, their lives were only inconvenienced. Families with small children were thrown into full-blown crisis mode the second and third weeks of March. It was a national crisis almost overnight. Entire sectors of the economy were suddenly without work. It became clear in the following weeks and months that the country's initial response to the international pandemic was critically insufficient. Largely forgotten in the national panic phases of March and April were the graduating high school seniors of America, the lost class of 2020. Those final months of senior year were just gone. Instead it was, "We piled the diplomas over there in the corner of the cafeteria. Congrats and welcome to this new hell. Good luck finding work. Take a gap year on the couch."

Every senior class has their favorite graduation songs. The class of 2020 had their favorite brands of hand sanitizer. Every generation has their favorite high school movies. The class of 2020 had *Dr. Anthony Fauci Stars in the Tiger King*. Most kids have senior proms, and senior pranks, and senior breakfasts, and senior skip days, and the signing of senior yearbooks, and those weekends when seniors tell their parents they're spending the night at a friend's house and instead they go to Tuscaloosa with fake IDs and get into Gallettes for the first time and then stumble to their friend's or older sister's gilded sorority mansion and eat waffles in the morning. Kids grow up together, laugh together, cry together, and play sports together, and the point of all that preparation starts to come into focus after everyone returns from senior spring break together with stories for a lifetime, and, finally, the goal of graduation is within sight.

Yeah, things were a little different for America's graduating senior class of 2020. Spring break came and then that was it, and for many seniors it all happened on the same day. The beginning and the end all wrapped into one thing like the alpha and the omega of a real-life Twilight Zone. The Coronavirus Quarantine Kids were on a rainbow bridge from high school to being alone with their parents for months.

When the high school graduating class of 2020 needed a champion, LeBron James was the natural leader to project a unifying message of positivity. After all, Mr. "More Than An Athlete" could actually back up his words with actions. He had already built a school in Akron, Ohio, for at-risk students in danger of being left behind. Having had his own life shaped by his time at St. Vincent–St. Mary High School in Akron, LeBron genuinely loved that time in his early development. It helped foster his innate gifts and point them in the right direction for sustained success. There is certainly a teacher out there in northeast Ohio who helped set the foundation, through selfless love and service, for James's future impact on the world, and that person is truly the closest thing we'll have to a perfect American hero. In a partnership between the LeBron James Family Foundation, XQ Institute, the Entertainment Industry Foundation, and a whole bunch of people across the entire country, King James, after a lifetime built on integrity and hope, put his name behind and hosted *Graduate Together: America Honors the High School Class of 2020*, a television special on May 16, 2020, on every major television network and online.

An advocate for education, the face of the NBA, an international celebrity and a rags-to-riches success story like few others in American history, King James was told to stick to sports in an attempt to obscure an image he had been crafting long before Donald Trump wrapped himself in an American flag. The power of truth is the strongest of things, though. LeBron's inherent message of a principled life rooted in hard work was built step by step with a determination that radiates the power of American possibility. King James actually is the ideal of American success that Trump told the country had been lost. Name another figure in contemporary America who comes anywhere close to matching LeBron's lifelong triumph of "American values." There are none. *Sports Illustrated* put him on its cover when he was a junior in high school and called him "The Chosen One." He then far surpassed that hype with substance, and even had the tattoo "Chosen 1" inked between his shoulders. Here is the thing that's special about King James, though, that might be lost on people who are more familiar with college football than the NBA. LeBron's greatest gift of all on the court and in his life was always his ability to make the people around him better. He was a pass-first superstar who then blossomed into a positive voice for the country, an entertainment icon, and a business mogul.

The reality in 2018 and then again in 2020 was that LeBron's message to America was far more powerful than that of his detractors, and every time someone took a shot at the King it just made LeBron stronger. In 2020, King James became Captain America. His graduation special to the class of 2020 was just another assist to teammates that no one else could have made.

"It's time to chase every dream, accept every challenge, strive for greatness, honor every promise, and recommit to your community," James said during the simulcasted television event.

The program featured "The Star-Spangled Banner" performed by high school seniors and a bat-phone emergency contacts rundown of A-list celebrities, including sports stars Shaquille O'Neal and Megan Rapinoe, actors and actresses Zendaya, Yara Shahidi, Julianne Moore, and Timothée Chalamet, and musicians Pharrell Williams, Bad Bunny, Dave Matthews, and Loren Gray. Barack Obama, the 44th president of the United States, was a speaker, too, and the music for the event, of course, included a slate of high-school-graduation, coming-of-age tunes like a soundtrack through time. The Platt Brothers (Jonah, Henry, and Ben) somehow blended together "Memories" by Maroon 5 into "Graduation (Friends Forever)" by Vitamin C into "Forever Young" by Alphaville into "In My Life" by the Beatles into "See You Again" by Wiz Khalifa into "Good Riddance (Time of Your Life)" by Green Day into "Congratulations" by Post Malone *back into* "Good Riddance (Time of Your Life)" that was flawless like they were some kind of magical wizard a cappella DJs from another dimension. YouTube it. It was wonderful stuff, and the recording of it likely will be played at graduations throughout the United States for many years to come.

LeBron's "Graduate Together" event also featured performances by luminaries Alicia Keys ("Underdog"), H.E.R. ("Sometimes"), and Cordae ("Broke as Fuck"). The special was beautiful, poignant, and a triumph of production during the pandemic that emphasized the importance of education and sticking together through tough times. One Heartbeat. One Mission.

One really long list of well-known superstars.

It was more than enough star power to light up America for the summer ahead, but some of the truest words of the simulcasted show were performed by an artist whom many in America might not have been familiar with before May 16, 2020. They wanted some bars from Alabama in LeBron's TV special, it was decided, because there was this ultra-talented 23-year-old woman from Montgomery who had things to say, and always had the courage to believe in herself and see it through. Roll Pride.

Jane Chika Oranika, a graduate of Montgomery's Booker T. Washington Magnet High School, goes by the stage name Chika, and, beginning with a social media post that went viral the day after Donald Trump was elected, willed herself into a spoken-word conduit of young Americans who grew up with Barack Obama in office, and then felt disenfranchised and alienated by his successor. Chika, who is Black, applied white makeup concealer to her face in a post on Twitter while brilliantly using humor to present social commentary on what it felt like to be Black through the voice of someone white and entitled who had never considered that viewpoint.

(Like Atticus Finch said to Scout in *To Kill a Mockingbird*: "Climb into his skin and walk around in it.")

(Like Alex Leatherwood wrote for Nick Saban to say: "Until I listen with an open heart and mind, I can't understand his experience and his pain.")

In her video, cut together in quick edits, Chika white-voiced:

African-American? [*chuckles twice sarcastically*] Never felt that. Never heard that. Uh, never tasted that. Never smelled that…Caucasian? I don't know what y'all talk'n…Never…
[BREAK]
Barack Obama? [*chuckles twice again*] Is that some kind of sauce?…I just…I don't…
[BREAK]
[*singing*] "You can take a ride on my big green tractor"…
[BREAK]
"Ketchup is a spicy, spicy food."

"Big Green Tractor" was a No. 1 country hit for country singer Jason Aldean in 2009, which…well…yep. Chika got 'em. So many delicate, victimized people reported her Twitter post to the Twitter police that the social media application suspended her account for five days. She put it on Instagram and from there her celebrity as a budding rapper and activist grew. Later, in an interview with *Teen Vogue* magazine, Chika said she only made the video to cheer up her friend.

Teen Vogue's interview with Chika presented the sophisticated perspective of a Black 19-year-old from Alabama after Trump was elected:

> **Teen Vogue:** What do you want to say to people who don't think racism had anything to do with this year's election?
> **Chika:** I feel like everyone knows this year's election had everything to do with racism. If they don't, they're so far gone and deluded, that I have no advice for them but to soul-search. No one wants to say it because to admit there's a problem presents the responsibility of creating a solution. Too many people would be inconvenienced by addressing institutional racism, so they'd rather sit on the issue. I think it's selfish and eye-opening.
>
> The only way to fix a corrupt system is to dismantle it and rebuild it. I feel like this election brought a lot of us together, and in doing so hopefully gives us the courage to try to mend a broken nation. But it has to be a group effort.

Words spoken in 2016 by one Alabamian were echoed by the state's all-powerful college football team almost four years later.

One heartbeat. One mission. One team.

In the lead-up to *Graduate Together*, LeBron James used the social media hashtag "#MoreThanAnAthlete" to promote the television special, but really it was the continuation of his call to America's team of athletes of all sports to answer the challenge of using their platforms for a higher purpose. In February 2018, Fox News's Laura Ingraham told King James to shut up and dribble. He would not, and then when LeBron was being interviewed by CNN in August of that year about opening his own school in Akron for marginalized children he said what America should have already known since Colin Kaepernick was villainized for a peaceful protest against police brutality. The president of the United States was using sports to split the country in half.

"What I've noticed over the past few months," James said, "he's kinda used sports to kinda divide us, and that's something that I can't relate to."

LeBron James became one of America's greatest athletes of all time by melding together the talents of his teammates and making everyone around him better. His greatest gift was never scoring. It was knowing that the extra pass was more important, and then having the vision to assist his teammates. King James used his voice and his vision and his platform to bring together celebrities and young people from all over the country for messages of togetherness and the importance of education when the country was about to be divided by a summer of plagues. He was the facilitator of that arena, too, and it was an achievement in the spirit of Jesse Owens, Jackie Robinson, Muhammad Ali, Colin Kaepernick, and Megan Rapinoe. In a sports-crazed country driven by capitalism, the players always have the inherent value to shape the country even if they're not getting paid. Chika, the artist from Montgomery, Alabama, and a first-generation American of Nigerian descent, then performed a song for King's TV special on every major network, entitled "Crown."

From the song:

And I don't blame your brainwash'n on you, G
It took me nineteen years to finally start to believe

LeBron James was anointed "The Chosen One" much younger than that, and he dedicated his life to honoring that call through service to others.

An enormous fan of LeBron for most of his young life, Alabama center Chris Owens, no longer a backup for the Crimson Tide, had his fingers on the heartbeat of American sports from August 2020 until a night in February 2021 when the dean's list journalism major summed up our entire saga with, once again, the perfect tweet: "Imagine a cycle of sports seasons where Tom Brady, LeBron James, and Nick Saban all win rings."

America's teams delivered the goods when a country of dedicated sports junkies needed it most.

CHAPTER 9

"WHAT DO YOU SEE?"

Five days after George Floyd gasped for breath and then died under the knee of Minneapolis policeman Derek Chauvin...

And 97 days after Ahmaud Arbery ran for his life and two white men chased him down in a truck in Brunswick, Georgia, and then shot him to death in the street...

And eight years after Trayvon Martin died for wearing a hood...

And 28 years after the acquittal of the four Los Angeles police officers who beat Rodney King...

And 55 years after John Lewis of Troy, Alabama, was brutalized on Selma's Edmund Pettus Bridge by Alabama state troopers for stopping to pray...

And 57 years after Bull Connor ordered the use of fire hoses and police dogs against Birmingham children...

And 64 years after six sticks of dynamite exploded outside the window of Fred Shuttlesworth's bedroom window...

And 119 years after champions of white supremacy seeking "purity of ballot" used voter fraud and racial terror in the Black Belt to pass a new Alabama state constitution to ensure that a framework for self-perpetuating, mutating, cancerous systemic racism would stunt the potential and growth of freed slaves and their descendants...

And every year that Alabama is ranked near the bottom of the national education rankings...

And health care...

But definitely No. 1 in recruiting football players...

And one day before another Alabama artist back in Birmingham would make a speech that took down the most divisive Confederate monument in Alabama...

And two weeks—just two short weeks—after appearing on LeBron's TV special for the graduating high school seniors of 2020, young Jane Chika Oranika of Montgomery, Alabama, was in the streets of Los Angeles with thousands of other young people once again protesting racial inequality and police brutality.

LeBron's *Graduate Together* special was on May 16, 2020, and George Floyd was murdered by Minneapolis policeman Derek Chauvin nine days later. Protesters wanted justice, and a summer of change had found America. With the country at a tipping point, President Donald Trump used his platform to push it over the edge. He didn't call for peace in the summer of 2020, or promote that message. He called for "law and order" and framed protesters as the enemy. Instead of trying to address a fundamental problem of American society, the long history of police violence against minorities and the policies that cause it, Trump leaned hard into America's original team, white supremacy.

The amnesia of America is a mystifying thing. How can people live entire lifetimes dotted with one social event after another caused by police brutality, and then allow themselves to ignore the reason why things repeatedly happen, or, more likely, just simply forget it ever happened at all? The Statue of Liberty is a forgetful idol. The seven-pointed halo atop Lady Liberty's head radiates hope to all the edges of the earth, but the head that wears the crown can't remember the eternal heartache of her own people. As Chika said in her song, maybe it's all the brainwashing.

In 2020, the messaging of people like Colin Kaepernick and LeBron James was so easily bent and distorted that Trump supporters who refused to listen simply started calling advocates for social justice reform "woke" or, counterintuitively, racist themselves. "Systemic racism" and "police brutality" and "brainwashing" are nebulous ideas that can be difficult to understand or easily dismissed. Here is a very real example of how evil men used all three of those things to shape the history of Alabama, and how their perpetuating legacy caused new voices like the ones of Chika and the Alabama football players to speak out so many years later.

On April 10, 1956, another supremely gifted Black artist from Montgomery, Nat King Cole, was singing to an all-white crowd at Birmingham Municipal Auditorium when four white men reportedly associated with the KKK rushed the stage during the third song, toppled the singer, and laid upon him until police pulled them away. The problem for those *righteous defenders of a just society*, victimized by Cole's mere presence, wasn't so much that he was Black. It was that they couldn't stand the thought of white people loving him, and men in power had convinced Cole's assailants that the penalty for that was nothing short of death. Reportedly their plan was to kidnap Cole, who was just a few months away from becoming the first Black man to host a national TV show.

The radicalized men were just the instruments of terror placed there by leaders of a group called the Ku Klux Klan of the Confederacy. The group was formed by a former Birmingham journalist, who had already been fired from a radio station for broadcasting his openly racist thoughts. A gifted communicator, Asa Carter later figured out all he had to do was change the wording and everything would be fine. *States' rights, baby.* A leader of the KKK faction implicated in the attack against Nat King Cole, Carter was the guy who would later write George Wallace's infamous "segregation now, segregation forever" inauguration speech in 1963.

Unfortunately, Alabamians are not taught these important history lessons in high school. As Chika inferred in her famous YouTube video, a history of racism is hard to see from the "big green tractor." Brainwashing does not happen in a day, though, and the modern-day framework of systemic racism was put in place purposefully to split society along color lines by white supremacists of the Klan.

"In the name of the greatest people that have ever trod this earth," Wallace said in the speech written by Klan leader Asa Carter, "I draw the line in the dust and toss the gauntlet before the feet of tyranny and I say: segregation now, segregation tomorrow, segregation forever."

If they can't use racism anymore to divide the country, then they'll just find some other way to exploit emotions. In sports, they call it bulletin-board material.

Nearly four years after successfully turning Colin Kaepernick into the enemy of America, President Trump took the stage in front of Mount Rushmore on July 4, 2020, framing a scene of flags and fireworks and patriotism that would stir the hearts of any person who loved the United States, and said these words:

We want free and open debate, not speech codes and cancel culture...Those who seek to erase our heritage want Americans to forget our pride and our great dignity so that we can no longer understand ourselves or America's destiny.

History's wicked axiom: Privileged people will make you believe they are being crucified so they can kill people who make them feel uncomfortable. Or, worse, they convince you to do it under the belief that it's the best thing for your children. History's purest axiom: Only mustard goes on hot dogs.*

⎯⎯⎯

Trump spoke of "heritage" and "pride" and "dignity" in his call to white supremacy on the Fourth of July 2020, but this is the history that America must never forget: Nat King Cole's assault in Birmingham by radicalized young Klansmen in 1956. Cole was beaten by Klansmen because white people loved the Black crooner. A few months later, on Christmas Day 1956, white supremacists bombed the home of Fred Shuttlesworth, pastor of Bethel Baptist Church in Birmingham, because he was about to lead an effort to integrate buses. When Shuttlesworth miraculously emerged from his home after its bombing, there was a Birmingham police officer already on the scene. He didn't ask Shuttlesworth if he was OK. The cop told Shuttlesworth that if he knew what was best for him, he would get out of town real quick. Shuttlesworth was the problem, not the bomb. The system of racism was just fine the way it was, and Shuttlesworth needed to die.

⎯⎯⎯⎯⎯

* Mustard goes on hot dogs unless you're in Birmingham; then it's mustard, onions, sauerkraut, hot beef, and Birmingham sauce, and don't get shit twisted. Run down to Gus's on 4th Avenue North or Gus's in Irondale, order one with a Buffalo Rock Grapico and some Golden Flake Sweet Heat BBQ chips, and try to not reflexively start slapping the person who brought you into this world. Don't get us writer types started on the Birmingham hot dogs, y'all, or the many uses of possessive tense therein, or we might never get to the football season. Roll Tide.

Years later, after all the blood and all the violence, and after the Civil Rights Act of 1964, and the Voting Rights Act of 1965, George Wallace used the Alabama state troopers in Birmingham, Huntsville, Mobile, and Macon County, as noted by Alabama historian Jeremy Gray of the *Birmingham News*, "to close schools rather than integrate."

"We are not fighting against the Negro people," said Wallace on Labor Day 1963. "We are fighting for local government and states' rights."

Pointed out by Gray, Alabama's famed archivist and preserver of the truth, Wallace later said that people critical of his decisions "just don't know their history."

One thing is certain. It would be nice if they taught these things in Alabama's schools so that future politicians of the state would fully understand their heritage.

Some of these things might be painful to read, but the telling of them is necessary to remember why the Alabama football Crimson Tide stepped out of the Mal Moore Athletic Facility on August 31, 2020, walked to the front of Foster Auditorium, and said this wasn't the end, but the beginning.

You Want Bama? Well, you got it now.

The Black community of Alabama wanted the Alabama football Crimson Tide to stand up for so long, and they finally did.

On that day, Jermaine "FunnyMaine" Johnson, the Alabama superfan, made the necessary personal decision to leave his home in Birmingham during the pandemic and drive to Tuscaloosa to see history for his state firsthand.

Why risk exposure to COVID-19 to be there?

"Because for people, I would say a lot of people in the know, that has been a conversation for decades, especially in the Black community. What would happen if they took a stand?" Funny-Maine would say months later.

"The most powerful entity in the state…we knew that would be monumental and it was…It really resonated because it allowed the conversation to happen and to talk about things that were uncomfortable. It was all the athletes.

"When you see Nick Saban leading the line with that team, and Najee and them, it was powerful and started the conversation. I would love to look back on that day and say this was the moment…I can legit say it has been better here. The Twitter conversation has even changed. And the success of all the sports since then, it's like it broke a curse that was put on the university by people in the past.

"We know about George Wallace, and the university took his side. Bro, it has been so many good things that have happened for this state, and that university since that moment, since they took a stand."

We Want Bama.

"I remember when George Wallace stood in the schoolhouse door at the University of Alabama to bar entry to Black students," Dan Rather tweeted. "I remember when the University of Alabama had a football team that was all white. This strikes me as significant."

We Want Bama.

George Wallace made his "segregation now, segregation forever" speech in 1963 after being elected Alabama's governor. What's actually more significant than that speech, and Wallace's little bit of theater to gain national notoriety in front of Foster Auditorium, is that Bull Connor's use of police brutality and the Klan's use of Bull-blessed racial domestic terrorism in places like Birmingham, Selma, and Anniston were the things that kept the entire system in check, and turned Wallace into a champion of states' rights. Otherwise inherently good white Southern people looked away in silent complicity while "law and order" gave the system the legitimacy it needed to demonize and vilify Blacks who were, obviously, breaking the laws codified by a government fraudulently built on white supremacy. It was just privileged people being made to feel generally uncomfortable.

Can we all just consider walking around in the skin of an Alabama football player, or do we want the Crimson Tide to just shut up and pound the country into oblivion so the state's Confederate sympathizers can continue thinking Alabama football is just some kind of bizarre extension of the Lost Cause? It's no secret within the state's borders that for the better part of the 20th century this is what the success of Alabama football represented to many.

Alabama's love of football isn't the problem. The state's real social handicap is this: The legacy of mythologizing Confederate heroes and pro-Confederate champions over the last 140 years still allows those in power to deceive otherwise inherently good people into having guilt-free consciences for going along with terrible things and maybe even feeling like self-righteous victims when they sit down and put ketchup on their hot dogs.

It can't just be that the Alabama football Crimson Tide marched to the schoolhouse door with their famous coach. The legacy of the players of 2020—who didn't even have to play that season, and yet no one opted out, and everyone wore Apple Watches when they slept, and even got the 70-year-old Saban COVID-19—is making sure the people of the state of Alabama understand the terrible and awful history that made that protest march significant in the hopes of it being a touchstone moment for the University of Alabama in its effort to help heal the state.

The actions taken by Alabama's players of Nick Saban's

"ultimate team" must live on in the form of telling truth to power and explaining the pain, all the terrible pain, and all the lies, and all the compromises for money, and all the sin, and leaving nothing out, in order to move forward. The state of Alabama remains stuck in its past by ignoring these things and being nice. It was built through racial terror and with police brutality. It was built through alienation and stealing welfare checks. It was built like America was built, because let's not act like education opportunities for underserved communities and police brutality against minorities in the name of law and order are any better in New York, Los Angeles, or wherever. In Alabama, though, it was formed by taking away schools. Steeled by denying votes. Everything is connected, and there are no perfect heroes, but there will always be young people who hope and love the hell out of some football and "Dixieland Delight" and Yellow Hammers down at Gallettes. Refusing to experience the pain is the nice Southern cousin to "shut up and dribble."

And Jane Chika Oranika of Montgomery, Alabama, rhymed on every single major television network, "Just wait and God will tell you when the time's near / But if I never jump then I die here."

America's team, y'all.

America's team of athletes rallied for unity in the summer of 2020, and the Alabama football Crimson Tide made sure it was going to do its part. Their 2020 season was already perfect before the games even started, and then they went out and laid waste to earth with hellfire going 13–0 to make the telling of their story more meaningful. The team had a dozen preseason, freshmen, or full All-Americans. It was anchored by the best offensive line, and National Freshman of the Year defensive end Will Anderson Jr., whom no offensive tackle could keep out of the backfield. The offense featured three of the top five recipients in votes for the Heisman, including the majestic wisp of a receiver DeVonta

Smith, who won the award after being the team's second option at receiver until the fifth game of the 10-game regular season.

"For equality," Smith said in Alabama's video of players reading teammate Alex Leatherwood's essay, "for greater understanding."

It was Smith who was given the last line of the video: "Because all lives can't matter until Black lives matter."

For a better tomorrow. For a better world.

For correcting a system that has left Alabama's Black community behind.

President Trump wasn't the cause, y'all. Trump was just the two-bit TV con man who took advantage of the country's weakness, which is racism. It bears repeating, so don't ever forget that this was the headline in the *Montgomery Advertiser* the day after the constitution of 1901 was voted into law: "THE CITIZENS OF ALABAMA DECLARE FOR WHITE SUPREMACY AND PURITY OF BALLOT."

That constitution is still in use.

In Autauga County, where distance is measured in time down country byways, it is not hard to see back through the decades. Not too terribly long before former Alabama tight end O. J. Howard attended a "segregation academy" because it was the best option for his education in an isolated community, his grandmother Lauretta Parker-Tyus was educated in a schoolhouse that was funded penny by penny from the Black community in Autauga County. Parker-Tyus, Queen of Southern cuisine, and pillar of love who used food to unite Black and white, attended Autauga County Training School in Autaugaville, and the school was a piece of Booker T. Washington's legacy. Autauga Training was a Julius Rosenwald school, and not only that, but the first of its kind in the state.

Julius Rosenwald was a philanthropist and part owner and leader of Sears, Roebuck and Company. Booker Taliaferro

Washington, one of America's most famous educators, was the founder of Tuskegee Normal and Industrial Institute (later Tuskegee Institute and now Tuskegee University) in Tuskegee, Alabama. Washington and Rosenwald teamed up to build rural schools for Black communities in the South after white supremacy took away their rights with those new post-Reconstruction constitutions. In a dollar-for-dollar match, Julius Rosenwald's Rosenwald Fund helped bankroll construction of schools specializing in industrial and agricultural training. This was Washington's great gift to the South. The original Tuskegee Institute was built by its own students by actually making the bricks and growing the crops. Pure subsistence living and learning, not unlike the philosophical models of education now used by all the modern-day Montessori schools throughout America. The building agent for the Rosenwald schools in Alabama was M. H. Griffin, and helping the Black community of Autauga County raise funds for their school was how he began his career. From author James D. Anderson's *The Education of Blacks in the South, 1860–1935*:

I have never seen greater human sacrifices for the cause of education. Children without shoes on their feet gave from fifty cents to one dollar and old men and women, whose costumes represented several years of wear, gave from one to five dollars... Colored men offered to pawn their cows and calves for the money and they did do just this thing.

Their last $2, in other words.

Autauga Training was built for $12,000 in 1921, and it was the type of country schoolhouse that if the teacher didn't like your name, she would just change it. Lauretta was born Laura Etta, but the future restaurant owner had her name cooked together in the Rosenwald Fund country schoolhouse. Good things come by combining different ingredients. Gumbo, for example, and pecan pie. And no one wants that imitation crap that takes out all the filé and the fire and the sugar. It is all inedible heresy, and an affront to Southern culture.

The 1954 U.S. Supreme Court decision *Brown vs. Board of Education* was supposed to give Black children equal rights and integrated classrooms, but that's not reality, now is it?

Suburban cities were formed, county vs. city boards of education drew lines through neighborhoods, and, essentially, any new school district could be segregated. A later case, *Milliken vs. Bradley* in 1974, made it so, and turned cities like Birmingham into school-district maps that look like a plate of al dente noodles spilled upon the floor. Systemic racism. Ketchup on spaghetti. States' rights and sin.

National civil rights icon John Lewis was educated at a school in Brundidge, Alabama, that was first built with the Rosenwald Fund. He credited his early education at Pike County Training School for instilling in him a love for reading. He tried to apply at Troy State University (now Troy University), but was ignored. He wrote to Martin Luther King Jr., and King set "the boy from Troy" on the path. It was a painful journey, and Lewis never stopped fighting for civil rights.

John Lewis was beaten in South Carolina (May 9, 1961), Birmingham, and Montgomery during the Freedom Rides, and fire-bombed on a bus in Anniston. A Klan-led mob viciously attacked him and others in Birmingham with Bull Connor looking away, and then he was knocked unconscious at the bus station in Montgomery. He was 21 in 1961 and understood at an early age the use of state-sponsored police brutality and racial terror to protect the South's carefully constructed system of racism. Four years later he was beaten again in Alabama, this time on the Edmund Pettus Bridge. It was March 7, 1965.

In a protest for the right to vote, Lewis and 600 others planned the first of three walks from Selma to Montgomery. John Lewis and his friends stepped out on the Edmund Pettus in the name of something better. So it was in 1965, and so it had to be in March 2020. Only a few weeks before America shut down because of the COVID-19 pandemic, Lewis was back on the Edmund Pettus Bridge for his last walk across in commemoration of a necessary sacrifice for civil rights and the future of America. It was One March Twenty and Twenty, and John Lewis let everyone know it would all be done together.

"Listen up!" they screamed on the bridge that day. It was time to let the songbird sing.

John Lewis's words:

Fifty-five years ago, a few of God's children attempted to march from Brown Chapel AME Church.

Across this bridge.

We were beaten. We were tear-gassed. I thought I was going to die on this bridge. But somehow, and some way, God Almighty kept me here. We cannot give up now. We cannot give in.

We must keep the faith. Keep our eyes on the prize.

We must go out and vote like we never, ever voted before.

Some people gave more than a little blood. Some gave their very lives.

I say this to each and every one of you, especially you young people. The fraternities and sororities. You look good! You look colorful!

Go out there! Speak up!

Speak out. Get in the way.

Get in good trouble. Necessary trouble. And help redeem the soul of America.

May each and every one of you believe.

I'm not going to give up! I'm not going to give in!

We're going to continue to fight. We need your prayers now more than ever before.

Let's do it. We can do it!

Selma is a different place. America is a different place. But we can make it much better.

We must use the vote as a nonviolent instrument or tool to redeem the soul of America.

Thank you very much. Good to see you.

Police broke Lewis's skull on the Edmund Pettus Bridge in 1965, and 16 others were hospitalized. Many more were injured. Lewis spoke his profound words on March 1, 2020, with Stage 4 pancreatic cancer. He died on July 17, 2020, and the last trip across the bridge, his coffin's hearse pulled by two horses, was on July 26.

There were many words written by John Lewis about civil rights during his lifetime, but perhaps the most haunting are the ones he never got a chance to say. The famous March on Washington on August 28, 1963, is credited with assisting the Johnson administration to later pass the Civil Rights Act of 1964 and the Voting Rights Act of 1965. The youngest speaker that day, 23-year-old Lewis had been beaten in the service of those two pieces of future legislation, and he was scheduled to address thousands from the Lincoln Memorial right before Martin Luther King Jr. In total, Lewis was arrested over 40 times during civil rights protests that started in Nashville. His job was just getting started, he knew, and there would be more of his blood on the street.

"The boy from Troy" wanted to be more critical of the federal government for not protecting protestors from racial violence in the South. He understood intimately at a young age this system set up in America, and the role "law and order" played in allowing police violence to uphold it. The original version of Lewis's speech for that day is not the one thousands heard in front of the Lincoln Memorial. There were too many hard truths within his words, and older civil rights leaders, worried that his speech would anger the Kennedy administration, edited it on the fly in a security room behind the Lincoln Memorial. According to Lewis's memoir, *Walking with the Wind: A Memoir of the Movement*, his speech was tempered down after Robert Kennedy had apparently expressed disapproval for its imagery of using nonviolent protests to move through the South "burning" down the system like Union general William Tecumseh Sherman burned a path during the Civil War. It was a war for civil rights in the South, and Lewis was a soldier in that fight, but he couldn't say it.

Lewis also wanted to open his address by saying the Student Nonviolent Coordinating Committee rejected the Kennedy administration's civil rights act because it wasn't going to do enough to prevent police brutality. Instead, that part of the speech was edited to this: "It is true that we support the administration's civil rights bill. We support it with great reservation, however." Lewis was right, of course, but no matter how any of it was worded the path of the South would have found its way to our history's greatest sin, making the villains feel like the victims and letting the Lost Cause win.

George Wallace was a bit of a stooge, and he later, after living with a guilty conscience for everything he did and represented, would apologize for his role in driving the wedge of systemic racism deeper in Alabama. Nick Saban and his football players gave Alabama new imagery to celebrate in front of the Foster Auditorium.

But the real legacy of the 2020 Alabama football Crimson Tide should be its choice to speak out against the use of law enforcement and police brutality to sustain an unjust system. The positive example they presented through working together to create the ultimate team can be a model for something better. Ignore Wallace's fiery words, really, when remembering the Tide's new stand. Instead focus on Bull Connor, the policeman with Klan ties to his native Selma who endorsed Wallace for governor. In the South and in Alabama, the real enemies are not the war birds circling overhead. Beware the soldiers who cry victim while whistling the South's oldest tune, turning groups like the National Association for the Advancement of Colored People and the Congress of Racial Equality into villains.

Bull Connor on Wallace in May 1962, taken from the *Centerville Press* in Bibb County:

> Let us unite behind this great son of Alabama and have four years of peace, progress and segregation. I think I know better than any man in Alabama which chip the NAACP and CORE are hiding. The filthy hands of the NAACP and CORE are spreading over this state like a black cloud. You know who they are against...I don't want to see Alabama taken over by them.

The new sons of Alabama, who spoke of "unity" and actually meant it, endured a long, emotional summer to make it to the schoolhouse door, and that didn't include the brutal, unprecedented seven-week camp they were fighting through at the same time.

Even the hardest players at Alabama could only survive so many practices against "Terminator" Will Anderson Jr., it turned out. He was an "alpha" from the day he arrived, according to those in camp. The 6-foot-4, 235-pound freshman defensive end from Hampton, Georgia, was the breakout star of the summer, and that was before he started holding his own against the senior-laden offensive line that would emerge as the nation's best. The savage nature of Alabama's camps are legendary among players, and units are pushed to the point of mental and physical exhaustion. Players snap. There are fights. Many, many fights, which is normal for football practice, but one time defensive end Isaiah Buggs punched Jalen Hurts "clean in the jaw" during an Alabama practice, and Hurts was an "off-limits quarterback." Imagine what the other guys do during camp. Former linebacker Rashaan Evans once said it best: Alabama's preseason practices are designed to make players want to kill each other for food "like hungry lions eating."

A Roll Pride emerges and feasts upon its Southern dominion.

Midway through it all, with the country electrified and exhausted from months of the pandemic and national unrest (and Trump spewing hate over all things), Jacob Blake of Kenosha, Wisconsin, a Black man, was shot seven times on August 23, 2020, by a white police officer. Blake was attempting to step into his car, and his three children were in the backseat. Police originally were responding to a call by a woman who said her boyfriend had taken her car keys. During protests of the police officer's use of excessive force (Blake was never charged with a crime and was paralyzed from the waist down), two individuals involved in the demonstrations were shot and killed by a 17-year-old armed with an AR-15 after a local alderman issued a post on Facebook calling for the formation of a local militia of "patriots willing to take up arms and defend" Kenosha. Like the Alabama high school football announcer calling for people to be lined up and shot for kneeling during the national anthem, Trumpland's alternate reality had cultivated civic-sponsored brainwashing for the use of violence. Only this time, horrifically, it was real.

That was the breaking point for the sports world. Players felt the social responsibility to stop playing games in protest of a country fighting and killing itself in the streets. The next night, in protest of the police shooting of Blake, and in the spirit of unity with their community, the Milwaukee Bucks refused to take the court for Game 5 of their first-round playoff series against the Orlando Magic. The NBA was inside its pandemic bubble at Disney World after restarting its season. In solidarity with the Bucks, the rest of the NBA players competing in the playoffs went on strike. Within hours of the Bucks' protest, athletes in the WNBA, MLS, and MLB joined the movement and games were canceled or suspended.

A report by Rachel Nichols of ESPN captured perfectly the acute sense of anguish for players and coaches of the NBA, describing the desperate words by coach Doc Rivers as "raw emotion and a thunderbolt cry for justice."

Said Rivers, "All you hear is Donald Trump and all of them talking about fear. We're the ones getting killed. We're the ones getting shot...It's amazing, we keep loving this country, and this country does not love us back."

Former president Barack Obama praised the NBA and Rivers for "standing up for what they believe in," and then calling for "all institutions to stand up for our values."

We Want Bama.

Some of Alabama's younger players wanted to protest in that moment as well, and from that collective consciousness of a United States of American sports came the well-crafted plan to instead make a larger statement to the world and walk in protest together with all athletes at the University of Alabama to Foster Auditorium. The initial idea was later credited to Phidarian Mathis, but many people played roles in the planning. Marches of protest to Foster had happened before at the University of Alabama, most notably when students protested the segregated sororities and fraternities in 2013, but having the football team make a stand would send a clear message to the state and country. Team leaders called a meeting, and, according to multiple accounts, Najee Harris, Daniel Wright, and Mathis were instrumental in organizing the plan and taking it to Saban. U.S. senator Doug Jones, in office at the time, was briefed in Washington a couple days in advance, and he said he would fly down to walk with the players if that was something they wanted. Players discussed it, according to Jones, but relayed a message back to the senator that they wanted the protest to be focused directly on the players and Saban. Jones said he agreed. The team was protesting with or without Saban, but they wanted him to join. When Harris and others met with Saban, the coach's reported response was the perfect answer.

In an interview with award-winning videographers Wes Sinor and Laura Goldman and beat writer Michael Casagrande of AL.com, Harris would later say the scene in the coach's office felt like "it was a movie."

"And this is for real," Harris said. "Saban was like, 'I was waiting for you guys to do something like this because if I say it as a coach, it wouldn't be as genuine. I wanted the players to come do it.' So Saban was all in."

Saban told the players he was proud of them like a father. It wasn't the first time in his life, though, that he had been around young people in college who needed to have their voices heard. The world is not a Disney movie, and that lesson was retaught to the country in 2020 in case anyone had forgotten. Saban had not. In 1970, he was a freshman at Kent State University and present on campus for the massacre there of students by the Ohio National Guard. He has carried that day with him his entire life. In the back of his mind, it is always there. Yes, of course, he would walk with his players, because he would be their shield.

Harris, the senior running back, made the announcement on Twitter, alerting the various social channels and their digital environs that the Alabama football Crimson Tide would be walking back in time in the spirit of a better future.

"Alabama football—players and coaches—are marching from the Mal Moore Athletic Facility at 4 p.m. Monday to meet at the schoolhouse door at Foster Auditorium. We want our voices to be heard as we strive to enact social change and rid our world of social injustices."

With an addendum: "We want all Alabama athletes to join us. This isn't a fan day... this isn't a football game... this is about lasting CHANGE!"

Supporters were later encouraged to attend because y'all already knew that nothing was going to keep FunnyMaine away. It was to be a statement to America, but also the University of Alabama's way of publicly rebuking the sins of its past, and that admission cannot go underrepresented. The hardest thing for people to do is admit that they are wrong. Former U.S. senator Jones would later say that he was "in awe that the players would do this, and that the university would sanction this." A graduate of the University of Alabama, and a diehard Alabama fan, Jones is a season ticket holder, and tries his best to dutifully stay until the end of games.

Najee Harris, a native son of Northern California who grew up and out of poverty through the help of his community and the love of a devoted mother, came of age as a running back for Antioch High School in Antioch, California, during Colin Kaepernick's success with the San Francisco 49ers. Harris was a senior in high school in 2016 when Kaepernick began his protest against police violence during the playing of pregame national anthems. Charismatic, with a genuine soul, Harris embodied Kaepernick's bold stand to kneel. One might even say he jumped at and over the opportunity to lead the march.

Harris made a reputation for himself in college for clean leaping over whole defenders, which is quite the physical accomplishment for a 6-foot-1, 232-pound back built in the mode of the beast, Marshawn Lynch. In 2019, Harris hurdled South Carolina Gamecocks defensive back R. J. Roderick in Columbia, South Carolina, after already shrugging off linebacker D. J. Wonnum at the 30-yard line. After the three-yard leap from the 18- to the 15-yard line, Harris rushed all the way into the back of the end zone inside Williams-Brice Stadium and struck a pose that would become notable. He was imitating a goal celebration by international soccer star Megan Rapinoe of the U.S. Women's National Team.

Later known simply as "the pose," the goal celebration was made iconic in the 2019 World Cup after Rapinoe said in an interview that she wouldn't be going to the "fucking White House" if the United States won the World Cup. Trump responded on Twitter, saying Rapinoe should "win first" before "she talks," and added that Rapinoe "should never disrespect our Country, the White House, or our Flag, especially since so much has been done for her & the team."

With her back straight, feet together, and arms outstretched like wings presenting artistic commentary, Rapinoe's goal celebration was her official response. She would later say in an interview with *ESPN FC* that "it really wasn't my celebration, personally. It wasn't just for me, but it was like, you and nobody will take our joy, you won't take our passion, you won't rob this from us, you won't take our happiness. We're going to stand up with a smile with our full chest exposed and really kind of just put it all out there, and, like, this is what we want the world to be. This is the kind of openness and vulnerability and passion and just kind of unbridled joy that we want in the world. So, it kind of felt like I was doing it with everyone, for everyone, and people feel free to use it. Take it with you. If you're in your office and something needs to happen, you can just bust it out and everyone will know what the deal is."

When Harris struck Rapinoe's pose, it was immediately celebrated by Alabama fans, who of course took the silhouette of his touchdown celebration and crafted it into those charming, sorority-style game-day buttons popular among SEC fanbases.

After going 11–0 and winning the SEC, Harris explained before the January 2021 Rose Bowl in Arlington, Texas, that his tribute to Rapinoe was out of respect for her courage to speak out, but "first of all" her being from California and listening "to Nipsey Hussle, one of my favorite rappers, too. She gave a shout out to him." Killed on March 31, 2019, Nipsey Hussle was a California-based rapper beloved for his activism and thought-provoking lyrics. Harris also explained that he was inspired by Rapinoe's stands against social injustices and unequal pay for women. Rapinoe responded to Harris publicly by writing, "Najeeeee Roll Tide!!!!! (Did I do it right? [crazy-face emoji]) Be Great, get those [roses]," and "hurdle someone for me."

Wait, wait, wait…Megan Rapinoe wanted Bama?

Behold, America, the awesome power of sports. Nothing in this world is impossible if there is love and emojis. She gave a leap of faith, and then the most brilliant thing happened in the melding of American sports since Bo Jackson, Wayne Gretzky, and Michael Jordan teamed up to be the ProStars and save the world from (and this is the actual name of their most fiendish adversary) Clockwork Delaronge. In one of the most memorable moments of the 2020 season, Harris hurdled Notre Dame cornerback Nick McCloud in the first quarter of California's COVID-displaced Rose Bowl. In that moment, the impossible was made real, and joy won.

We Want Bama.

LeBron James . . . Well, LeBron James did not want Bama, and never wanted Bama. King James was silent in Alabama's moment of 2020 perfection, and it was well understood why. There are no perfect heroes, y'all, but Ohio State fans always cry.

"Get in good trouble," John Lewis cried out from the Edmund Pettus Bridge on One March Twenty Twenty. "Necessary trouble. And help redeem the soul of America."

For the August 31 protest in front of Foster Auditorium, Harris wore a T-shirt that read, "Defend Black Lives." It was a simple statement and a plea. Honest and genuine just like Najee.

There was nothing sinister about those words. They were a humane course correction, which had been breathed into existence by so much incredible pain. "Defend Black Lives" was the answer to a statement made more than 57 years before them by George Wallace, who told America that Black lives did not matter, and Blacks were the enemy for even thinking it.

Where Black students Vivian Malone and James Hood once had the courage to walk through those doors, Najee Harris took a stand to tell everyone that they had a duty to speak:

First and foremost, me and the team want to thank everyone for uniting and standing in solidarity at this peaceful protest. The past few months have brought a great focus to issues that have been prevalent in society for years. Black men and women have been undeserving victims of racism. It has been evident in many different ways, including policy brutality and hate crimes. This is not a problem that will simply come and go in a news cycle. It is not a problem that will eventually dissipate without action. Being here today is a huge step. But I ask you, what's next? ... For certain, we can't let this momentum die. This has to be an ongoing movement until change happens. We must do more as a team and as individuals to keep this movement going.

Chris Owens, our backup center from Texas by flood of New Orleans, had crafted the perfect answer to Najee's call.

I just want you to take a moment to look at the people in front of you. What do you see? People of all races and ethnicities coming together to form a team. In sports, a team is a place where everyone has equal opportunity to be successful, and in order to get things done on the field of play, we must all come together and unite as one. We must understand the mission that we are trying to accomplish and take the necessary steps to reach our goals. Now, look at the status of our country. Unlike the example of our team, our country is not a place of equality and unity at the moment. Because of this, we are unable to accomplish the goals of a just society.

America's team wasn't formed in a summer, but was built by generations of brave leaders who sacrificed so much to put this great power of Alabama football in the hands of determined young people who became men.

The season of hope was either beginning or just ending, depending on your frame of reference. Either way when this history is viewed, everyone who knew anything understood that the Alabama football Crimson Tide wasn't losing. They loved each other like brothers, and they enjoyed being around each other like friends. Their strength was earned the lion's way, and America's team used its great power to bring their world together.

CHAPTER 10

WE WANT BAMA

There are myths and there are legends in Alabama where they play football in the fall...

Monsters be there, red teams and blue,
and memories of 4th and 2.
Bo Jackson soared and Tim Tebow cried and Cam
    Newton parted the water,
but no one really knew what to think when Mississippi
    State hired a seafaring marauder.
There are secret money bags and no moral snags and
    everyone's always been a cheat'n.
It's just about the greatest place on earth when the leaves
    they are recede'n.
There are no perfect heroes there in that land of air thick
    as butter.
Ole Miss and Arkansas were once both good, but they
    can't share Houston Nutter.
Tiger Bait is LSU and Aggieland is always yell'n.
When they get together it's damn near sure that Bubba's
    catch'n a case or a felon.

When Ole Miss plays the Tide the Rebels don't wear
  clothes of power hue.
It's actually just the color of guilty fear, and in the South
  we call that haint blue.
Men in Mobile and the Flora-Bama called their wives one
  day and said batten every hatch.
Nick Saban, crazy as it be, just left paradise for a cotton patch.
The Shulas were super pissed and of course they had all
  the reason.
It's not every day that an honest man sets to do'n treason.
It was the Dolphins that wanted Bear all those many years
  ago,
and now his son had harpooned Flipper and set off for the
  Gulf of Mexico.
Mal Moore looked out the window and said, "Should I call
  you Skipper?"
Nick Saban said call me never and you're going to need to
  write down what we want for dinner.
The great writer Monte Burke said that Saban was really
  only good at 'croot'n.
The West Virginia Wizard had other things in mind and
  turned into a modern-day Rasputin.
Saban did not tell the truth and of course that means he
  lied.
They played banjos on the radio as he stealed away with
  his bride.
There are no absolute villains in the place of Archibald's
  and good eat'n,
but the myths are better for impressing children who dip
  white bread in sauce and say, "Hey, what's that there
  you read'n?"

If the SEC is poetry, and "We Want Bama" is the muse,
every Forrest Gump from Eutaw to La Batre only wants
    to hear good news.
Rat poison is the writer's pill, and of this we all agree,
but pay attention and lean in for down-home truth tell'n
    and clean eyes to help you see.
Be wise for you to close them if you refuse to know the
    light,
but what makes mystical creatures of Alabama ain't all the
    wins. It's when the Tide finally loses the fight.

In the Deep South, there is reality, and then there is college football. We have left reality behind, and are now set adrift in a different realm of magical possibility where the smoke of slow-cooked whole hogs rises from holes in the dirt, and the steam of crawfish boils opens portals to truth. Firefly vodka Saturday punch dances with the light of outdoor possibilities in a Dixieland Delight dreamscape of Southern angels, their beaus, and thousands of other tailgate parties all crammed into college campuses throughout the Southeast. This is the world of SEC football, and it is an ecosystem unlike any other. Lives are built around it, families grow from it, and tourists from all over the world now travel to the South to experience this unique slice of American culture. But beware: A terrible thing lords over it all. It is the malevolent ruler of this fairy tale, and it comes like a summer storm into every campus to drown away all of the dreams and the tailgates, too.

The terrible malevolence is *Bama, and you do not want it.*

Megan Rapinoe and her international squad of shit-kicking super-heroes do not want this Bama.

Dan Rather's wisdom does not want this Bama.

Jules Winnfield's wallet does not want Bama.

Vladimir Putin's Twitter bots do not want this Bama.

Bruce Lee's karate does not want this Bama.

Supermodel casino sex does not want this Bama.

The THC levels of Elon Musk's hybrid space weed do not want this Bama.

And NCAA compliance does not want this Bama…

Oh, and President Trump's motherfuck'n tweets definitely did not want Bama.

The guys at *SEC Shorts* tried to tell y'all in 2017, but apparently no one was listening.

Alabama has lost 15 games from 2009 to 2020, and during that span Ohio State only lost 19, but the Buckeyes also forfeited every win of an entire season (12 in 2010) and paid four different people to be the team's head coach. Since the 2009 season, Ohio State has played in two national championship games. Alabama has played in eight.

Alabama hasn't lost to SEC East rival Tennessee since the iPhone was invented.

Alabama has had three Heisman Trophy winners since 2009. Florida has had four coaches since 2009.

There were 196 iterations of the AP Top 25 Poll from 2009 to the end of the 2020 season. It's not that Alabama was ranked in every single one, and it's not that Alabama was outside the Top 10 only five weeks during that time. It's that Alabama was ranked either No. 1, 2, or 3 in the country in 158 weeks over those 12 seasons. In that time, the combined total of top three appearances in the AP Poll of USC, Oklahoma, Notre Dame, Ohio State, Texas, and Florida State equaled exactly 158. Teams in Alabama's division, the SEC West, combined to make 55 top three AP Poll rankings from 2009 to 2020. The SEC East totaled 43.

From 2013 to 2020, upstart Clemson, which is coached by

former Alabama receiver Dabo Swinney, was ranked either No. 1, 2, or 3 in the AP Poll 71 different times. Pretty good. Alabama was ranked among the top three teams in the country 108 times during that same span, falling out of the top three eight times. Every single time, some genius made the mistake of writing off Nick Saban and his Crimson Tide dynasty.

We Want Bama.

There is no equivalent in sports to seeing the Alabama football Crimson Tide lose a game. For fans, each loss is like watching Marlon Brando's famous scene opposite Martin Sheen in Francis Ford Coppola's *Apocalypse Now*. Sheen's character, Captain Willard, was sent into the symbolic heart of darkness to kill Brando's Colonel Kurtz, a decorated U.S. Army officer in Vietnam who had gone rogue and turned himself into a homicidal jungle god.

"Where are you from, Willard?" Brando asks Sheen.

"I'm from Ohio, sir," Willard replies.

"Are you an assassin?" Brando asks calmly.

"I'm a soldier," Sheen says.

"You're neither," answers Brando. "You're an errand boy... sent by grocery clerks... to collect a bill."

We Want Bama.

This is how myths and legends are built in the South where they play football in the fall. The essence of the phrase "We Want Bama," three simple words that have come to define and shape college football in the time of Nick Saban, is a representation of everyone's greatest effort or best team or most talented gift ringing with flawless confidence and then wanting to test that craftwork against the best that ever lived and getting housed 55–0 in the first half.

And therein lies the true power of We Want Bama's lion-prided dominance. When Saban actually loses a game—and sometimes it happens—Alabama's loss is bigger news than the team that actually won the game, but usually it's the biggest news event in all of college football that season. That mystique fuels the sport, and has turned one of the country's greatest traditions, college football, into a cultural influencer that aligns all things and turns Saturday mornings on ESPN into the greatest four hours in television.

Everyone in the South, and maybe beyond, still knows where they were in 2014 when Ohio State upset Alabama in the semifinals of the first College Football Playoff. If someone strapped electrodes to every meaty temple in the Southland and stimulated our minds with torture, only the liars and the displaced Buckeyes that have somehow rolled yonder way could answer where they were when *the* Ohio State University won the next game.

———

No one understands this tug of influence better than Rece Davis, who is the host of *ESPN College GameDay*, and also a native of Muscle Shoals, Alabama, and a graduate of the university. Roll Pride. Muscle Shoals is a folktale musical mecca for rock and roll musicians, and Rece Davis walks with this vibe and speaks its coolness into existence. "Muscle Shoals has got the Swampers," Lynyrd Skynyrd sang in "Sweet Home Alabama" about the Shoals' legendary studio band. College football has Davis and the game's Saturday morning rhythm section.

Davis's position in college football as a television journalist is a fascinating one. *ESPN College GameDay* originates from the campus of the week's best game in the country, and the show's brilliance is that it uses college students as living, screaming, drinking props to create iconic scenes of Americana every weekend. It is more than must-watch TV for fans. It is part of the culture of college football, and every single week it gives the sport that fresh youthful feel of endless possibility. *GameDay* is like an *Animal House*–style backyard concert picnic toga party thrown by Norman Rockwell's black sheep middle child who's in his fifth year of school but still a sophomore and doesn't ever go to his art philosophy or English classes but, like his father who still loves him, can paint the most brilliant things but on cardboard and then glue sticks to those pieces of cardboard and hold the clever signs for the country to celebrate as national works of joy. Because the solar system is perfectly weighted by God, Rece Davis—Alabama grad—is paired on the set with analyst Kirk Herbstreit, who is a graduate of *the* Ohio State University and played football there as a quarterback.

Of the people who analyze things for money in this country, and this includes the Pentagon's whiz children saving the world every day, no one is better at their chosen field of contextual understanding than the man they call Herbie. He can tell you who's going to win the national championship in three years in casual conversation without a thought and, of course, be correct, but he caught holy heck early in 2020 when he rightly surmised that college football was in trouble of not happening because of the coronavirus pandemic. Herbie sounding the alarm early was one of the things that helped save the season, and the entire state of Alabama should now appreciate Ohio State simply for that reason. Herbstreit's buddies and fellow analysts on *GameDay* are Desmond Howard and the wise sage himself, Lee Corso. Howard, one of the most famous players in college football history, was a receiver and return specialist at Michigan and is from Cleveland, so that perspective alone makes him one of the country's leading authorities on life and why it matters: for experiencing all things through every prism, and then posing questions to educate the masses. Corso is that grandfather you just want to hug and squeeze for hours.

This is the level of love and devotion nearly every person living in the seven-county Greater Birmingham, Alabama, area feels about *ESPN College GameDay*. It is well watched. "We Want Bama" allows things like *SEC Shorts*, a sketch comedy internet show about the wild kingdom of the SEC, to not only exist, but thrive to the point that those guys could actually quit their jobs and focus on that full-time. The Alabama sports information department noted before the 2021 College Football Playoff national championship against Ohio State that games including Alabama had been featured as the host site for *ESPN College GameDay* a record 50 times. Every single one was like public relations gold nuggets. Per Alabama, "The 41 appearances in the Saban era are 10 better than Ohio State (31) for the most GameDay appearances since the 2007 season." During that span, LSU was second most among SEC teams in *GameDay* appearances at 24. (*And Saban built LSU, too!*)

ESPN College GameDay *definitely wants them some Bama.*

Rece Davis on "We Want Bama" and its effect on the sport:

You measure yourself by that. I love this sport ever since I can remember in 1971, and there has never been a dynasty like this. None like this. Even fans from other programs can recite every loss. It's because "We Want Bama." Everyone wants to topple them from their spot on top of the sport. When they lose, it's the biggest most gargantuan story. There is no greater compliment than that. "We Want Bama" created for our show and created for our sport something to chase and something to want to topple.

Alabama's football players and other athletes harnessed that power in 2020 and bent it to their will, and Davis, as a native of Alabama and graduate of the university, said he felt a deep sense of pride watching it all unfold.

"Something poetic and symmetrical and meaningful," is how the great man of words described the scene, "that they went to that spot to make sure their voices were heard."

"There is so much in the history of the university that is regrettable," Davis said. "And the way in which those statues have been honored and for that landmark. And for the players to grasp that in their moment and tie in the future, and as a moment to mark that spot where things changed drastically."

To get to that moment in history, though, where "We Want Bama" was answering a hero's call instead of representing the ultimate villain, the phrase first had to become a multilayered metaphor for courage ubiquitous with American sports. The meme of our time, in other words, and the public expression for the challenge of a lifetime.

When Alabama defeated Florida for the 2020 SEC championship game, it was the Crimson Tide's 31st victory in a row against teams in the SEC East. Alabama entered the 2021 football season winners of 98 consecutive games against unranked opponents. That might be the greatest streak of all. There are no bad weeks of practice and inexplicable losses like Urban Meyer's Ohio State going down against Iowa in a burning heap.

The organic cries of "We Want Bama" from stadiums began in earnest around 2010 or 2011. If a team had a big win, that team's fans were chanting "We Want Bama" at the end of games. Ohio State, Penn State, Florida State, Central Florida, LSU, and on and on. When Kansas in 2014 upset Iowa State and chanted it while students shimmied up goalposts to pull them down, it was already several years a standard-bearer for the charming allure of how college football makes dreamers out of us all.

Noting that victory by Kansas, college football writer George Schroeder of *USA Today* penned a feature story on "We Want Bama" before the inaugural College Football Playoff in 2014:

> Earlier this month, in the waning moments of the Big Ten championship, Ohio State fans chanted the phrase. Shortly after winning the ACC championship that same day, Florida State players said they, you guessed it, wanted Bama.
>
> "I want to play them real bad, and I look forward to that game," said Jameis Winston, the Seminoles' quarterback. "It's amazing."
>
> No, what's amazing is the context. Florida State had just notched its 29th consecutive victory, and is the defending national champion. The Seminoles beat an SEC team last year in the BCS title game.

Winston, who is from the Birmingham-area municipality of Hueytown, wanted Bama after previously not wanting Bama. Nick Saban recruited the quarterback, but he instead chose FSU and Jimbo Fisher, a former Saban assistant.

The phrase is still evolving, and maybe always will, but "We Want Bama" can mean all of these things, and then some of them at the same time: belligerent bravery, obscene stupidity, the handle of a shrimping boat, self-effacing sarcasm, clout-chasing recognition, school spirit, social commentary, good jokes, bad ideas, declarations of war, regrettable overconfidence, shoutouts from the stands at the 2014 World Cup in Brazil, pride of achievement, alcohol poisoning, unbridled celebration, the birth of a child, requesting the return of an animal, and, most often, arrival to the weigh-in as a contender. Signs on Davis's *ESPN College GameDay*, the best live TV show in the country, played a large role in making "We Want Bama" part of the broader American culture beyond college football.

This is why.

From 2009 to 2020, a dozen years of dominance, beating Alabama in the SEC was like the combination of winning the Super Bowl and the heavyweight boxing world championship, and losing your wedding band in the Gulf back in 1999, but then landing a 1,200-pound blue marlin 15 years later, and after fighting through seven hells in the sun, and pulling the big sea creature up alongside the watercraft, Marvin the Marlin flips you something with its bill and says, "You lost this, ya prick," and then falls back into the depths of your imagination.

There is one exception to this rule, and that is Auburn. Auburn does not give one fuck about Alabama, but then at the same time gives them all away by the millions. When it comes to college football, Auburn operates inside of its own constant state of denial.

Time for all the Stat-y McStat-stats, y'all.

From 2009 through the 2020 season, the Alabama football Crimson Tide had 141 wins to only 15 losses with a scorecard against SEC opponents of 85 victories and 11 "world-imploding in Alabama but baby-making nights somewhere else" losses. Outside of the fantasy world that is the SEC, Alabama's 12-year run had only four other losses, and three of those were to Ohio State (2014) and Clemson (2016 and 2018) in the College Football Playoff. The only other loss by Alabama outside of the SEC and the College Football Playoff in 12 years was to Oklahoma in 2013 in a throwaway Sugar Bowl. That November, Alabama had lost the "Mother of All Iron Bowls," as famed *Birmingham News* sports columnist Kevin Scarbinsky called it, in a game we now just know as "Kick

Six." It's not the wins that built "We Want Bama." It's the defeats. And for spoiled Alabama fans, even the close wins are like losses.

The best high school recruits in the country definitely want Bama. Alabama has had the top-rated recruiting class in the country nine of 11 years since 2011, including a 2021 class rated higher than any class since recruiting services have been assigning value to such things. Over 12 years from 2009 to 2021, Alabama had 96 players drafted by NFL teams, and among those were 33 players selected in the first round. Las Vegas Raiders running back Josh Jacobs, one of the best offensive skill players in the NFL in 2020, was never actually a full-time starter for Alabama. He was behind Damien Harris (New England Patriots) the entire time. During his three years in Tuscaloosa his highest rushing total was only 640 yards his junior season. The Raiders drafted him 24th overall in 2019 to be their featured back in their new city.

The 2020 NFL season ended with six former Alabama running backs on active roster, and then Alabama's Najee Harris was selected No. 24 overall by the Pittsburgh Steelers in the 2021 NFL Draft.

Beginning with its undefeated season in 2009 and ending with its undefeated season in 2020, Alabama played for a national championship eight times in 12 years. That sustained dominance connects Alabama's ability to recruit the best players year after year despite constant turnover among assistant coaches. Another big pitch that no other team can come close to claiming: Every recruiting class of Saban's since his time at Alabama has won at least one national championship. In 2020, a year when 69-year-old Saban had to use a Zoom app to recruit, he lapped the field. Here's the perfect summation of the West Virginia Wizard's ability to recruit, as noted by former AL.com college football reporter Matt Zenitz on December 23, 2020: "Alabama's recruiting class now includes the top-ranked players from Texas at these six positions: tackle (Tommy Brockermeyer), running back (Camar Wheaton), wide receiver (JoJo Earle), quarterback (Jalen Milroe), inside linebacker (Kendrick Blackshire), center (James Brockermeyer)."* Most of these kids will probably toil in relative anonymity for years in the Mal Moore Athletic Facility for Turning Boys into Lions before emerging as All-American candidates who still might not start until their junior or senior years.

"Nick at his core is about doing what's best for his players," said Davis, the host of *ESPN College GameDay.* "Everything they do there is aligned with trying to give their players a way to be successful in some walk of life. That's the secret to their longevity. It's not about breaking records. It's about those who are there winning the moment every day and not in that coach-y way. What can make you better today? What is it that I can do for you?"

Eventually, Big Nick Energy gets everyone in its orbit talk'n like the Sun God of the SEC.

Those were the positive numbers, but this now be the pain.

No player representing the University of Tennessee in the varsity sport of SEC football has ever tasted the sweet sensual aroma of a well-crafted victory cigar in the 14 years since Nick Saban has been the coach at Alabama. The East Tennessee Hill Tribes have been playing fiddles and sticks of sorrows down in their Appalachian hollers for many, many moons. They call the Alabama-Tennessee rivalry the Third Saturday in October, but it's just an early Halloween of horrors for the Volunteers. Then the SEC usually gives Nick Saban an off week for his birthday (October 31), and everyone in the Deep South celebrates it by paying homage to the things that scare us most of all.

---

* No wonder Texas requested to join the SEC in 2021: The Longhorns were sick of Saban stealing all of their state's best recruits. In response, Texas poached Saban's offensive coordinator of the 2020 championship season, Steve Sarkisian.

When perpetually tragic Tennessee ran off former Saban assistant coach Jeremy Pruitt in the winter of 2021, the Vols' fresh sacrifice, Josh Heupel of UCF, represented the 49th head coach at an SEC school since Alabama was rejected by then–West Virginia coach Rich Rodriguez. That snub allowed former Alabama athletics director Mal Moore (and, yes, Paul Bryant Jr.) to save Alabama by hiring a coach who was raised on hard work and football in the small Appalachian coal-mining town of Monongah, West Virginia. A symmetry of coincidences are woven into the story of what led Saban to Alabama, but there is something more powerful there, too. He chose to coach at Alabama to win and chase history, but his devotion to helping and protecting young people in college is a calling. Saban's recent years have revealed that more and more. As he walks through his career's doorframe of dictatorial champion into a place of deeper wisdom, his higher purpose points backward to a tragic beginning.

In 1970, Saban was a freshman at Kent State when the Ohio National Guard, called in by Governor Jim Rhodes, fired their rifles upon students who were peacefully protesting the conflict in Vietnam. Four were killed, and they were Allison Beth Krause (age 19), Jeffrey Glenn Miller (20), Sandra Lee Scheuer (20), and William Knox Schroeder (19).

"To have students on your campus shot, killed and—actually, didn't see it happen, but saw the aftermath, right after it happened—it made me have a lot of appreciation for a lot of things," Saban said on September 21, 2016. At the time, the sports world was defending Colin Kaepernick's right to peacefully protest.

"So, nobody could ever quite figure out how that happened," Saban went on. "It seemed pretty unnecessary, but I had class with one of the students that were killed, Allison Krause. I didn't know her or anything that well, but it was a pretty chilling experience and something that makes you view things a little bit differently, and certainly have a much better appreciation of not taking for granted life itself."

The evening prior to the slayings, Ohio's governor labeled the young people un-American during a news conference, and said they were dangerous and worse than communists.

"We've seen here at the city of Kent especially, probably the most vicious form of campus-oriented violence yet perpetrated by dissident groups," Rhodes said. "They make definite plans of burning, destroying, and throwing rocks at police, and at the National Guard and the highway patrol. This is when we're going to use every part of the law enforcement agency of Ohio to drive them out of Kent. We are going to eradicate the problem. We're not going to treat the symptoms.

"And these people just move from one campus to the other and terrorize the community," Rhodes continued, "they're worse than the brown shirts and the communist element, and also the night riders and the vigilantes. They're the worst type of people that we harbor in America. Now I want to say this. They are not going to take over campus. I think that we're up against the strongest, well-trained, militant, revolutionary group that has ever assembled in America."

The dead were students, and none older than 20 years old. Analysis of the massacre determined that the average distance between the Ohio National Guard and their victims was 345 feet.

At his core, Rece Davis said, Saban does what's best for his players, whom he views as his children. Maybe the greatest college football coach who has ever lived just realized when he was with the Miami Dolphins that it was turning him into a man he did not want to be, and that the man from West Virginia had to mine something richer. Few remember this so many years later, but Saban took a pay cut to return to the college game. He is now the builder of men and he protects them from the real monsters of this world through education and tough coaching. There are no perfect heroes here, but there are leaders moved by life experience and faith and that thing they call the Holy Spirit. It pushes determined people to be better tomorrow than they were before they went to bed.

Saban told Alabama to have faith back in 2006. That perspective of Saban is lost or ignored on the many fans of football who are clouded by tribalism and, of course, Saban's well-crafted public demeanor. According to the journalist who broke the news that Saban was leaving Miami for Alabama, Saban had his agent, Jimmy Sexton, tell Alabama to be patient and let him finish his season with the Dolphins before making a final decision. Alabama, according to former *Birmingham News* columnist Kevin Scarbinsky, got antsy and worried Saban was going to "leave them at the altar." Mal Moore then went after Rodriguez, only to be turned down. It was at that point that Moore checked back with Sexton about Saban's interest.

Said Scarbinsky, who attended Troy State University and then the University of Florida for journalism school, "Alabama got in touch with Sexton and Sexton called Saban. Saban had just walked off the practice field. He said, 'If they had listened to me in the first place they wouldn't be in this predicament. Get me the fucking job.'"

Nick Saban definitely wanted Bama.

But now for the truth about this thing we love called "We Want Bama," and Alabama's current role in American culture. It's not about the winning at all. It's about the losing. And it's about Auburn.

In the 12 seasons between 2009 and 2020, Alabama won six

national championships. It is the highest achievement in college football history, but during that time span the Crimson Tide only had one more SEC championship. Surviving the SEC, in other words, prepared Alabama well. The seven-team SEC West wild kingdom bested the lion king almost half the time. Inside the SEC West is the greatest rivalry in American sports, and that's the football game between Alabama and Auburn. Bo Jackson and Pat Dye changed everything together. Before Jackson arrived at Auburn in 1982, the Tigers had lost nine in a row to Alabama, but were 19–4 against the Crimson Tide dating back to 1959. Since the 1982 Iron Bowl they call "Bo Over the Top," a reference to a famous goal-line touchdown, Alabama actually has a losing record to Auburn (19–20) after the Crimson Tide's most recent Iron Bowl victory in 2020.

The origin of "We Want Bama" is a difficult one to trace because spoken-word storytelling is an organic collective of people's folklore and culture, but the significance of the phrase was never more important to the future of the Iron Bowl—and that game's power to change a state—than in 1989 inside Georgia's Sanford Stadium. It's impossible to fully understand Alabama without knowing Auburn. For all of Saban and Alabama's amazing records and championships and statistical feats between 2009 and 2021, the Crimson Tide was just 3–3 inside Jordan-Hare Stadium. The Tigers are the kings of that immaculate jungle, and don't ever doubt it. Since the Iron Bowl was removed from Birmingham's neutral-site Legion Field in 1989 by force of will and Pat Dye, Alabama is 5–10 against Auburn in Jordan-Hare.

Alabama did not want the game moved away from Birmingham, but Dye, also Auburn's athletics director, fought through all the hollow threats and bluster to bring the Iron Bowl to Lee County every other year. Alabama briefly threatened to once again discontinue the game. The city of Birmingham threatened legal action to try and keep the game at Legion Field. Dye, who was an All-American at Georgia and never lost to Georgia Tech as a player or coach (10–0), understood deeply how to win rivalry games and shape a school. Can't do it, he reckoned, in pro-Alabama Birmingham. He was right, and the state of Alabama and the SEC, and maybe America, is better for it.

Auburn was making the turn at its Amen Corner, which is of course a reference to the Masters at Augusta National, but also the nickname for the part of Auburn's schedule when it must play Georgia and then Alabama in the span of three weeks. With its game in 1989 against Georgia well in hand, Auburn's fans inside the Bulldogs' stadium began chanting, "We Want Bama! We Want Bama! We Want Bama!" According to an account by sports reporter Tommy Hicks, then at the *Anniston Star*, Dye tried to quiet the crowd, but the Auburn fans persisted. For them, it was already the schedule's eve of the first game against Alabama at Jordan-Hare.

"We Want Bama!" the Auburn fans cried out.

"We Want Bama!" they demanded.

Three words shouted inside Georgia's Sanford Stadium by Auburn fans that shaped college football forever. And that is how two different things with mutual, common purpose pushed an entire state into a better future.

Auburn wanted Alabama, but the Tigers were not scared
    one bit of the Tide.
Bo Jackson of Bessemer had already trampled that beast,
    and given Auburn unmovable confidence and pride.
Alabama was ranked No. 2 in the country when its
    players' cleats first touched the grass.
No. 11 Auburn won 30–20 and Pat Dye said kiss my ass.

The greatest rivalry in sports had entered a new plane of
cosmic chance.
Big Hurt, Barkley, and Bo looked on with happiness, and
led everyone in a dance.
Time can even stand still for a second or two in this new
place of wonder.
When the Iron Bowl is at Auburn the Tigers always have
the power to push balance asunder.
The beast lurks for Nick Saban in Jordan-Hare, and he
could never deny it.
Give Auburn one second and you know they're going to
try it.
The force of nature that is Alabama can't refute the facts.
Saban started 3–4 in the jungle with a collection of dirty
slacks.
Auburn miracles are real and the magic is not some devil's
fix.
It's Touchdown Jesus who lives there and he moved us to
faith with Kick Six.

Auburn's "We Want Bama" chant is a testament to the glory
of college football, and the Alabama football Crimson Tide would
not exist in this modern form of domination without its counter-
weight within its own state. In the 10 seasons from 2009 and 2018,
either Auburn (two) or Alabama (seven) played in every single season's national championship game except one (2014, when Alabama lost to Ohio State in the inaugural College Football Playoff
semifinals). Cam Newton led Auburn to the 2010 national championship with an undefeated season, and the Tigers would have had
another national title after the 2013 season if not for Florida State's
quarterback from Hueytown, which is about a 10-minute drive

from Bo Jackson's Bessemer. (Bobby Bowden, FSU's legendary coach, is from the east Birmingham neighborhood of Woodlawn.)

When they say college football is religion in Alabama, Bobby Bowden remains the high priest of Birmingham ball. This game makes believers of everyone who lives in the curious and confounding little state between Georgia and Mississippi, and even the transplants convert to their new denomination over time. Robert Clay, an Auburn fan who rushed the field after Kick Six, is a believer in the mystical energy and power of the SEC, and he has the banknotes to prove it.

He doesn't wager on sports, but how he makes a living is going to sound like he's a riverboat gambler. Need an overnight sketch comedy on "We Want Bama"? Clay and his buddy Josh Snead are the guys for that service. They have channeled the uniqueness of the Southern experience that revolves around SEC football and turned it into a thriving business that could not exist anywhere else. Their story of professional success is the absolute manifest-destiny essence of what the SEC means to the people who love it. And that is everyone in the Deep South. Clay and Snead are the *SEC Shorts* guys, and they are more popular than an unmarried preacher on spaghetti night.

To completely wade yourself into the Alabama white sauce* alternate universe that SEC football occupies inside the culture of the Southeast, attempt to imagine your first thought if a spouse or son or sister mentioned over dinner that they were quitting their well-paying jobs and going all in, and betting on themselves, to earn a living making sketch comedy with their friend for an audience online around scripts like "Alabama fan still wishes they had hired Rich Rodriguez."

---

* "Alabama white sauce" is barbecue sauce that was gifted to this world by Big Bob Gibson of Decatur, Alabama. Fuck what you heard about North Carolina, Kansas City, or Memphis. When it comes to barbecue, Alabama is the King and Birmingham is the Mecca. Try a sandwich at SAW's in Avondale. Their "Roll Tide Sauce" is a mix of red and white together.

SEC Shorts posted that sketch online three days after Alabama defeated Ohio State for the 2020 college football national championship.

"It sounds ridiculous to say out loud," said Clay, who attended Shades Valley/JCIB High School in Irondale, and then Auburn University for undergraduate studies before attending film school at the University of New Orleans. Snead, who's like Robin Williams with a Southern accent, is a professional actor who attended the University of Montevallo. Located in Shelby County, it is Alabama's only public liberal arts college.

Google their stuff. Absolutely fucking hilarious. They are the enlightened magnolia minstrels of a New South. They are peach and pecan ice cream through the nose funny. Their work is so perfect that when they go to games around the South the home-team fans are always disappointed to learn they're not actually fans of their team. It's like *Saturday Night Live* but for the South.

Like FunnyMaine with Alabama fans, Clay and Snead embody the South's quirky, innocently delightful charm in their work. They have teamed up with FunnyMaine in the past, too. *SEC Shorts* and FunnyMaine are two of the best things in modern-day Birmingham, and they make people laugh with jokes about college football (and make nice livings doing it, too).

SEC Shorts started in 2014 when Birmingham sports radio host Paul Finebaum joined the SEC Network. They wanted people to send in video "fan rants" in the early years of the show, and Clay and Snead submitted a sketch about the quarterback battle between Alabama's Blake Sims and Jacob Coker.

"You would have thought we won an Academy Award," Clay said. "They were trying to find Josh so he would call in to the show. 'Who are these guys?' We just wanted to be on TV. That's the embarrassing truth. We were so vain. Like videoing fireworks on the Fourth of July. Why?"

They sent in a video once a week for free. Great deal for ESPN. Of course, the network would repay them for their work eventually. Their sketch comedies are now featured on the SEC Network's version of *ESPN College GameDay*. They quit their full-time jobs in 2018 "to go out on our own." They were worried about finding sponsors, but they were underestimating themselves. Renasant Bank, a regional financial institution, now sponsors their shows that run online. Clay, who is 37, says his mother almost had a "nervous breakdown" when he told her what he was going to do with his life. When Alabama lost to LSU in 2019, they sketched out a joke about LSU burying Alabama's final hope of making the College Football Playoff. They put out a call for help on Facebook, and a guy in Moody with a backhoe dug a hole in his yard. The *SEC Shorts* guys worked through the night. In the hole went Matt Scalici, who is a managing sports producer for AL.com. Scalici and colleague Ben Flanagan are two of the most knowledgeable college football fans in the state.

"It was freezing," Clay said. "We were out there for five hours. The guy grew a bunch of legal marijuana."

That dude definitely was an Auburn fan. Roll Tide.

Robert Clay is an Auburn fan by way of several generations of Auburn grads. He knows all the history and all the games like any other Alabama native would. Without hesitation, he names Kick Six as his favorite Iron Bowl victory of all time. It ended with a walkoff kick return of 109 yards after Nick Saban called for Alabama kicker Adam Griffith to attempt a 57-yard field goal with one second on the scoreboard. Auburn coach Gus Malzahn put returner Chris Davis in the end zone just in case, and Davis took it to the house. In an instant, the stadium's scene went from suspended in suspense to frenzied hysteria. Like taking your foot and kicking off the top of a fire-ant mound.

What made that game the best Iron Bowl ever, and possibly the best ending to a college football game in the sport's history

(Tua Tagovailoa and DeVonta Smith might disagree), wasn't just the finish, and it wasn't just the stakes (the winner was going to the SEC championship). It was that Auburn defeated Saban's Alabama in the most unlikely way imaginable to win the most insane rivalry in American sports (and after Auburn's immaculate-reception victory against Georgia a couple weeks before).

Scarbinsky, the sports columnist who coined the name "Prayer at Jordan-Hare" for Auburn's victory against Georgia, was on the field for Kick Six and had to fight through thousands and thousands of belligerent Robert Clays to reach the postgame news conference.

"I might have given someone a forearm shiver along the way," Scarbinsky said.

Vanity license plates—00:01, KICK6, K1CS1X, KIK 6, GIVEM1, and so on—celebrating that Auburn victory against Alabama are common throughout the country. Tattoos are a given. This is how myths and legends are made where they play football in the fall.

And this is how great stories end.

Robert Clay, future creator of *SEC Shorts*, and lifelong Auburn fan, was an employee of the University of Alabama at the time, and not only that, but his job as a videographer meant his workstation was in an office located in an end zone of Alabama's Bryant-Denny Stadium. Unlike just about every other Auburn fan in Alabama, Clay could not spike the football on Monday at work. He was also an adjunct instructor at Alabama before joining the school's documentary team.

"I had to mellow out real quick," Clay said. "But I will still to this day go watch Kick Six. 'Watch the groundskeepers react to Kick Six?' Yes, please, and I will watch that shit four times."

The SEC is not just about the teams or the coaches. It's also about the fans, and then, most devotedly, the people who chronicle it for the South and the country. And everyone stops everything they are doing to watch the unicorn of an Alabama loss as it walks out of the Talladega National Forest and into oncoming traffic. For reporters covering the SEC, seeing an Alabama collapse in person is the rarest of events, but "We Want Bama" to lose is always the pachyderm in the press box. Actually picking against the Tide and being correct sets apart the Hall of Famers from the rest.

EDWARD ASCHOFF, ESPN *SPORTSCENTER*, OCTOBER 30, 2019:

In the bye week before the next game of the century between LSU and Alabama all eyes are on Tua Tago-vailoa's surgically repaired ankle...While Tua is expected to return to practice on Wednesday, Nick Saban said he didn't have a crystal ball to predict his status against LSU. The Crimson Tide believe they'd be in good hands if backup Mac Jones had to start again with cornerback Patrick Surtain telling me, "We knew he could do special things. He knows what to do in big-time games and he's poised to do anything."

In Tuscaloosa, I'm Edward Aschoff, ESPN.

EDWARD ASCHOFF, REPORTING ON "NEXT" GAME OF THE CENTURY, SATURDAY, NOVEMBER 9, 2019, 10:03 A.M.:

I'm now picking @LSUfootball simply because of [Marcus Spears's] opening chair slam. But seriously LSU 34, Bama 31 #GeauxTigers #RollTide.

[2:56 p.m.] One-on-one and it's ALL Jamar Chase for the TD. No chance on that one. My goodness.

[3:05 p.m.] An SEC defensive assistant to me on LSU vs Tua: "Make him have to move in the pocket but not make the throw. He is one of the best improvising and right now he's coming off that ankle injury so he's gonna have to figure out if that ankle can hold up." LSU making Tua move a lot.

[3:21 p.m.] Man this game has been fun.

[3:31 p.m.] Alabama's secondary just looks totally overwhelmed against LSU's WRs right now.

[3:56 p.m.] Oh boy [DeVonta] Smith just dusted [Derek] Stingley on that one. Ohhhhhh man those legs were churnin!

[4:23 p.m.] LSU is dominating Alabama on offense and defense. Utter domination by the Tigers right now.

[4:37 p.m.] LSU linebacker K'Lavon Chassion to me before the season on Alabama: "I promise you, nobody here thinks Alabama is better than us—we all know that. It's far from a talent level, it's far from the schematic level." Tigers were CLEARLY the much better team in the first half today.

[5:11 p.m.] Bama creepin…

[5:31 p.m.] Man this fourth quarter should be fun in Tuscaloosa. Bama getting some momentum on both sides. Pressure mounting for LSU. What a game.

[5:38 p.m.] Ooooooohhhhh boy Bama.

[5:51 p.m.] What a response from LSU on that drive. The Tigers absolutely needed that touchdown.

[6:18 p.m.] That should do it. [Joe] Burrow will get the Heisman praise but Clyde Edwards-Helaire had a helluva game. He ran over, through and by Alabama defenders all day.

There are some who paint in medium tones, and others
    whose brushstrokes be United States blues,
but never was there a poet with more colorful Godzilla
    socks behind his shoes.
Ed Aschoff with words that danced off was there for Tebow
    and Percy.
He even cried out this one time on Bourbon, "Help me,
    Jesus, Lord Have Mercy."
He described Gators winning title belts,
then moved to Atlanta and ate one or two patty melts.
Met a Bayou Queen who stole his heart.
Went to L.A. to make a new start.
He loved the SEC more while away,
which is the Southern song that will forever stay.
With Oxford blood and Gainesville training
there was no one better for SEC explaining,
But when it came to cover'n the Tide,
he could not hide his underdog pride.
If Ed had to pick or choose,
he would tell you "We Want Bama" means for them to lose.

In memory of Edward Carmichael Aschoff. There was no one better.

b. December 24, 1985.

d. December 24, 2019.

Rest in pride, my friend, and we'll see you in the press box on the other side.

CHAPTER 11

VOICES OF GOLD AND THUNDER

We stand together against racism," said Alabama quarterback Mac Jones in the offseason video of teammates reciting the essay by offensive tackle Alex Leatherwood.

And there was absolutely nothing that could stand against Alabama's offense the entire season after that.

If things like hatred and racism were the defensive secondaries of the Southeastern Conference in the unforgettable season of 2020 for the Alabama football Crimson Tide, then discriminating against people for the color of their skin and being different, and making laws against them, and putting ketchup on spaghetti would have been blasted into a million little pieces of ashen dust and blown away down I-20 in Alabama and on and on until it passed the magnolias in Mississippi and floated over Lake Pontchartrain and then out into the Gulf forever to be food for the little things of the sea called phytoplankton that work their way up the food chain until one day Marvin the Marlin gobbles all that sin right up and saves your marriage, too.

Michael McCorkle Jones of Jacksonville, Florida, and his Squadron of Lion-Hearted Receivers incinerated with extreme prejudice every single defense it faced in 2020. The games were not contests. They were the physical manifestation of historical repudiation. It began with a Week One victory at the University of Missouri and did not stop until all of the ashes were blown out of Hard Rock Stadium in Miami Gardens. Roll Tide.

Jones had waited and waited and waited his turn at Alabama because that's what they do there, and then he unleashed all of his enhanced gifts and acquired knowledge upon the world. Paired with coordinator Steve Sarkisian's advanced offensive schemes week after week, Jones, his elite receiving corps, and running back Najee Harris feasted upon every defense they faced. Some were shorthanded, and that made it all so much worse. Games felt like never-ending highlight clips. One dared not look away for a moment. Sweet merciful mother of lion meat, the throw and catch from Jones to Jaylen Waddle in the first quarter of the first game could have been the offensive highlight of the season at any other school in any other year. And there it was right at the beginning. After a spring and summer of hell and a seven-week fall camp that was worse, it was finally time to eat. Jones let loose a tasty thing and Waddle got vertical and then horizontal between two defenders, solved a Rubik's Cube, made the catch, did a helicopter spin after contact, and held on for the positive advancement down the field of 46 total yards. First down, Alabama. Roll Tide. Waddle caught two touchdown passes that game—final score: Alabama 38, Mizzou 19—and was well on his way to being the most electrifying receiver in the country. It was not to be, of course, but before his ankle injury on the opening kickoff of the fifth game of the season (Tennessee), Jaylen Waddle of Houston advanced the ball down the field farther per catch (22.28 yards) than any other receiver in the country with just as many receptions (25). There was no one better, and Waddle's combination of size and speed and quickness was the reason. In the spring of 2020 he trained with his old mentors at Fast Houston, and they prepared him well.

In their early years, Waddle and his teammates called Mac Jones "Joker" when he was the scout team quarterback. It's because he laughed like Batman's comic book archnemesis. By their senior seasons together, Jones and his primary receivers (Waddle and DeVonta Smith) had formed strong bonds that reached much deeper than on-field chemistry or practice hours together. After the season was over, and while they were preparing for the 2021 NFL Draft, Smith and Waddle both said they would prefer Jones as their quarterback over Tua Tagovailoa. When Tagovailoa was at Alabama he was an outsized celebrity. Jones was the All-American Couch Potato Quarterback his senior season, confined to his apartment and the training facility because of the pandemic. During the pandemic, Jones and Alabama's receivers would hang out on the practice fields after hours and play catch because that's all they could do for fun.

"Why were they so incredible?" said Jones's mother, Holly. "They won all their games and they were arguably the best ever, and how could they do it all under those circumstances? I think it was because they all came together. They put everything aside and they put all their different backgrounds together, and said we're going to put everything into this hat right here and we're going to play for each other.

"Not only does it take that affirmation, but it also takes doing it. Those are two different things. Because I think a lot of teams made that their goal. To put 'me' before 'we' is really hard for this generation of kids, but they showed they were young men and not kids."

Moms, y'all, proverbial wisdom factories of love and pride. It took families to get through 2020, and it took moms, and they saved us all. They worry a lot so maybe their children can do that less.

Holly was worried going into Alabama's first week that her son might have a bad game and then be put into a quarterback battle with backup Bryce Young, who was the No. 1 quarterback recruit in the country the previous year. Mom Jones, whose maiden name is the McCorkle of "Mac," had been reading too much stuff on the internet like everyone else. From the beginning, McCorkle Jones was dug in like an Alabama tick,* to borrow a phrase, as the Crimson Tide's starter. He proved that his ability to lead had not diminished since the end of the 2019 bowl season. Against Missouri, he had a clean 18 completed passes on 24 attempts with a positive advancement of 249 yards by way of forward pass. By the end of it all, after going 13–0, Jones, an afterthought quarterback for years at Alabama, would finish one of the more challenging seasons of football in the sport's history, and certainly the most bizarre, as the national and SEC quarterback leader in most every statistical category. They were: pass completions (311), pass completion percentage (77.4), passing yards (4,500), passing yards per attempt (11.2), passing efficiency rating (203.1), and total yards per play (10.3).

Jones (seven), receiver DeVonta Smith (three), and running back Najee Harris (five) combined to lead the country in 15 individual offensive statistical categories in 2020. It was an abusive amount of offense. They couldn't get Smith out of the game against Kentucky with a 53-point lead in the fourth quarter. Two games the entire season flirted with being close in the fourth quarter, the 63–48 victory at Ole Miss and the 52–46 victory against Florida in the SEC championship. The 11 other games, including the two in the College Football Playoff, were like exhibitions.

---

* Movie trivia time: Who used this line in the all-time classic sci-fi flick *Predator*? Answer: Blain, played by Jesse Ventura.

Alabama smoked Tennessee 48–17 and Tennessee coach Jeremy Pruitt said, "I can assure you the gap is closing."

Jeremy, what?

Tennessee fired Pruitt with cause in an attempt to not pay his buyout.

In one of their sketch comedies about the health of SEC football teams after the 2020 season, the guys at *SEC Shorts* delivered some hilarity about the Volunteers' annual autumn heartaches. More than any other fanbase, says *SEC Shorts*, Tennessee fans love the jokes about their team and are in on the gags. This short was in a doctor's examination room with the SEC doctor offscreen and a Tennessee fan sitting on the table.

> **Doctor:** Your symptoms are inflamed hope…
> **Tennessee:** Yep.
> **Doctor:** Festering losing streak…
> **Tennessee:** Uh-huh. [*nods head with tired acceptance*]
> **Doctor:** And fan fatigue…
> **Tennessee:** Bingo.
> **Doctor:** Yep, you're still Tennessee.

Alabama has outscored Tennessee 537–177 since Nick Saban's first season in 2007. That is, on average, almost two whole points more than the sum total of three touchdowns, three extra points, and a field goal. There is no prescribed treatment that can cure that moonshine punch-drunk stupor.

After Jaylen Waddle was carried off the grass inside Neyland Stadium on October 24, 2020, Alabama's offense had a quick huddle. It was time for backup receiver Slade Bolden, a redshirt sophomore with three years of training behind him, to take the field, and for offensive coordinator Steve Sarkisian to adjust personnel.

DeVonta Smith and John Metchie III, a sophomore, were now the primary targets for Mac Jones.

It worked out.

Jones started the game with 11 perfect completions, which, when combined with the eight passes in a row he had used to kill off Georgia the game before, set a new Alabama record for consecutive completed forward passes (19). The Joker had 387 passing yards in the 48–17 rout of the Vols, and at the halfway point of the 10-game season, DeVonta Smith did not lead Alabama in receiving yards. He had seven catches for 73 yards against Tennessee. It was Metchie, the Canadian born in Taiwan, who had 151 yards on seven receptions.

Mac Jones even had a rushing touchdown against Tennessee, which is significant because it points to perhaps the quarterback's greatest stat above all the rest. Jones led the country in total offensive yards in 2020, which is phenomenal, of course, but that total was just 14 yards more than his accumulation of measured distance by throw. In other words, he only advanced the ball on the ground with his legs for 14 total yards of positive offense over 13 games. The Joker stood and delivered, and his one rushing touchdown came, of course, against Tennessee.

He was an unstoppable terror of reckless abandon on the ground that day. He had four whole yards.

For those of us whose brains might spin on different axes than the rest, and with hindsight now being 20-20, watching Jones in his senior season allows for a what-if-type question about the history of Alabama football. Just what if Bart Starr had not been hazed at Alabama back in 1954 before what was supposed to be his breakout junior season. In those days, players were paddled for initiation into Alabama's varsity A-Club, and Starr, in an account of real events hidden for 62 years, was brutally beaten to the point that it fractured his spine. His wife, Cherry Starr, told AL.com in 2016 that her husband's back looked like "raw meat," and the lingering effects of the injury were so severe it even disqualified him for military service after he graduated. Indeed, according to unearthed military records, the Montgomery native was medically disqualified from the Air Force by the commanding officer of Eglin Air Force Base in 1957. Only then did the Green Bay Packers take a flyer on Starr as a favor from one coach to a friend. The sliding doors of what-ifs there are endless, but this is certain. Mac Jones in 2020 didn't have to punt and throw like Starr, so actually Holly's son got off lucky.

Had Starr been healthy his senior year at Alabama, it likely would have changed the course of history for both Alabama and the Green Bay Packers. In that regard, Starr might have more in common with Mac Jones's predecessor at Alabama, Tua Tagovailoa. Both Jones and Starr were afterthoughts at different points in their careers, but they also share something more lighthearted. Before he ever took a snap in pro football, Michael McCorkle Jones had one undeniable thing in common with one of the greatest NFL quarterbacks ever to come out of Alabama. Bryan Bartlett Starr had an incredible middle name, too.

We are all connected through time and space and silly things that make us cry, and don't ever forget it.

———

Edward Carmichael Aschoff was so right, too. He was right about everything. He knew back in 2019, and he tried to inform everyone with his reporting. The man's talent will live forever. He called Mac Jones's future breakout in a live report on *SportsCenter*, and also made note of Tua Tagovailoa's inability to scramble. That report came just one game before Tagovailoa's injury against Mississippi State, which was one of the worst days in Alabama football history for a quarterback since Starr's abuse by his own teammates. Tagovailoa's surgically repaired ankle affected his performance badly in the first half against LSU in 2019, and then the next week against Mississippi State the nightmare happened. Still playing in the game after his offense scored five touchdowns in five possessions, Tua scrambled to his left on 3rd and 4 inside State's Davis Wade Stadium but could not outrun his pursuers. Defensive lineman Marquiss Spencer and weak-side linebacker Leo Lewis landed on him, knifing Tagovailoa's knee into the turf at a flexed position. Later described as trauma common in a car crash, the blow forced the ball at the top of his femur out of its cupped socket and then through bone.

Injuries to key players derail national championship hopes every season in college football. In 2020, Alabama endured despite some major ones. Analysts predicted a major fall for Alabama's offense after Waddle's regular-season-ending ankle injury. Didn't happen. Rimington Trophy–winning center Landon Dickerson went out with his knee injury before the College Football Play-off. Despite that devastating loss, Alabama's fulcrum in the middle held. With Mac Jones's first option taken away, receiver DeVonta Smith went on to win the Heisman Trophy. Dickerson was a scratch and dean's list backup Chris Owens had been waiting five years for the opportunity to be a permanent starter. Elite depth is just another view through the sliding doors of what made this group Saban's "ultimate team." Smith strongly considered leaving for the NFL after his junior season. What if then?

"I'm so proud of him because I know it was a tough decision for him at the end of last season to come back," Sarkisian said before Alabama played Notre Dame in the Rose Bowl in Texas, "but clearly him coming back has been worth his while, and I'm sure it's been very gratifying for him.

"Clearly we've benefited from that as well, from a football standpoint for our team. So all in all, I think it's been a win-win, but really proud of Smitty, his leadership that he's displayed, the work ethic he displayed and ultimately the play-making ability."

Sir Smitty, the "Slim Reaper," Lord of the Catch and Keeper of the Records. The trim and always dapper Heisman Trophy winner finished the 2020 season with national-leading marks in receiving yards (1,856), receptions (117), and receiving touchdowns (23). For his career, he set SEC records in the advancement of offense down the field by way of catch (3,965 yards) and number of times one of those catches forced very weary digital media professionals inside stadiums to add six more points next to Alabama's scoring totals. Smith set a new SEC record for touchdown catches (46) in a career.

And somehow the suits he wore during the awards season and the playoffs in 2020 and January 2021 were just as fresh as his game on the field.

The third point of Alabama's perfectly angular offense was Harris, the deep-thinking, honest-talking, ultra-competitive running back from Northern California. He was a smasher of a ball carrier with breakaway speed, and, as he was quick to inform people before the 2021 NFL Draft, possessed an underrated ability to catch passes. Consider Alabama's first scoring drive of the season against Missouri, and then Harris's game against Florida in the SEC championship. The greatest offense in the history of Alabama football didn't begin with a lightning strike, but with Najee's constant thunder. He had seven tough carries for 35 yards and gave Alabama its first touchdown of the season with a pounding one-yard war. It was vintage Nick Saban smashmouth "Murder-Ball," as it was coined by fans during Derrick Henry's heyday. Harris slammed home three hard-earned rushing touchdowns against Mizzou that day. Sixty total team touchdowns later, Harris had three touchdowns by way of catch and two by churn against Florida in Atlanta's Mercedes-Benz Stadium. That day, Harris proved without question that he could do it all.

This was a question posed to Harris after that five-touchdown masterpiece against Florida, and then the back's quick rebuff of a criticism that wasn't even there.

> **Question:** Your coaches always told me you were a great receiver. Now you hold the single-season record for running backs. Is that one of the reasons you came back, to show everybody you can catch the ball?
>
> **Harris:** No, man. What? I've been catching the ball since birth. What are you talking about, man? People don't expect it because of the running back name. The slogan is, "Can he catch?" I've been catching the ball since I was in the fetus position. C'mon now. [*laughs*]

Najee had been uncommonly motivated to succeed since then, too. All told, in one of the most impressive *all-around* seasons for an offensive skill player in college football history, he led the country in five major statistical measures: rushing yards from scrimmage (1,891 yards), touchdowns from scrimmage and total touchdowns (30), rushing touchdowns (26), and points scored (180). He finished his four-year career, during which he considered transferring (as many at Alabama do), with an SEC record in career touchdowns (57) and a terrestrial accumulation of measured advancement of a ball shaped like a tater that put his name, fittingly, at 13th all-time among those men who went against the best collection of defenses in all of college football and crushed it like Jell-O shots at Gallettes.

The Top 13 SEC career rushing leaders (measured in yards): Herschel Walker, Georgia (5,259); Nick Chubb, Georgia (4,769); Darren McFadden, Arkansas (4,590); Kevin Faulk, LSU (4,557); Bo Jackson, Auburn (4,303); Ralph Webb, Vanderbilt (4,178); Errict Rhett, Florida (4,163); Dalton Hilliard, LSU (4,050); Charles Alexander, LSU (4,035); Anthony Dixon, Mississippi State (3,994); Emmitt Smith, Florida (3,928); Benjamin Snell Jr., Kentucky (3,873); and Najee Harris, Alabama (3,843).

This list is significant for two reasons. One, Harris became Alabama's career leader in raw, cold rushing yards during the era when offenses in college football got all sophisticated with their RPO offenses, spread formations, and general modes of tater advancement to make Nick Saban's face grimace with reluctant acceptance for a game that will never be like it once was. And, two: Harris finished his time at Alabama with more than twice as many touchdown catches (11) as all but one player on that list. Hilliard of LSU had six. More honest words from the SEC's all-time greatest running back among those who were also pass-catching infants:

> **Question:** [after the SEC championship game, via Zoom] You have a lot of confidence in your receiving skills. Have you ever sort of went to [Steve Sarkisian] and said, "Throw me the ball?" Or he just saw your skills...
> **Harris:** Pass me the ball? No. We always had amazing receivers. Look at who we got now. No point in saying, "Throw me the ball." We have all these weapons on the edge.

The reporters are always catching heat from players, who are brainwashed at Alabama to mistrust the "media," and from fans, who hear Saban rant and rave and want to be like their favorite coach. There is always one member of a team's "media" coverage at every SEC school who is immune to the strawman, boogie-dee-boo games that people play with journalists, and for the Alabama football Crimson Tide that man is Eli Gold.

———

Gold watches Alabama football games more intently than anyone else, and he also might be the state's greatest lover of words. He is certainly, everyone will agree, the greatest speaker of them. And for a state full of Southern oratory masters of spoken-word sciences, that's pretty good for a kid from Brooklyn, who recounted selling peanuts outside Madison Square Garden as a child in his beautiful memoir *From Peanuts to the Pressbox*. The players sacrificed for championship title No. 18, but they weren't the only ones. The "Voice of the Crimson Tide" was also an MVP in 2020. Saban's "ultimate team" even extended all the way up to the radio booth in 2020.

Want to talk about sacrifice? Let's talk about real sacrifice. Eli Gold, a 66-year-old bona fide national broadcasting legend even before 2020, sacrificed his health in more ways than one for Alabama football fans amid the historic college football season during a pandemic. After a professional lifetime of hauling radio equipment around the country for a career that has covered everything from NASCAR (41 years) to the NHL (Nashville Predators) to football and basketball, his arthritic shoulders gave up the fight in 2020. Gold did not. He had one shoulder replaced on August 4 and then another on November 3, Election Day, which came during Alabama's off week. He was then going to travel by car to Baton Rouge, Louisiana, for Alabama's game against LSU, but it was canceled due to, reportedly, coronavirus cases and contact tracing among LSU's players. Gold revealed the pain and his struggles to AL.com the week of the Iron Bowl, and called it "debilitating, impossible," and "agonizing." He could not fly to the season opener in Missouri, so he was driven to Columbia. His colleagues in the press box turned over his elaborately detailed spotting charts after possessions throughout the season because the boards were too painful to lift. His voice never quavered or winced except for maybe when receiver John Metchie laid out Florida defensive back Trey Dean III in the SEC championship game, forcing a key turnover moments after Mac Jones threw an interception.

"Metchie just lowered the boom on him," said Gold during his call of the famous play.

Gold is the modern-day Homer of Alabama football who is not a "homer" on the radio. He is a fabulist and an oral storyteller. He's also the ultimate pro, and tells it like it is supposed to be told instead of how some announcers and reporters know fans or readers would rather hear it. His words through the years and decades have tied together the history of families in Alabama, and woven richness into a Southern state's culture and consciousness. In 2020, with many fans stuck at home, his work was more needed than ever. He knew it, too. So he scheduled that surgery amid the pandemic and then never took off any work after the other. Shoulder replacements are major surgeries, and among the most painful. He understood that his service and sacrifice for others was more important than even his own health. There is a lesson there for everyone. On the dedication to his craft, Gold said, "I am a professional describer...but those descriptions week in and week out, you build up a relationship with the fans and the listeners that cannot be replicated in any other form of media. So, the job I have, I take it so damn seriously."

In 33 years of calling games for Alabama, he only missed one from 1988 to 2020. That's the one when he had COVID-19 the week Alabama was at Arkansas on December 12. Alabama won

52–3, and Gold was back in the booth the next week for the SEC title game in Atlanta.

"I work for the fans and I owe it to them to give them the best, as bizarre as the season has been," Gold said before the Iron Bowl. "On top of everything else and all the craziness, I've had to deal with that, but you do the best you can. You play hurt as the players do. I'm no different.

"My bosses have been wonderful. They said, 'Can you do the talk show?' I said, 'Sure, my mouth isn't broken. I'll be fine.'"

Nick Saban is never a closer public representation to his true self than when he's in front of a microphone with Eli Gold on Thursdays during the season.

Gold offered Alabama fans artful descriptions of the opener against Mizzou and the 52–24 victory against Texas A&M, and then it was time to prepare his body for another road trip.

But not just any road trip. It was the one every Alabama fan, and probably every college football fan in the country, had been waiting for ever since SEC commissioner Greg Sankey announced there would be a dime's worth of SEC competition for every team in the league. It was Alabama at Ole Miss on October 10, and, as if it were sent to the Deep South for that very orgasmic calamity of cultural suspense by some supernatural element, the wind started to blow and the thunder came down from low Southern skies. There was a whole lotta fresh water coming up from the Gulf for Saban's first game against his ol' buddy Lane Kiffin.

Asked about the game being affected by Hurricane Delta, Alabama center Landon Dickerson joked, "As you guys know, I'm a business administration major, not a meteorology major."

But everyone in Alabama knew a guy who was.

When curtains of clouds gather, and the air starts smelling like earth but means rain, and the storms come up in Alabama and around the Deep South, people need help and important information, and that includes Nick Saban and the SEC. Alabama meteorologist James Spann goes to work when everyone else goes inside for bad weather, and residents love him like an uncle or a father. If there were a Top 5 list of most universally respected or beloved people living in Alabama, it would probably go in some order like this: Charles Barkley, Nick Saban, James Spann, Eli Gold, and... coming up with a definitive fifth for this Mount Rushmore plus one is tough, so let's go with whoever is the current pitmaster at Archibald's.

Like Gold and Archibald's pitmasters, Spann has dedicated his life to the service of Alabamians, and people appreciate that genuine love of the community. The best local weatherman in the country—brag'n rights!—Spann is from Greenville, Alabama, which is in Butler County. By and by, Butler County might as well be considered the heart of the Black Belt. The Southern Shakespeare himself, Hank Williams Sr., is from Butler County, and the 2005 movie *Sweet Home Alabama* was set in Greenville (although not filmed there). Bordering Butler County to the west is a touch of Monroe County, which is where Alabama authors Harper Lee and Truman Capote became childhood friends. James Spann, who now lives in Shoal Creek outside of Birmingham, adores Greenville with all of his heart, and his best friend is the mayor.

James Spann the Weatherman pretty much loves five things the most in this world, and they are God, his family, the weather, baseball, and teaching people about all those things. His internship program is nationally renowned by young meteorologists, and he takes it just as seriously as Gold takes storytelling and Nick Saban takes turning boys into leaders of men. Ginger Zee, the national chief meteorologist for ABC News, is Spann's protégée.

The appreciation that James Spann has for Nick Saban is palpable and there are a lot of similarities between the two Alabama icons. They're both from small country towns and they're both hardwired for greatness. Spann says he sleeps about three hours a night, and the only person in the state who might sleep less is Saban.

"He studies, he does his research and his homework," Spann said of Alabama's coach, "and I wish everyone would be like that, and the world would be such a better place. There is too much mediocrity in this world."

What Spann loves most about Saban is the coach's "integrity," and Spann, who teaches Sunday school to children at his local church, is a man of integrity, too. They also both like winning, and spot winners, and then help mentor those young adults for the perpetuation of a better world. Spann tells a fun story about how he knows if a young meteorology intern is cut out for television. He takes his interns to the Wal-Mart in Adamsville, Alabama— "the most diverse cross section of people in the state"—and if they can't socialize and interact with everyone there, then they're going to need to go into research. There is a popular T-shirt in Alabama that reads, "James Spann is my homeboy," and that's how most Alabamians feel about the chief meteorologist for Birmingham and Tuscaloosa's ABC 33/40, who wears famous suspenders, has important catchphrases like "respect the polygon" for tornado warnings, and possesses a street-level memory for the geography of just about every town, big or small, in Alabama. If Spann is talking about a storm near the intersection of Wesley's Boobie Trap on Highway 78 in Dora and starts rolling up his sleeves, it's time to pay attention. When Spann rolls up those sleeves, people in Alabama know that the weather event he is discussing on the TV is not to be ignored. He rolls up his sleeves for Nick Saban pretty much every game week when weather might be a factor. It is little known to anyone outside of the Mal Moore Athletic Facility, but Spann regularly sits in on conference calls with Saban's staff and gives the team detailed weather reports.

That's right. James Spann is Nick Saban's homeboy.

"Not the type of stuff for the general public," Spann said.

Let's just say if the day comes when frogs and fish fall out of the sky in Alabama, Spann will be letting Saban know before anyone else. Spann calls Saban a "weather nerd" who wants to know specific things like if it's going to rain one and a half inches or three inches in the first half, because if it rains three inches they're going to have to change everything, so it needs to be correct the first time and as specific as possible. It should be noted that Spann helps Saban at no cost. He does, however, give game-day weather reports for fans inside Bryant-Denny Stadium for their rides home. The week of the Ole Miss game was a little different than the typical only-for-Saban weather report, though. There was a hurricane twirling in the Gulf.

The specter of Hurricane Delta had already disrupted LSU's home game against Missouri (moved to Columbia), and Ole Miss coach Lane Kiffin, according to Spann, wanted to move the date of his first game against Alabama. At the beginning of that week, Kiffin told reporters they were considering Friday, Sunday, or another weekend. None of those things ended up happening. Saban wanted the game played on Saturday because why wait during this season being played amid a pandemic? Who knows what could happen one week to the next, and someone had Spann on speed dial, aight? Also, and this valuable context, Ole Miss had just survived a pretty wild overtime game at Kentucky the previous Saturday.

The SEC had a conference call about possibly moving the game, and it was determined that Hurricane Delta would be beyond Oxford, Mississippi, and into Tennessee about an hour after the originally scheduled kickoff time of 5 p.m. The game was pushed 90 minutes. On that call was James Spann. Get ready for the storm, Joey Freshwater, because the Tide is coming.

A couple days before the Saturday game, Kiffin told reporters that "the latest now is just really, really heavy rain by the time it gets to us. We're anticipating playing. They're moving it back, they're going to announce today, to like 7:30 at night or something. But we're still on."

It was a mess of a game, and by that we mean there was more offense than rain. The teams combined for several SEC offensive records for a non-overtime game: 15 touchdowns, 1,370 yards of offense, and 111 points. Ole Miss's 647 yards of offense were the most ever conceded by an Alabama defense. Fans wanted defensive coordinator Pete Golding fired that night. Just leave him in Mississippi with Kiffin. Alabama put the game away late in the fourth quarter with a 15-yard touchdown pass from Jones to Smith, but Kiffin was given a standing ovation by Vaught-Hemingway Stadium for putting a scare into Alabama. It's the little things, aight?

There for the game, Holly Jones knew it was going to be a long night from the very beginning. The mother of Alabama's quarterback said she looked up "and the skies were circling."

"It was exhausting," said Gold, the dedicated Hall of Fame play-by-play radio announcer who had to call it all without being able to lift his arms because his shoulders hurt so badly.

Did a weather report give Alabama the edge in the fourth quarter? We'll have to leave that one up in the air. Here's what you need to know about Spann, though. He's a diehard Mississippi

State Bulldogs fan and alum. The sworn enemy of Ole Miss. The SEC plays by different rules, y'all. Roll Tide.

"I can't even remember who won the game," Spann would later say.

It's not that James Spann, great Southern weatherman, wanted Bama to win. He just maybe wanted Hail State not to lose.

CHAPTER 12

BIG NICK ENERGY

He did not really want to meet Nick Saban at all, and it was suddenly his job to perhaps be the one person in Saban's office more than anyone else. Fuck my life, he thought. This was his living hell. He had gone from being just fine with his very anonymous food-service job at the University of Alabama to suddenly being cast into the inner sanctum of every ring of a hateful Iron Bowl inferno.

What Oliver Grimes did to deserve this torture he was about to endure of giving Nick Saban, head football coach of the Alabama fucking Crimson Tide, shit like chewing gum to put into his dirty Alabama mouth, and then have to do things like clean out the mini fridge in Saban's office when the crap inside it started to mold, and then restock that mini fridge with other extremely specific junk that Saban probably would not eat or drink, or, worst of all, SO MUCH WORST OF ALL, stockpile the little fancy tricolored, individually wrapped Dove's chocolates in the bowl by Saban's couch to impress all the recruits whom Oliver Grimes, the new official Saban food-stocker guy, would later want to all fucking lose in every damn game...how all this came to pass, he'll never know. He'll never know what he did to find this fate. Just being really good at his job, probably, because the people making him do this knew he would be the one guy who definitely would not fuck it up, but dammit to hell, why him? Oliver Grimes was not impressed "one goddamn bit" about any of it, and that electronic office door of Saban's could "go straight to hell," too. You see Oliver Grimes was an Auburn fan by birth and by blood and by hard living, and now this shit was put on his War Eagle soul.

That's what Oliver thought in the beginning because that's what he knew in the beginning. That's what every Auburn fan thinks in the beginning because this ain't no kindercare "who wants tater tots with ketchup kinda of place" for football fans. This is the proud state of Alabama, and it might not be ranked very high in all the other stuff, but its belligerence for the Iron Bowl is world class.

They say no one close to Nick Saban will ever talk about him. The people in his orbit do not speak. If you look hard enough, though, or maybe just luck up and play golf with the right guy, you can find the one. The one was found. His name is Oliver Grimes. He had stories to tell, and he was happy, oh, so very happy, to elaborate in neon, glowing paint smeared on sorority girls inside Gallettes. Eventually, all Alabama fans start talking and philosophizing and regurgitating coachspeak like Nick Saban. This is one of the rivers that flows from "Big Nick Energy," and it has shaped the state earnestly for many positive things in the areas of finance, job growth, population booms, civic responsibilities, and grant writing. All of that stuff makes Oliver Grimes appreciate Nick Saban, but Oliver Grimes wants one thing to be understood. Oliver fucking Grimes will think and speak like Patrick Fain Dye until the day Oliver fucking Grimes floats off to that big Jordan-Hare in the sky, aight?

"I will never be an Alabama fan," Grimes said.

Noted.

Don't tell Oliver Grimes his surname rhymes with Denny Chimes. He might knife you in the liver. Piss drunk at an apartment pool in Tuscaloosa, Grimes says he once walked up to Brodie Croyle before the Iron Bowl, Roman Harper flanking Alabama's quarterback, and told Croyle, "I hope they break your skinny bitch ass in half. War Eagle." Grimes was friends with Harper at the time. "It was my birthday," Grimes said. Croyle was then sacked 11 times, and Oliver Grimes went around screaming "Kick 'em in the Brodie" for about a year. Grimes is a full-grown adult now, and works for Delta Airlines in Atlanta, but he grew up in Tuscaloosa and hustled his way through the service industry there. "Never paid for a drink at Gallettes ever," he said.

Great dude with a solid mid-iron game into the green, but also just an enormous fan of Auburn football who, like maybe a couple football coaches at Alabama, communicates casually as if he were on the expo line of a restaurant calling for a medium rare steak that was 10 minutes behind schedule. Nick Saban's kinda dude, in other words, but in Alabama every last joule of Big Nick Energy is balanced by the nuclear-powered wattage of Auburn fans who want to hate him. Oliver Grimes was going to work for Nick Saban and his assistants, Glenda Edwards and Linda Leoni, but he was not happy about it. This was in the beginning.

Understand, Grimes wasn't some low-level errand boy working an entry-level position for Bama Dining. He was a manager for Aramark, which is the national food service company that contracts with universities, stadiums, hospitals, and other venues. His "real job" for Bama Dining involved things like purchasing inventory for all of Bama Dining's properties on campus. This new side project was, "out of the blue," added to his workday because he was so efficient at his job and logistically brilliant. For Saban and his administrative assistants, Oliver Grimes became "like a walking CVS."

"I was the only contact with Saban from our business," Grimes said. "I had access to more vendors than anyone on campus. I knew where to get any kind of random shit…If I couldn't find something I would just drop in the conversation that it was for Coach Saban, and it would get done for me immediately. It was like saying jump and how high."

Big Nick Energy.

As an Auburn fan with a busy job, Grimes was just annoyed that this was one more thing to do. When the head of Bama Dining called him on the phone one day and told him he would be there "in five minutes," and that he could tell no one about some new task that was about to be put on him, Grimes was not enjoying the Big Nick Energy one bit. He had known Big Nick Energy from before. Prior to Bama Dining, Grimes was a manager at Chuck's Fish in Tuscaloosa, a landmark restaurant in the city where all the football recruits and their families were entertained on official visits. It was at Chuck's Fish that Oliver Grimes first experienced Saban's power, but also learned that the only thing more powerful in Tuscaloosa than Big Nick Energy is Awesome Miss Terry Authority.

EAT AT CHUCK'S

Chuck's Fish is named in honor of Charles Morgan Jr., the civil rights attorney who represented boxer Muhammad Ali and civil rights leader Julian Bond. A graduate of Ramsay High School in Birmingham and the University of Alabama, Morgan might be best known in Alabama for his speech the day after the 16th Street Baptist Church was bombed in his hometown. Morgan was critical of the white community in Birmingham for remaining silent during the civil rights movement, and denounced white community leaders for feeding racial prejudice. Said Morgan, "Four little girls were killed in Birmingham yesterday. A mad, remorseful, worried community asks, 'Who did it? Who threw that bomb? Was it a Negro or a white?' The answer should be, 'We all did it.' Every last one of us is condemned for that crime and the bombing before it and a decade ago. We all did it."

The daughter of a West Virginia coal miner, Terry Constable Saban is the unofficial chief executive officer charged with managing the greatest college football coach of all time. Nick is the talent, and Terry is the person who has the authority to tell the talent what to do onstage (and sometimes uses it). Not all married couples can relate to the Sabans, but all those who are or have been married understand the dynamics of the relationship. Terry Saban keeps everything in good working order and calls the shots. She works with Nick's administrative assistants to coordinate his schedule, and knows everyone in the inner circle. Terry is tough, and Nick isn't shy about saying it, but she has a big heart like her husband, and the couple has helped to donate millions to Alabama charities through their Nick's Kids Foundation. Terry Saban's philanthropic passions include scholarships for first-generation college students, Catholic charities, and at-risk youth. The Sabans are high school sweethearts, and Terry is the biggest reason for her husband's professional success.

And she might be a better recruiter, too.

The better half of a college football power couple that will never be matched or duplicated, Terry Saban was the person in charge of impressing recruits at Chuck's Fish when Grimes worked there. If a railing had chipped paint she would point it out to one of the owners and, in so many words, say the problem needed to be corrected forthwith. If a chair had a splinter or a piece of wood out of place, Grimes said Terry Saban would have it replaced. All the Fathead wall decals of Alabama players in the stairwell had to come down, too, Terry Saban said. Not classy at all. Before food came out of the kitchen, Terry Saban was on the expo line checking plates. Awesome Miss Terry Authority and Big Nick Energy ain't ever losing to Tennessee, aight? When Terry Saban first saw Oliver Grimes inside the inner sanctum of the Mal Moore Athletic Facility, she said, "Who is that?" and Oliver Grimes, indomitable Auburn fan, was scared. Nick Saban is such an excellent recruiter of college football players in part because Terry Saban is a lioness and appeals to powerful women who produce good men. The vibe is strong between them.

Grimes said it was not uncommon for Alabama fans to "camp out" inside Chuck's Fish on the nights Nick Saban entertained guests. Saban's parties never ate in the main dining space, of course. Fans just wanted to watch him enter the restaurant and walk to the elevator. Big Nick Energy.

"It was like the ducks at the Peabody," Grimes said. "Oh my God. Worst nights for business. We would play the fight song when he came in, and everyone would fucking stand up and cheer and clap and he would go in and up the elevator."

Not the best working conditions for an Auburn fan whose parents both graduated from the university. Grimes understood the drill, in other words, before he walked into the Mal Moore Athletic Facility and met Nick Saban for the first time. Grimes wasn't completely unfamiliar with the inner sanctum either. It was at Chuck's Fish where he got to know, in passing, Cedric Burns, who is the football team's "athletic relations coordinator." Burns has seen a few things at Alabama since being hired at the end of Paul Bryant's tenure. On game days, he is the person everyone sees on TV who follows Saban around the sidelines, but in Saban's day-to-day world, Burns manages people who want things from Alabama's coach. He's not a bodyguard, but he knows how to get things done.

After their quick meeting, Oliver Grimes and his associate from Aramark, A. J. DeFalco, were going to meet the administrative assistants, Glenda and Linda, before meeting Nick Saban in his office. They were there to establish a business relationship with the most powerful person in Alabama not named Terry Saban, and take care of the food the coach of Alabama football wanted in his office in perpetuity. This mood was serious and the tightness in their guts was building. We're not talking kicker Andy Pappanastos type nervousness with the 2018 national championship game tied with three seconds left, but working stiffs only get one shot to make a first impression with the King.

After getting buzzed through the front door of the Mal Moore Athletic Facility and walking up the stairs, visitors to the inner sanctum must enter another electronically sealed door to begin the real journey through winding hallways to reach the suite outside the office of the coach. For an Auburn fan, the layers to reach the inner sanctum are not unlike the glowing road Neo had to travel to reach the final boss in the *Matrix* movie franchise. From the inner sanctum radiates the source of all incandescent evil that fuels the world of Big Nick Energy. The path inside "the process" to the final boss of Alabama football, as told by Oliver the Chosen One Grimes, Auburn fan protected at all times by the spirit of Patrick Fain Dye: "Keep going down the hall. Cedric's office is on the left. He's never in there. Then there is another countertop with really hot girls working. Then go left and down the hall where assistants work and then that opens up where Glenda's desk is located. Then go through a doorway and there's a smaller room with Linda Leoni. She has been with Nick since his days in Cleveland with [Bill] Belichick. She's salt of the earth. Couldn't be nicer."

From there, double doors must be penetrated for Neo to reach Agent Smith, the exacting and perfect code chain of the computer that controls all things. There are no blue pills that can be ingested at this point and save the soul of Pat Dye, aight? So don't get it twisted. Everyone who comes anywhere close to the inner sanctum of Alabama is eating the fucking red pills every day by the mouthfuls. Neo tricked Agent Smith in the end, but this isn't a movie. This is the Alabama football Crimson Tide, and the Matrix has like three backup servers and at least five of those wiz kid IT professionals who quit their jobs at the Pentagon and went to work for truth, justice, and the American way. Big Nick Energy. Roll Tide.

Before they even entered the building, Grimes said DeFalco warned him not to look into the light. Grimes recalled the conversation: "'You don't speak to Saban unless he speaks to you. Don't seek him out. Don't harass him. Handle him with kid gloves. If you have to ask for him, ask someone else to ask him on the football staff. Don't directly speak to him,' and I'm like are you fucking serious?"

DeFalco hands Linda Leoni a list, and Linda looks it over and hands it back to DeFalco. Nothing reaches Saban that does not first go through Linda Leoni. The doors to the office then open, and Grimes and DeFalco are led into the chamber of secrets. There is a couch and table off to the side, and opposite that lounging space a kitchenette. Saban's desk is a "gorgeous" piece of craftsmanship, one of a kind. Resolute. "His desk looked like the president's desk in the Oval Office," Grimes said. "Handmade by the facility department at the university. Gorgeous. Gorgeous. It was custom made for him. It even has a button on its under lip like the movies to open and close the door. Just over the top."

Grimes had eaten the red pills, and even though he didn't understand what was happening at the moment, the chemistry inside his brain was changing. Big Nick Energy.

Saban stood up, walked around the desk of champions, and shook the hand of an Auburn fan who had put drunken Iron Bowl voodoo upon Brodie Croyle's countenance and held many a novelty plastic cup filled with Yellow Hammers from Gallettes and never once paid for any of them. In Grimes's other hand was the sheet of paper, and he handed it to Saban. Saban looked it over. It was a grocery store list for the god-man of Alabama football. On that list were things like gum, juice boxes, and oatmeal creme pies.

When Grimes was in the holy-of-holies source of Big Nick Energy, Saban would only chew Dentyne Ice Peppermint Gum, but in the shape of squares. "He hates the stick," Grimes said. "He won't eat it. He literally pointed at me: 'I want the squares not the sticks. Are we clear?'"

Squares are more efficiently chewed than sticks. It's computer science.

———

The list was long, and the requests would change and become more elaborate over the years as the inner sanctum came to realize that Oliver fucking Grimes was a man who could get things done. He was confused at first, though, why "4.25" was written next to "cranberry juice cocktails." Grimes didn't know, and he wasn't about to question anything. " 'The bottles can't be any taller than

4.25 inches,' he literally said that," Grimes noted. "I said, 'OK?'" He would later realize that nothing taller than 4.25 inches could fit inside the mini fridge.

It was immediately communicated to Grimes that "I need to make this perfect." After that, he "just ran with the fact of if he's that anal, then I'm going to be that anal. I just went with the idea that I was going to make the client happy."

Big Nick Energy.

Even for someone who knows how to get things done, Grimes said the appetites of the inner sanctum sometimes presented worthy challenges. There was once a "wild crusade" for a specific kind of salad dressing. This was before Amazon could deliver anything and everything. Back in 2012, individually wrapped chocolate squares (not bars!) of Dove Silky Smooth Promises weren't always easy to come by. Grimes had to find someone at Publix next to the Houndstooth on The Strip to specially order a few items like Vernors ginger ale, a regional favorite around Detroit. Eventually, Grimes, like everyone around Big Nick Energy, began to sincerely respect and appreciate Saban. The red pills had changed him, and he knew it, too.

"And as time progressed, and I would check on things there and on him, he didn't even acknowledge my existence," Grimes said, "and at first it was enforcing that personality and notion you have of him because of how he is with the media. That he's such a prick. But as I was around him more, I understood that he's not being rude. He honestly didn't know I was there. Because his gears are going 1,000 miles an hour, and he's grinding, and he's always thinking about football. Always."

A man of logistics who is now in charge of such things for an international airline might even have learned a thing or two from Big Nick Energy, and that's the real power of the thing. People around Saban generally turn into better people if they have the potential to do so.

"He was so specific in what he wanted," Grimes said, "and he took the time to make it clear that this is what I want, and when he took the time from an efficiency standpoint, if he goes through that much detail with those specific things, then he doesn't have to worry about it again because he has so much on his plate."

Funniest story involving Oliver Grimes and Nick Saban? Grimes startled Saban one time in his office while stocking the fridge. Saban, per usual, had no idea Grimes was in his office, but Grimes kicked the mini fridge closed with his foot. Saban shouted, "Who's there?!"

Just the Walking CVS Auburn fan, that's all.

"Goddammit, Oliver," Saban said. "What the hell?"

"Whatever, Nick," Grimes said.

As Grimes was walking out of the office, Saban closed the electronic door on him, trapping his leg.

"I hear him laughing as I'm trying to pull my leg out of the door," Grimes said.

There is a soft side to Nick Saban, too, and of course the best way to understand that is through the universal language of food. He is not the final boss from the *Matrix* movies. A.I. don't have to have three squares. The very specific salad dressing that Saban wanted for his very specific salad—cubed (not strips!) pieces of Boar's Head turkey, romaine lettuce chopped, and cherry tomatoes sliced in half and surrounding the outer edge of the salad— which he ate every day when Oliver Grimes, Auburn fan, was fetching things for Saban was Maple Groves Farms of Vermont Fat Free Honey Dijon. Saban enjoyed it, but it did not agree with the olfactory nerves of administrative assistant Glenda Edwards. Edwards approached Grimes one day while he was checking on things within the inner sanctum, and she acted as if she needed help with a very delicate task. She wanted Grimes there with her when she suggested Nick Saban try a different salad dressing.

"Can we get a different kind of dressing?" she posited to Oliver. "I'm going to ask him right now."

The two compatriots addressed Saban together. Better a united front for these types of things.

"Nick, I got Oliver here, you want to talk for a second? So, I just wanted you to know, with Oliver being here, that he could get any kind of salad dressing."

"The look on his face was absolutely priceless, like a little kid," Grimes said. "Like, 'But I like that salad dressing.' In that same tone and vulnerable sense. Like we were going to take away a toy. That was his comfort zone, and his consistency that let him take care of everything else…As I got to know him, I really looked forward to seeing him because I liked him so much."

Oliver Grimes—let's get this clear, never an Alabama football fan ever even for a second—said "probably the coolest" experience he had inside the inner sanctum was when after he had moved away and returned a year later. He went for a visit.

"We're chatting it up," Grimes said, and catching up, and talking about North Carolina, and I'm going on about snow in Cleveland with Linda, and then all of sudden Nick's office door opens, and some kid who had to be 15 walked out, and they say their goodbyes, and Nick looks and he says, 'Oliver, how you doing? I haven't seen you in a while.' And that was cool. Nick Saban remembered who I was."

Now Grimes enjoys watching Saban's news conferences when he goes off on a rant about "rat poison" or whatever manufactured emotion is needed that day. Saban coined the term "rat poison"— famous among college football fans now—to describe the type of undeserving, gushing praise heaped upon his players by fans and media that could potentially fester into psychological hang-ups and prevent development.

"Everything he does is for a reason, and it's calculated and plotted, and I went from hating his guts to having tremendous amounts of respect for this guy and liking him," Grimes said. "The funniest thing now is I so enjoy watching his press conferences because I get why he's annoyed, and I love that about him."

Sooner or later, they all start talking and thinking like Nick Saban. Even the Auburn fans, and even the politicians. Former U.S. senator Doug Jones, who has loved the Alabama football Crimson Tide all his life, is an apostle of Big Nick Energy like all the rest. Eater of the red pills, Jones sounds exactly like Nick Saban when talking about the Crimson Tide.

Does Saban have the same leadership qualities as the guys in Washington?

"Probably better," Jones said. "He is disciplined, highly self-disciplined. That doesn't mean he won't snap someone's head off for asking a dumb question. No, but it's discipline in his process, and then the ability to adapt when appropriate, and then the ability to just instill confidence in his players. And I think the first two points lead to the third.

"Because if you're disciplined and can adapt, you demonstrate to others that you have confidence in what you're doing. And it's not cocky or arrogant confidence but reassuring. Taking that confidence not just for themselves, but to use that confidence for each other and having the ability for it to build that teamwork is so hard.

"Everyone can say it, but Saban can do it."

Big Nick Energy from the former U.S. senator of Alabama. Like really, really, really, BIG Nick Energy. Doug Jones, who went to school at Alabama, enjoys a good "Saban rant" just like everyone else.

"But I really do think it's important if you go back and look at his press conferences, and they're all consistent," Jones said. "The demeanor, and how he reacts are consistent. It's all part of that discipline, and process that he builds. And his process is not going to be for everybody."

Spoken like one of Saban's top recruiters.

Alabama's fans weren't so confident after the night Joey Freshwater poured gallons of cold panic all over the entire program. When Alabama's defense returned home from its near-death experience against Ole Miss, "the process" didn't seem to be agreeing with anyone. Lane Kiffin, according to Alabama sixth-year senior Josh McMillon, "knew he had a pretty good chance against us with his offense. He has the ability to call up the right play at the right time."

Added McMillon about Kiffin, "He gets under Saban's skin."

Maybe so, but Kiffin's play calling definitely found a way under, into, and behind Saban's secondary in the Ole Miss coach's first game against his old boss.

"This is the worst I've seen Alabama's defense play," wrote Aaron Suttles of *The Athletic*, one of the leading authorities on Alabama football and a favorite among fans of the team. "They are lost."

Added Tommy Deas, who is the SEC and Alabama sports editor for Gannett, a former executive sports editor of the *Tuscaloosa News*, and a past president of the Associated Press Sports Editors, "This has been the norm in recent years more than people want to remember. Clemson more than once. Auburn and LSU last year. Etc. It's been a while since Alabama has been a rock on defense."

Without question, many wanted defensive coordinator Pete Golding fired after the Ole Miss bloodletting and before the next game against Georgia—logic and reason be damned. Alabama built its franchise on defense before Saban ever arrived, and then the tough coach put together some of the best collection of defensive talent the game had ever seen. Now this? National prime-time embarrassment? Golding had to go. It was decided on Twitter that he would be fired before the team plane touched down in Tuscaloosa following the game. What did Saban see in this guy, and what did all this mean about Saban?

A tactically gifted student of the modern game of college football and an excellent recruiter, Golding was promoted from co–defensive coordinator to full defensive coordinator as a 35-year-old in 2019. He took over a young defense made even younger by the losses of interior linebackers McMillon and Dylan Moses before the season even started. They were replaced by a pair of true freshmen whom Golding had recruited from Baton Rouge. A native of Hammond, Louisiana, Golding has deep ties in the state. He was an easy target, in other words, and especially after Alabama's two-loss season in 2019. It was one thing for LSU's all-time-everything offense to run it up on Alabama's defense, but the final score of the 2019 Iron Bowl was still a fresh memory. Auburn won 48–45, setting a new record for points allowed by an Alabama team coached by Saban. The old record was set in that 46–41 loss at Bryant-Denny Stadium three weeks earlier.

After the 2019 Iron Bowl, *Sports Illustrated* college football reporter Pat Forde didn't hold back with a column headlined "Iron Bowl may portend new reality for Alabama: The Tide's dynasty may or may not be dead. But the era of dominance certainly appears to be over."

Put another way, after being exposed by first-year Ole Miss coach Lane Kiffin's gift for calling games, combined with Kiffin's thorough understanding of Alabama's defense, Alabama's defense was flying back to Tuscaloosa after having allowed at least 46 points in three of its previous five games against teams in the SEC West.

Jermaine "FunnyMaine" Johnson, the professional comedian and Alabama superfan, and voice of younger Alabama fans, perfectly expressed the animated, building shock and horror of a fanbase during the 63–48 Alabama victory. FunnyMaine's hilarious videos after each week's set of SEC games are shot in his home with him sitting on his couch. From his Week Three YouTube episode of *How Bama Fans…* after Ole Miss touchdowns:

[Ole Miss 21, Alabama 14 with 3:15 left in the first half]

Defense, y'all straight? You good? How your momma and dem? Maybe it's just slippery out there. You know, it's raining. It's slippery. That's what it is. It's slippery out there.

[At halftime: Ole Miss 21, Alabama 21]

We are tied up with Ole Miss at halftime. [*swaying back and forth in a daze*] What is going on? Now, Coach Saban, we know we ain't never told you to use no strong language, but whatever you got to say in that locker room, you go right ahead and we'll look away.

[Ole Miss 28, Alabama 28 in third quarter after a 68-yard passing touchdown]

Bruuuuuuu-UH! He was wide open. Man, we really tak'n this social-distancing thing serious.

[Ole Miss 35, Alabama 35 after a 75-yard, 10-play touchdown drive]

Not today, y'all. We cannot lose today. I've been talk'n too much trash on Twitter about other teams. Don't do this…to *ME*!

[Ole Miss 42, Alabama 42 with 11:41 left in the fourth quarter]

Defense! I love you. [*pleading*] I believe in you. We just need one stop. That's it. Just one. Just one.

[Final score: Alabama 63, Ole Miss 48]

FunnyMaine looked to his left while laughing, and said, "I knew we'd win. I knew we'd win," and then looked to his right, symbolically showing his real side, and muttered under his breath, "For a minute there I wasn't even sure."

He summed up Alabama's scare by saying, "But, but, BUT... we handled our business. Yes, we got to make some improvement, but we 3–0. They say them 'Dawgs com'n to town next week. We're going to get back to the drawing board, fix up what we need to fix up, and we'll be ready to roll. Roll Tide."

It was time to EAT ALL THE RED PILLS.

And eat those power pellets they did. They gobbled them right up.

Now, it would be fatuous, uncivilized, and beneath all the sophisticated forms of prescribed journalistic integrity to assume that what happened next to the Alabama football Crimson Tide was the thing that motivated Pete Golding's defense against "them 'Dawgs," so that will not be the thing suggested here in these pages forever and always. It will instead be presented as black fact. Nick Saban tested positive for COVID-19 after the Ole Miss game, and even though it would turn out to be a false positive test, that scare refocused Alabama's team in an instant. Suddenly, there was no time to question anything, but only produce results and right the season. Nick Saban, 69 years old in 2020, tested positive for the coronavirus four days before the SEC's biggest game of the year, No. 3 Georgia at No. 2 Alabama on October 17. In Alabama, losing Saban to quarantine immediately after an all-time defensive collapse to Lane Kiffin and the week Kirby Smart and new Georgia special teams coach Scott Cochran were coming to Tuscaloosa felt like being stranded on an alien planet but then learning that that alien planet was actually a glimpse of the future on Planet Earth and the Statue of Liberty had collapsed into the sea.

Look, out in the distance, what is this new horror?

———

Alabama was a bare-chested Charlton Heston, riding atop a horse with a beautiful, beautiful girl, a new girl, a fresh girl, a girl from Gallettes who had no idea what was happening when her space-lover dismounted his happy steed and gazed upward at the dystopian wreckage of Lady Liberty and a once beautiful America. It was an America that was better before and failed, an America that had no chance of being anything again. And Charlton Heston stumbled forward 10 paces through the unfresh water, jabbed Nick Saban up the nose with a PCR stick, and the horse knew the false truth immediately but told no one. In that moment, Heston saw toward his past and back into our future, and crashed his whole body into the surf. He could not look. Was it shame? Was it anger? Was it the white man's victimhood? We'll never know all the things, but Heston pounded his fist into the wet sand, and uttered, "My God. I'm back. I'm home. All the time…we finally, really did it," and screamed, "You maniacs! You blew it up! Damn you! God damn you all to hell!"

A season of hope was changing by a nasal swab. So, no, it will not be assumed that Saban's false positive before his team played Georgia scared the Alabama defense into an All-American form one week after it surrendered more yards than any defense in the history of Alabama football. That is exactly what happened, and the players saved the season and the past and the future and all the land where Liberty's torch shines in the darkness. The "ultimate team" would work harder than ever with their coach stuck at home. An initial retest for the coronavirus would come back negative, but Saban would need two more negative tests spread out over 48 hours to be cleared for the big game.

The *New York Times* questioned the ethics of it all in a large piece of reporting, but for some reason had not devoted the same energy to covering the football team's protest march to the schoolhouse door.

Others expressed shock and pretended to be offended that Alabama would fly Saban's final swab of snot to Mobile on Saturday morning for the fastest test possible, but none of those people lived in Alabama.

A validating truth was missed in the end, too. Critics of Alabama's effort against Ole Miss were all wrong. The process was not broken. In that game against Ole Miss, the process offered a definitive proof and affirmation of everything Saban had ever built at Alabama. It happened with two plays in the second half. The first came with the game tied at 35–35 and less than three minutes before the fourth and final frame. With Alabama's offense three yards away from the end zone, and the skies still mean from the storm, and something resembling haint-blue panties tied around Lane Kiffin's face like a pandemic bandanna, the symbol of collegiate scholastic achievement and sacrifice to a team came running onto the field for the Alabama football Crimson Tide. It was Josh McMillon, the sixth-year senior linebacker, but he was playing fullback on one of the most important plays of the game. The first-team player at that position, Carl Tucker, had gone down with a hamstring injury, and McMillon was ready. He was one of the top-rated linebackers in the country out of high school, and grinded through Alabama's system for five years until it was his turn to start in 2019. He tore his knee in the preseason and was done. Instead of leaving Tuscaloosa, though, McMillon returned to school for another year after petitioning the NCAA for a hardship waiver. He did this to be a backup, *again*, and later said he wouldn't have traded the experience "for anything." During his time at Alabama, he earned an undergraduate degree in mechanical engineering and then an MBA.

"It took a lot of effort," he said. "Long nights until 2 and 3 a.m. It was the same effort with engineering as football."

He added that his faith helped him when he had doubts.

"I was walking with Him," McMillon said.

And now Najee Harris would run behind McMillon. The power running play was called "South Stromboli," and the Memphis native made a path through Ole Miss's goal-line defense and into the end zone. Later in the game, with Alabama needing a final score to finally put away Ole Miss, McMillon had the key block on Harris's 39-yard score to send the limited number of Ole Miss fans who could attend the game back to their homes with nothing but images of an aging panty-faced former playboy and half-empty bottles of too-expensive bourbon.

The victory against Lane Kiffin gave Nick Saban 21 wins in a row against his former assistant coaches. After missing practice on Wednesday, Thursday, and Friday, Saban rejoined his team on Saturday for the SEC showdown of the season. Alabama won in a rout, 41–24, after trailing 24–20 at halftime. It was another second-half collapse for the Bulldogs against Alabama, only this one somehow seemed more raw and revealing than the 2018 SEC championship game (Jalen Hurts's comeback for Tua Tagovailoa) and the national championship of the 2017 season (Tua's comeback for Jalen). Compared to Alabama's ever-evolving schemes, Kirby Smart's team was left behind in 2020. Georgia would go on to lose to rival Florida 44–28 on November 7 in a game dubbed the World's Largest Outdoor Cocktail Party. It was not that in 2020 due to the pandemic, and Georgia's offense could only gain 277 total yards against the Gators. After creating so much attention for himself with his move to Athens, former Alabama strength and conditioning coach Scott Cochran kept a low profile in 2020's biggest games.

Alabama's defense held Georgia to 414 yards of offense. Those probably aren't sexy numbers for football fans used to Alabama's defense stuffing run-based opponents at the line of scrimmage, but they were Jurassic-era statistics compared to what the elite SEC offenses produced in 2019 and 2020. Alabama defenders Daniel Wright, Malachi Moore, and Justin Eboigbe had interceptions, and Alabama quarterback Mac Jones had three more yards passing (417) than the Dawgs' entire combined effort. The stars of the day, though, were Alabama receivers DeVonta Smith and Jaylen Waddle. Smith had 11 receptions for 167 yards receiving and two touchdowns while Waddle had 161 yards on six catches and a score as well. It was their last game together until the national championship.

The SEC championship matchup of the unprecedented 2020 SEC season was taking shape. Florida had more offensive yards against Georgia than Alabama (571 to 564), and Florida Gators quarterback Kyle Trask had 474 yards passing with four touchdown throws. The neutral-site rivalry game in Jacksonville did another thing for Florida, too. It fed Florida coach Dan Mullen's growing persona as the new Steve Spurrier-esque villain of the SEC East. The coach who once had Tim Tebow and Cam Newton in the *same* Florida quarterback room, and later coached Dak Prescott at Mississippi State, had put the SEC on notice by slapping around Georgia and Kirby Smart. Call it the curse of Justin Fields, whom Smart failed to retain after Fields's freshman season. Fields was also allegedly the target of racial slurs by a member of the Georgia baseball team, Adam Sasser, who shouted abuse at him from the stands during a football game, according to witnesses present for the incident. Fields transferred to Ohio State months later.

Keeping all that quarterback talent locked inside the Crimson Matrix from 2016 to 2020 despite four different offensive coordinators (Kiffin, Brian Daboll, Mike Locksley, and Steve Sarkisian) was Big Nick Energy in its most potent form. Jalen Hurts talked like Nick Saban for an entire season at Oklahoma after transferring for his final year of eligibility. Hurts was even calling things "rat poison" when he got to the Philadelphia Eagles. Saban's methods can be mimicked by his assistants who leave, and they can be studied by young coaches and business professionals. Everyone can benefit from some aspect of his disciplined work ethic and lifestyle, but Saban was 23–0 against his former assistant coaches after the first half of the 2020 football season for a very important reason.

The Force is strong in that one.

"Even Luke Skywalker couldn't defeat Yoda," said Doug Jones, the former U.S. senator from Alabama.

CHAPTER 13

THE JOKER HAS A BAT PHONE

The height of insanity in the state of Alabama in the year the coronavirus shaped America started on Wednesday, November 25, one day before Thanksgiving, two days before leftovers of Thanksgiving, and three days before things like family and Thanksgiving no longer seemed to matter so much because that person who you once thought was your younger brother—but are now questioning his DNA—had explained over mouthfuls of Auntie Irene's oyster stuffing how his in-laws, who were Auburn fans like his wife and children, were probably right about Alabama's football dynasty suddenly being over.

In addition to his opinions and devil children, your brother also brought his new electric car to Thanksgiving. You brought a gallon of gasoline called Wild Turkey 101.

Roll Tide.

———

Iron Bowl Week 2020 for Alabama fans was not a time for dressed-up things like fancy manners and expensive bourbon. It was a time for quick and raw terror and fevered sweats in the night.

On Wednesday, November 25, 2020, it was announced by the

University of Alabama football Hold Onto Your Crimson Butts that Nicholas Lou Saban Jr. had the coronavirus, or, more accurately, tested positive four days before the Iron Bowl and had "very mild symptoms."

Saban got the 'Rona the week of the Iron Bowl and Thanksgiving.

"That week it was clear it wasn't a drill," said Rece Davis, who was in Tuscaloosa making preparations to host *ESPN College GameDay* from, he would later say to open his show, "atop the Magnolia Garage with Bryant-Denny Stadium in the background."

The fences were down in Jurassic Park. The bloody-toothed beasts were in charge now.

After testing positive on Wednesday morning, Saban went into quarantine in his home, and it was from there that he would try once again to coach his team. This time, though, there were no extra tests or five-alarm, daybreak flights to Mobile. It was Thanksgiving with the bug and then the Iron Bowl on television just like any other ordinary college football fan during the COVID-19 pandemic of 2020. Question: In the week of the Iron Bowl, did doctors pump Nick Saban full of the convalescent plasma of Alabama fans for Auburn fans? Friends of science would say it does not matter, but the devoutest believers of that witchcraft know the truth, and it might be too much for any brain connected to our 5G network to handle.

Yes, bizarre theories of COVID-19 flourished in 2020, but any learned fool should know, too, that history teaches us all should be forgiven in the end. The making of fantastic myths is coded into the mortal experience, and this is what the Iron Bowl feeds the soul of a state every Thanksgiving Saturday of the year. We have our good myths and our bad. Is it so hard to believe? In Birmingham, where Lynyrd Skynyrd sang they loved the governor, the citizens tore down one myth in 2020 while another, cast in iron and standing atop Red Mountain, watched over all without any pants to even cover his ass.

Vulcan is Birmingham's 180-foot erection of random, iron joy. Why is an enormous statue of the Roman god of the forge smithing a spear above the city? Who the hell knows anymore, and who the hell cares? Build your own myth. The Vulcan Man is so adorably ugly that adopted-Southern folksinger John Prine himself went years and years trying to write the big guy into one of his songs. Prine finally did it two years before he died. Said Vulcan's head was "full of bumblebees," and "his pride hangs down below his knees." If the people of Alabama told their children it was Vulcan's forge that formed the Iron Bowl, then kids would believe it.

The Iron Bowl rivalry between Alabama and Auburn or Auburn and Alabama—the order in which the words are written or spoken carries meaning—is so hard-cast into the foundational culture of the state that many young Auburn fans who have come of age during Nick Saban's run of history now say "Roll Tide" as a lexical defense mechanism of sarcasm, derision, and reflexive wit. The phrase is used in everyday conversations as an interjection to describe events that are embarrassing or silly, but also uttered as levity for situations that speak to the specifically general red-naped hijinks of Southern folk who have their own ingenious ways of doing things or fouling things up. To the "S-town" podcast by *This American Life* that enraptured a nation unfamiliar with the complex, dark, but strangely beautiful sorrows of the small-town Southern experience, an Auburn fan might just say, "Roll Tide." Pee-Paw in Cullman trips over a cut in the shag carpet and throws a boatful of Thanksgiving red-eye gravy on the heads of his grandchildren and your new camera? Roll Tide. That clever black dog you rescued drinks your full beer? Roll Tide. Fly open on a first date? Roll Tide.

Alabama's coach has COVID-19 the week of the Iron Bowl? See, that is not a good example.

Not even an Auburn fan would wish that on Nick Saban, but if the latest Alabama kicker hooks another field goal, then most definitely, with gusto, followed minutes later by thousands of students and young alumni storming Pat Dye Field at Jordan-Hare Stadium. Roll Tide.

After Alabama kicker Joseph Bulovas missed wide left from 30 yards near the end of the 2019 Iron Bowl, effectively giving the game to the home team, Auburn played Alabama's favorite tune, "Dixie Delight," during Jordan-Hare Stadium's raucous postgame celebration. Moments like this become legendary in Alabama and fuel passion for the sport year-round.

Roll Tide.

———

Leading up to the 2020 Iron Bowl, vengeful Alabama had not played a meaningful game since the 48–17 victory against Tennessee on October 24.

After shutting out new coach Mike Leach and Mississippi State's air-raid offense on Nick Saban's birthday (October 31), Alabama went three weeks without a game and then beat the blue out of Kentucky 63–3 on November 21. In between those two games, the country's November 2020 COVID-19 bloom slapped the SEC in the face. Three games were canceled leading into the league's Week Eight slate of matchups originally scheduled for November 14: No. 24 Auburn at Mississippi State, No. 5 Texas A&M at Tennessee, and No. 1 Alabama at LSU in what was supposed to be the Crimson Tide's shot at revenge after its rare home loss to the Bayou Tigers the previous year.

Alabama's once worrisome defense wasn't much of a concern anymore after the Crimson Tide outscored Mississippi State and Kentucky by a combined total of—and this is not a typo—104 to 3. The offense had also improved despite receiver Jaylen Waddle going out with his ankle injury against Tennessee. Thrust forward by necessity as the clear No. 1 target for quarterback Mac Jones, receiver DeVonta Smith had—and these numbers are also somehow real—20 receptions for 347 yards and six touchdowns against Mississippi State and Kentucky. Alabama had even been moved up to No. 1 in the country after Clemson, playing without quarterback Trevor Lawrence, was upset 47–40 in double overtime by Notre Dame on the first Saturday in November. Lawrence tested positive for COVID-19 on Thursday, October 29, which forced him to sit out games against Boston College and the Fighting Irish.

Alabama's players were delivering on the promise they made to each other after the symbolic stand at the schoolhouse door— that an undefeated, national championship season would allow their heartfelt actions, words, and teamwork to resonate long after 2020—but now there was a new worry. They weren't going to have their leader on the field for the Iron Bowl.

The evening after testing positive on Wednesday morning, Nick Saban joined Eli Gold, the voice of the Alabama Crimson Tide, on their weekly radio show, *Hey Coach*, to try his best to project an image of confidence. The "media guest" on the show that night was ESPN reporter Marty Smith, who also was in quarantine due to coronavirus contact-tracing measures. (Someone in Smith's family had tested positive.) Both Saban and Smith joined Gold for the live show via Zoom. Maybe somehow Saban's presence on the popular call-in show for fans could reestablish a form of continuity for a week of Iron Bowl and Thanksgiving that every year presents challenges. At that point, it did help that Alabama's players were isolated from their families and other "outside distractions," as Saban always liked to characterize anything beyond the sphere of football that might occupy the attention of his players. Having already gone through the same quarantine-related situations before Georgia certainly helped, too. That first coronavirus scare now seemed, bizarrely enough, like a practice run for the real thing.

Saban did not look well in the video, but he reassured Gold that he was feeling "not any different." He did report having "a little head cold, a little bit of a runny nose," and "every now and then I have an occasional cough." During that initial exchange with Gold at the top of the show, it almost seemed like Alabama's coach was trying to hold back a cough while speaking.

Smith asked Saban what the coach's "role" would be with his team while in quarantine. "Will you be in the meetings and whatnot?" Smith said.

"Well, I do everything," Saban said. "You know, I went through this for three days before the Georgia game, you know, when I had the false positive I was actually quarantined and tested out. So, I do exactly everything that I do in a day. Um, you know, at two o'clock today I'm in the meetings with players, special teams meeting. Go in with some part of the team, most of the team [defensive backs]. Um, you know, watch the entire practice. Have communication on the field.

"You know, I can tell somebody that they didn't do right and we can repeat the play or whatever. Uh, I Zoom the team afterwards when we call everybody up. Um, so, I did recruiting calls from practice until now and I'm going to do some more when I get done with this, so, nothing really changes.

"Tomorrow morning, 7:30 in the morning, we always watch today's practice, you know, because tonight is kind of recruiting night, and I'll watch it with the defense, I watch it with the defense, and then we'll do two-minute and two-point plays, so we just do what we do.

"And, you know, I ratchet things up for the players. Talk to the team. Had a team meeting today to inform them. You know, I didn't want them to hear it from anyone else, so, you know it's just kind of business as usual, but, you know, now the biggest difference is going to be I can't be involved in the game, and you can't have any electronic telecommunication or anything with the sidelines, or anything at halftime, which to me is…I mean, if you're not there, you should at least be able to communicate maybe some kind of way maybe with the press box or at halftime with your team or whatever.

"I mean, you're not going to give anybody…unless this stuff spreads over the phone or something, or over a Zoom call, so who knows? But it is what it is, and we'll just have to work it out the best we can."

Now, in case you just rightly skimmed through that long quote, here is the biggest takeaway from those rambling, head-cold-coronavirus words: Nick Saban, 69 years old and the winner of six national championships, said he was going to call recruits on the night before Thanksgiving while being sick with the 'Rona.

So, yeah, who wouldn't want to go play for that guy? But never forget this: The Wizard of West Virginia is always recruiting.

Saban's unflappable veteran players were the difference in the Iron Bowl just like they were the difference throughout the entire season, and just like they were difference makers in front of Foster Auditorium. They won everything in a blowout. All of it. Final score from the 85th playing of the Iron Bowl with Nick Saban in quarantine: No. 1 Alabama 42, No. 22 Auburn 13.

There were still five games to play and win to be national champions, but that Iron Bowl was the crowning achievement in the reign of college football's new undisputed king, and it was Saban's first game he missed in his career as a head coach. His attendance streak ended at 607 games, and the one he missed was the magnum opus. He had prepared them all so well, as fathers do, for when he could not be there, and they knew it, and they were ready. They had all the confidence, and it came by way of hard work and sacrifice, which is the only way to achieve anything worth doing. They would win for the legacy of their coach, and what he had built to change his little part of the world. The Crimson Tide had transformed itself into an unstoppable offensive and defensive cannonball express of staggering youthful genius.

"It was as if you could still feel his presence on the sideline with that team," said Davis, the host of *ESPN College Football GameDay*, and a University of Alabama graduate, "and it took him seeing that, and it really underscored how much he enjoys it but also how he needs it."

Davis, another Hall of Famer in the making, was on the sideline for the 2020 Iron Bowl after hosting *GameDay* that Saturday morning. It could not be confirmed at press time if he sang the words to "Dixieland Delight" by the band named Alabama from Fort Payne, a town in northeast Alabama with its own proud musical history to rival Davis's northwest Alabama roots.

Saban had two TVs in the room for the game. One had ESPN's broadcast, and the other had the full-field feed that coaches use. Terry and Nick Saban, the dream team, watched the game together, just not in the same room. Terry was downstairs and Nick was above. The coach ate chili dogs at halftime, reported Chris Lowe of ESPN, and Saban hollered in his colorful West Virginia parlance when Mac Jones didn't throw the ball where his coach thought it should go. That's pretty much every fan in Alabama, and the really devoted ones have been known to do things like physically remove their shoes after bad plays and throw them at their TVs.

"When there was a bad play, I was cursing the TV," Saban told ESPN. "When there was a good play, [Terry] was screaming, so we were kind of polar opposites. And sometimes, I'd hear her cheering and would wonder, 'What in the hell is she cheering about?'"

That's called being a fan, Nick. That's what fans do.

They weren't perfect, but quarterback Mac Jones and his receivers managed to link together some throws for the accumulation of positive yards downfield. Steve Sarkisian's offense averaged 8.4 yards per play against the defense of Alabama's principal rival. The Tigers had 4.3 yards per play by comparison in Auburn coach Gus Malzahn's final Iron Bowl. Mac Jones threw five touchdowns passes, tying an Iron Bowl record set by Tua Tagovailoa in 2018. The first touchdown pass on Saban's TV, a score down the middle of the field by DeVonta Smith, was a picture of how dominant and unstoppable Alabama's offense was in 2020. Eli Gold's call on the play from Jones to Smith: "Play-action fake, then he pumps. Throws long! DeVonta wide open! He is so wide open it is unbelievable! *Touchdoooowwn* Alabama! Sixty-six yards! I mean, folks, seriously. He was so wide open he could have stopped and read *War and Peace* and they wouldn't have been able to catch up with him."

Saban's Zoom call with reporters after the game was, of course, framed with his house's "recruiting room" in the background. There was a pool table behind him, and Crimson Tide–themed artwork on the walls. Hanging on the far wall was the likeness of an elephant's head, tusks and all. The coach said Terry had decorated the room. The Crimson Tide Foundation, Alabama's booster club, paid off the Sabans' mortgage on the home in 2013 after Alabama walloped Notre Dame in the 2013 BCS national championship. At the time, it was reported that the University of Texas's well-heeled boosters might have been trying to lure the Sabans to Austin. Years later (2019), former University of Texas regent Tom Hicks,* a billionaire investor from Dallas, said in the podcast *Your Turn with Colby Davidson* that Saban's agent, Jimmy Sexton, had expressed interest for his client in perhaps leaving Alabama for Texas after the 2012 season. Nothing came of the talks, Hicks said, because former Texas coach Mack Brown, who played at Vanderbilt and Florida State, didn't want to retire and then see Saban win a national championship with players Brown had recruited.

Hicks said on the podcast that Sexton told him, "If Saban was a business guy, he's what you would call a turnaround artist. He's not a long-term CEO. He likes to go someplace, fix it, win, and go on. He knows he will never catch Bear Bryant's legacy in Alabama, but he'd like to create his legacy that he won more national championships at more schools than anybody else. He's already done it at LSU, he's already done it at Alabama, and he knows he can win a national championship at Texas. He knows he can."

Thankfully for Alabama, commonwealth of, the Sabans stayed in Tuscaloosa and won three more national championships. Turns out it was good for the entire SEC too: Had the Sabans left for Texas in 2014, then maybe Texas and Oklahoma would have remained in the Big 12 instead of defecting for the conference Saban helped turn into a superpower. Alabama's dynasty was written off for dead at least twice from 2017 to 2019, but Saban's exacting attention to his program's every last detail, and his ability to manage all of his new assistant coaches, and his enormous back-of-the-house staff making red-laced smoothies every day, and the coach's talent for communicating efficiently to assistants, and dedicated boosters to

---

* Tom Hicks, sports nut, once owned 50 percent of Liverpool F.C., in addition to the Texas Rangers. Nothing happens at Texas without his input, and that includes the selling of Bevo's soul and sirloins to the SEC.

fund the recruiting trips set the standard against which all other future college football dynasties will now be measured.

None will achieve what Alabama's players accomplished in 2020, though, and hopefully the state of Alabama's future continues to bend toward better for everyone because of them. Like the great Paul Bryant before him, Saban's mark on history now reaches far beyond the football field. He passed Bryant in national titles with a championship from the most extraordinary year in college football history. The players gave each other everything they had thanks to their own courage, Saban's leadership, and the legacy built by the Bryants. There are no perfect heroes, and there will never be, but there was a perfect team where they play football in the fall, and a perfect season, too, and things happened there more powerful than people of power could ever have imagined.

"This was the best team," said Saban, addressing a few thousand fans in Bryant-Denny Stadium following the 2021 spring football A-Day Game. Traditionally, Alabama would have had a victory parade after a national championship, but the pandemic did not allow for one. Never a coach to publicly compare championships or players or much of anything really, Saban was still inspired by the power of 2020's accomplishments all those months later. His "process" does not pause for reflection, but he was still looking back in the spring of 2021.

"I'm not saying we had the best players," he went on in a video recorded by AL.com. "This was the best team that was committed to a standard of excellence and to each other to accomplish something of significance, and winning the national championship is something that will stay with every one of these players for the rest of their lives."

They said it was just the beginning in front of Foster Auditorium, and then they made it so.

The full weight of accomplishment in 2020 for the Alabama football Crimson Tide walks forward with momentum.

"I just want you to take a moment to look at the people in front of you," Najee Harris said in front of Foster Auditorium. "What do you see?"

A whole lotta badasses. America's team.

They walked through many fights, and lost at none.

━━━

Most poetically to the history of college football's best rivalry was the perfect Iron Bowl revenge game delivered in 2020 by one unassuming, once overlooked former child model turned quarterback with the fun name McCorkle Freaking Jones.

In 2019, Mac Jones and his mother, Holly McCorkle Jones, were trying to enjoy the holiday week together in Tuscaloosa before Mac's first start against Auburn. Enjoyment was not to be in the apartment where Mac would later spend so much time bubbled off from the world in 2020. There are no perfect family holidays, but this one was a Thanksgiving stress soufflé.

The Joneses' 17-year-old family dog, Chanel, was not thriving, and the pup would later pass away after the Iron Bowl. Caring for the ailing animal created a stress level in the apartment that maybe wasn't the best environment for an inexperienced former backup quarterback elevated to QB1 after Tua Tagovailoa was injured against Mississippi State so badly that he needed to be flown by helicopter to Birmingham's St. Vincent's Hospital for emergency surgery.

Anxiety in the apartment was made worse, though, by the constant, uninterrupted ringing of Mac's cell phone. It would not stop, and Holly McCorkle Jones very much wanted it to stop. Ring. Ring. Ring. Ring. All night.

"Are you going to answer?" Holly said. "What is going on?"

Mac, nicknamed the Joker by his buddies on the team, had

already moved the cell phone to another room in an attempt to distance little Chanel from the constant buzzing.

"Yeah, those are the Auburn fans, and they're leaving me hate messages," Mac said.

Before the biggest game of his life, someone from Jones's high school, Jacksonville Bolles, had passed along his cell phone number to Auburn students. It was the next generation's Oliver fucking Grimes on the phone, and he had things to discuss with McCorkle Jones. Roll Tide.

"I mean, they were as mean as possible," Holly said, "and I couldn't believe it."

Turn the phone off, Holly said.

Not possible, Mac said. Alabama's coaches do not want players turning off their phones under any circumstance, and especially before the Iron Bowl. This might have been an exception, but Mac Jones wasn't breaking protocol. The Joker never clowned around with Saban's process.

Before the 2020 College Football Playoff semifinal against Notre Dame, a 31–14 victory won with ease, Saban allowed everyone on the team to go home for Christmas break. Even then, after not being around family for so long, Jones remained in the kitchen, mask on, studying his playbook.

It's just Notre Dame, his family said.

That set Mac off, and he channeled his Big Nick Energy with a speech about all of Notre Dame's quality players and how no opponent can ever be overlooked and especially before the one and only Rose Bowl in Texas.

If Mac couldn't turn his phone off, then it had to be silenced somehow, Holly said.

"So I got up and took the phone into the kitchen, and I put it inside a container, and then inside the cupboard," Holly said. "I said,

'I'm in charge of this phone right now, and you're not going to have that phone anymore. I'm going to get you a new phone tomorrow.

"The phone lived in the kitchen. 'You are not to have that phone.'"

The next day, true to her promise, Momma Jones went and bought her son a new phone. She took the old one away, and turned it off. It had never stopped ringing.

"I will give it back to you after the Auburn game," Holly said to her son.

"So, now there is the Bat Phone," Holly said after her son got his revenge against the Tigers. "It's just for his coaches, and then his old phone is for everybody else."

The Joneses weren't able to be together before the 2020 Iron Bowl, but Mac talked to his mom one last time before devoting all of his focus and energy to the pregame preparations in the team hotel.

"Oh," he said. "The Auburn fans are calling me again."

"Well, you know what to do," Holly said. "Turn it off and use your Bat Phone."

The Joker had a Bat Phone for the Iron Bowl.

"It doesn't matter how long ago anything was for Auburn," Holly Jones said. "Auburn always remembers."

And the SEC never forgets.

The cell phone harassment aimed at McCorkle Freaking Jones by the students of a rival school was a bit of perfect symmetry for those well taught in contemporary SEC football folklore. Jones is a proud Florida–Georgia line Floridian who grew up a fan of the Gators and another standout Jacksonville-area quarterback, Tim Tebow. Jones idolized Tebow and made it a personal goal for himself as a young quarterback to one day be as tough as Timmy. Maybe in his own way, Mac Jones turned out even tougher. In 2007, Tebow's sophomore year, students at LSU got ahold of the young quarterback's cell phone number and called him relentlessly the week of the Florida-LSU game, leaving voice messages as tasteful as a pineapple upside-down cake, no doubt, until Tebow changed his cell phone number. The Florida-LSU game was at Tiger Stadium that year, and it arrived with all the color and flare of a classic SEC rivalry game in the making. LSU's students did their part, too, selling hundreds of "Teabag Tebow" T-shirts on campus. There are plenty of rowdy fanbases in the SEC, but none come close to touching LSU's toothy game-day revelers.

It was No. 1 LSU (5–0) vs. No. 9 (4–1) Florida, which was the defending BCS national champion after veteran Gators quarterback Chris Leak, with Tebow as his backup, gave Florida coach Urban Meyer his first national championship with, naturally, a 41–14 blowout of coach Jim Tressel's Ohio State in the previous season's BCS title game. On that second Saturday of October 2007, the Gators were coming off a 20–17 loss to Auburn in which the Tigers' Wes Byrum of Fort Lauderdale St. Thomas Aquinas High School kicked a game-winning field goal inside the University of Florida's Ben Hill Griffin Stadium at the final gun, and then streaked down the field doing a reverse Gator Chomp.

AH, THE GLORIOUS SEC

Sidebar: Byrum would later kick Auburn's championship field goal against Oregon to win the 2010 season's BCS national championship, and truly kick-start all kinds of insanity in the state of Alabama.

Double sidebar: Major Wright of St. Thomas Aquinas was the Gators' starting safety for three years. His younger brother, Daniel Wright, was a starting safety in 2020 for Alabama.

Triple sidebar: Fort Lauderdale St. Thomas Aquinas was the high school where some of Don Shula's grandchildren went to school when Nick Saban was coaching the Miami Dolphins. When Saban left for Alabama, effectively replacing Mike Shula, the Hall of Fame athletics director and football coach at Aquinas sent Alabama athletics director Mal Moore a letter informing him that Saban was banned from their campus.

The fourth and final sidebar before we get back to Sir Timmy: Alabama's championship secondary in 2020 featured four South Floridians: Wright (Lauderdale Lakes Boyd Anderson), cornerback Josh Jobe (Miami Columbus), All-American cornerback Patrick Surtain II (Plantation American Heritage), and Jordan Battle of Aquinas.

South Florida football players are raised on community football fields that impart them with a perfect mix of talent, confidence, desire, and swagger. Said Battle before the 2020 season's national championship in Miami Gardens, "We come out, we run, just run straight out of our moms. We run. That's what we do. So that's how South Florida prepared us for moments like these."

No. 1 LSU defeated No. 9 Florida 28–24 on October 6, 2007, but not before Tebow showed the world for the first time that he wasn't just a perfect angel after all. After throwing a short touchdown pass in the second quarter to give the Gators a 10–0 lead, Tebow ran into the end zone toward LSU's student section and vigorously punched buttons on an imaginary cell phone and held it up to his helmet. Tebow would later get his revenge just like Mac Jones, but in 2007 LSU went on to blow out, naturally, Ohio State for the 2007 season's BCS championship. The Bayou Tigers wouldn't win another until 2019.

Coming off its emotional victory against Auburn in 2020, the Crimson Tide suddenly had double revenge set out before them on plates of cold iron. SEC commissioner Greg Sankey had waved his magic wand and put LSU back on Alabama's schedule after its Week Eight cancellation. It was a brutal reckoning of truth for LSU. Coach Ed Orgeron might have had an all-time team in 2019, but his sloppy 2020 team showed the difference between an SEC castle built on granite and one raised on sand. Final score: Alabama 55, LSU 17, with receiver DeVonta Smith delivering one of the best catches of his untouchable, Hall of Fame college career.

Eli Gold's call of the play: "Mac claps his hands. He gets the snap. Mac stands in, throws, back of the end zooOONE... High... DeVonta, oh my goodness! Touchdown Alabama! DeVonta Smith goes up, makes an unbelievable touchdown catch. I mean even LSU fans are applauding him right now."

DeVonta Smith's Heisman Trophy pose was taking shape—he was no longer a long shot to win the most famous MVP trophy in American sports. How could he be? He had eight receptions for 231 measured yards of positive accumulated distance down the field against a team that featured All-American cornerback Derek Stingley Jr. Smith's three scores pushed his school and SEC record for career touchdown catches to 38. Smith would go on to have an 84-yard punt return for a touchdown against Arkansas in the final week of the COVID-altered season, and then 15 receptions for 184 yards and two touchdown catches against Florida in the SEC championship game. That performance, which set a personal record for receptions in a game and also a new mark for the SEC championship, gave him the Heisman. He then had a legendary first half in the College Football Playoff national championship game that will go down as two of the finest quarters of football in college football history: 12 receptions, 215 yards, three touchdowns. Smith dislocated his finger at the beginning of the second half and then spent 20 minutes in the sideline medical tent enduring, no doubt, unholy levels of pain. When he emerged from the collapsible structure, he threw his helmet against the sideline bench in disgust as he walked toward a tunnel leading out of Hard Rock Stadium's bowl and to the locker rooms within.

There are players every season at Alabama who most resemble the human form of their coach's energy-emanating persona. Defensive backs Minkah Fitzpatrick and Eddie Jackson were Saban clones. DeVonta Smith was Big Nick Energy incarnate: small-town country tough, slight of frame but fearless, and, most of all, motivated by savage self-discipline in the pursuit of perfection.

It was legendary *Tuscaloosa News* columnist Cecil Hurt who asked Saban about Smith's diminutive size after Alabama's second of two pro days in 2021. Saban's answer on Smith summed up his own personal code.

"I'll be honest with you, when we recruited DeVonta he weighed 159 pounds. I wished he was bigger. And now he weighs 179 pounds, and I think people at the next level are probably saying, 'I wish he was bigger,' aight? But I'm saying all that to say this: There are bigger people who don't perform anywhere near how he performs. There are people who are bigger than him who don't have the competitive spirit that he has, nor the competitive toughness. I mean, tell me how many receivers are tougher than he is—that block better, that play more physical than he does. So, I think maybe there is a time when you say maybe this guy overcomes the fact that he's not the biggest guy in the world, and he really plays the game really, really well."

One moment during the 2020 football season summed up DeVonta Smith's unrelenting character, and the ethos of Saban's entire "ultimate team." It wasn't during the championship game, or against LSU or Auburn or Florida. It was in the fourth quarter of Alabama's Week Seven blowout of Kentucky. The Crimson Tide won 63–3 against its short-staffed opponent, and Smith had nine catches for 144 yards and two touchdowns. His final catch of the game went for an 18-yard score to give Alabama a 49–3 lead with 3:58 left in the third quarter. With the Iron Bowl one week away, Nick Saban then pulled all the starters, including Smith.

Later in the fourth quarter against Kentucky, with a limited crowd all but gone and Alabama leading 56–3, Kentucky's offense was struggling against Alabama's backups. DeVonta Smith was not on the bench with a towel around his neck, or joking with the Joker, Mac Jones. Smith was watching intently from the sideline alongside his friend Patrick Surtain II, the All-American cornerback who was Smith's backup at punt returner in 2020. Kentucky went three-and-out, and Smith popped on his helmet and fastened his chin strap. He leaned over and said something to Surtain. Surtain laughed, and maybe thought Smith was making a joke. He was not. Smith had just pulled rank and was preparing to go back into the game to return the upcoming punt. It took an observant assistant coach to notice what was happening and call Smith off of the field.

Similarly, after Landon Dickerson tore his ACL in the SEC championship game, the captain suited up for the national championship game just to go through warm-ups. He then ran onto the field at the end of it all to be with his brothers for the season's final two plays. It's almost like they knew what a special piece of history they were, and they didn't want it to end. That's true love, because 2020 was a helluva year. Alabama's 52–24 obliteration of Ohio State was a curtain call and a victory lap. Surviving the unprecedented season in the SEC was the real test, and the ultimate challenge. After replacing Dickerson against Florida, backup center Chris Owens, patient and true, rushed off the field after the

SEC championship game and toward his homecoming in the one and only Rose Bowl ever to be played in Texas.

Owens screamed out the significance of the SEC's all-time accomplishment while in the tunnel of Atlanta's Mercedes-Benz Stadium. His words carried the same power as a similar moment described by SEC commissioner Greg Sankey months and months earlier on the day sports stopped in America due to the quickly spreading COVID-19 pandemic. It was March 12, 2020, and Sankey had to catch his emotions from spilling out on live television during his news conference from Nashville ending the SEC basketball tournament. Sankey recalled the words of a Georgia basketball player after winning the 2008 championship tournament that was almost canceled by a tornado hitting the Georgia Dome. "This is the best day of my life," the player cried out while celebrating through the halls of Georgia Tech's arena.

"I don't know if y'all know," Owens shouted into a camera after Alabama won the 2020 SEC football championship game 52–46. "It's only 14 teams! And we done beat 11 of them! And we one of them!"

Roll Tide.

Owens had waited five years for that moment. Alabama had waited decades and decades for that team. The adopted son of Arlington, Texas, sent away from New Orleans by the worst natural disaster in U.S. history, returned to school for the 2021 season to take advantage of the NCAA's free year of eligibility. A rare sixth-year senior, he would be a bridge from a season like no other to everything ahead.

Nick Saban, famous for never looking back, and a man who considers reflection on yesterday anathema to his "process," ended his news conference after the spring football 2021 A-Day Game with an unprompted reminder of the splendid team that he nurtured and coached and came to love during the pandemic season of 2020 and the summer of social awareness before it. Alabama's coach, wearing a dapper pink suit with checks that no doubt was designed by "Miss Terry" Saban for the new spring of hope, wanted everyone to love that team the way he loved that team, his ultimate team.

People had to know what happened there. That this one was different. This one was a rare flower growing in the middle of the river. Those guys gave everything they had for each other during a season that had to happen at all costs, but then gifted history a priceless treasure.

And on a side note, Saban wanted to send a message to those students who attended the 2021 A-Day Game and tell them how much their attendance was appreciated. Everyone is a part of the team, and the process. If those drinks they call Yellow Hammers are calling out from Gallettes in the fourth quarter of some blowout in the sun, please just stay a few more minutes to sing about the other Yellowhammers in the "Rammer Jammer" song. The recruits are there and they need to be impressed. *We told them that Alabama isn't for everybody.*

Nick Saban, April 17, 2021, Bryant-Denny Stadium:

I'd like to thank all the folks that came out today, especially the students. I think there were a great number of students there today to support our team, and also to support the championship team. Like I said out there, I don't think people really realize the disruptions that that team had to overcome and they never skipped a beat, you know? They handled it better than anyone else. They continued to improve. It was almost like, "So what? What's next?" Whether we had a game canceled…we had coaches not there. I was not there. It really didn't matter.

They had a great sense of purpose. We had great leadership on that team, and it's something special. And I hope people certainly have an appreciation for that, and don't take it for granted, and I certainly appreciate all the people that came out today to honor that team and support our players this year. Thank you.

ACKNOWLEDGMENTS

This book and a career of writing would not have been possible without many faithful and loving people. I would like to thank my family for their support, but especially Doctor Captain Chili Pup Mountain Mama, Rufus, Frodo, Crumb, my brothers, Iris, Marty and Sue, Jet and Tom, Mary and Jim, Sandy and Bill, Glenda and Sam, and Anne and Jim. Special thanks for Daniel Greenberg, Sean Desmond, Bob Castillo, Roland Ottewell, John Talty, Izzy Gould, Kelly Ann Scott, Michelle Holmes, David Magee, and Tom Bates. Patient mentors and teachers along the way: Guin Clifton, Sister Judith Diane, Sister Mary Leo, Adam Rubin, Ron Ingram, Tom Arenberg, Dr. William Hutchings, Stan Voit, Doug Segrest, Kevin Scarbinsky, Roy S. Johnson, John Archibald, Jorge Rojas, Alex Mena, Lydia Craver, George Richards, Michael Wallace, Michelle Kaufman, Susan Miller-Degnan, Linda Robertson, Greg Cote, Israel Gutierrez, Dan Le Batard, and Edwin Pope. Sheila Rule of the *New York Times* gave me the confidence to grow, and Gene Miller of the *Miami Herald* baptized me into the American newsroom with these words: "This ain't no fucking Wal-Mart." Forever grateful and thankful for Manny Navarro, Shandel Richardson, Steve Gorten, Ethan

Skolnick, the Miami Heat, Mike McCall, Andy Staples, Wright Thompson, Edward Aschoff, Brian Windhorst, Tim Bontemps, Ben Hochman, Mike Rodak, Matt Zenitz, Laura Goldman, Wes Sinor, Lauren Sisler, Matt Scalici, and Matt's buddy, comic book expert Michael Casagrande.

INDEX

ABOUT THE AUTHOR

Joseph Goodman was an industrial painter, like his father, before pursuing a career in journalism. To break into the business while in school with a young family, he commuted from Birmingham daily to work at small-town Alabama newspapers. After stints at the Jasper *Daily Mountain Eagle, Cullman Times,* and *North Jefferson News,* Joseph was awarded a fellowship at the *New York Times.* He respectfully declined to cover high school football for the *Miami Herald.* Joseph then covered the Florida Gators and the Miami Heat as a beat writer for the *Herald.* He returned home to Alabama in 2015 to work for the *Birmingham News,* his hometown newspaper. He is now the sports columnist for the *Birmingham News, Mobile Press-Register, Huntsville Times,* and AL.com. Joseph was born in Mobile and raised by Irondale. His lifelong best friend is Kevin "Skinny Bandit," aka El Flaco, aka Bryant "Get Me Something Cold to Drink" Jackson. Joseph is married to Sarah Goodman, who encouraged him to write from the beginning. They have known the love of three children. This is Joseph's first book. It was written in the Jesuit tradition.